Circling crescents of pink-tinted shrimp. Tiny, tender scallops. An assortment of fresh vegetables—peppers, mushrooms, eggplant, sweet potatoes. All are dipped into batter, placed in deep fat, and in minutes are crispy and delicious. The result is called tempura, and it is one of Japan's great delicacies. Low in calories, high in protein, it's a dish to delight the most Western of families. See how to do it on the following page.

Your FREE packet of Recipages!

TEMPURA: A DELICATE DELIGHT

1 Shell and devein shrimp, leaving shell on very tip of tail. Drop shrimp into boiling, salted water to cover; bring back to boiling. Reduce heat; simmer, covered, 5 minutes. Drain; cool. Drop scallops into boiling, salted water to cover; bring back to boiling.

2 Reduce heat; simmer, covered, 3 minutes. Drain; cool. On large serving platter or tray, arrange shrimp and scallops in attractive pattern, with parsley, eggplant, sweet potato, green pepper and whole mushrooms. Refrigerate, covered, until ready to cook.

3 Make batter: In a large mixing bowl, with wooden spoon, combine the egg yolk with the ice-cold water and baking soda. With a wire whisk, stir in the unsifted flour to make a smooth batter; it will be thin. Use the batter soon after it is made; it should not stand.

4 In deep-fryer or heavy skillet, heat oil (at least 3 inches deep) to 375F on deep-frying thermometer. With tongs, dip shrimp, scallops and vegetables, one by one, into batter, to coat lightly. Deep-fry, a few at a time, until lightly browned—about 3 minutes.

5 Make dipping sauce: In small saucepan, combine sherry, beef broth and shoyu; bring to boiling. Divide into six individual bowls. Place on tray with three small bowls filled with grated radish, horseradish and ginger root (guests add to sauce to taste).

6 Tempura is best served immediately, cooked at the table. Serve a combination of seafood and a variety of vegetables to each guest, along with a small bowl of sauce for dipping. Makes 6 servings as a main course, 10 to 12 servings as an hors d'oeuvre.

TEMPURA

½ lb large fresh shrimp
1 lb sea scallops
6 large parsley sprigs
½ small eggplant, cut
in 2-by-¼-inch strips
¾ lb sweet potatoes, pared
and sliced ⅛ inch thick
1 large green pepper, sliced
lengthwise in ¼-inch strips

½ lb small fresh
mushrooms

BATTER
1 egg yolk
2 cups ice-cold water
⅛ teaspoon baking soda
1 ⅔ cups unsifted
all-purpose flour

Salad oil for frying

SAUCE
½ cup sherry
½ cup beef broth
1 cup shoyu or soy sauce
Radishes, freshly grated
Horseradish, freshly grated
Ginger root, freshly grated

8604-1

An elegant holiday favorite is this Pâté Maison—chicken livers blended with Cognac and light cream, seasoned with onions and herbs. And leave it to the French to make food as decorative as it is savory: Egg-white flowers and pimiento trim the pâté (we've added a wreath of greens). Spread on French bread, Melba toast or crackers, it's a festive hors d'oeuvre with champagne or cocktails. For the recipe, turn to the next page.

PÂTÉ FOR THE PARTY SEASON

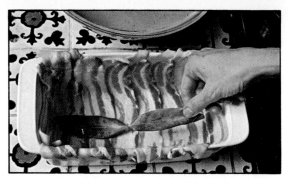

1 Day before: Wash livers, trimming any white part; dry on paper towels. Cut in half. In hot butter in skillet, sauté onion with dried herbs until onion is golden. Add livers; sauté, stirring, 5 minutes. In bowl, mix livers, Cognac, cream, eggs, salt, and pepper.

2 Puree in blender or food processor, one-third at a time (do not over process). Preheat oven to 400F. Line a 9-by-5-by-3-inch loaf pan with bacon. Arrange bay leaves in bottom. Pour in liver mixture; place in pan of boiling water (1 inch deep). Bake 1½ hours.

3 Remove pan from hot water; cool completely on wire rack. Refrigerate, covered, overnight. Next day, unmold: Loosen edge with spatula; turn out on wire rack on a tray. Remove bacon and bay leaves; smooth surface with spatula. Chill until glazing.

4 Prepare glaze: Sprinkle gelatine over ¼ cup water in small saucepan; let stand 5 minutes to soften. Add wine, tarragon, parsley; stir over low heat until gelatine is dissolved; strain. Set pan in ice water; stir, until slightly thickened (starts to "jell")—15 minutes.

5 Use half of glaze to cover completely. Chill to set glaze—½ hour. Decorate: Halve egg crosswise. Remove yolk; mash with ½ teaspoon soft butter. Cut pimiento into strips ¼ inch wide. Cut each olive into 8 slices. Place pimiento and olives around edge.

6 Cut 10 ovals for egg white petals. Slice pepper to make 2 stems and 2 leaves. With capers, use to make 2 daisies on pâté as pictured. Reheat remaining glaze and any on tray; rechill. Spoon over; repeat with any remaining glaze. Chill. Makes 40 servings.

PÂTÉ MAISON

3 lb chicken livers
6 tablespoons butter
⅓ cup chopped onion
1 tablespoon dried savory leaves
1 tablespoon dried tarragon leaves
6 tablespoons Cognac
½ cup light cream
5 eggs
1½ tablespoons salt

¼ teaspoon pepper
8 slices bacon
2 bay leaves

GLAZE
1 tablespoon unflavored gelatine
1 cup dry white wine
½ teaspoon dried tarragon leaves
½ teaspoon chopped parsley

DECORATION
1 hard cooked egg
½ teaspoon soft butter
1 jar (4 oz) pimiento, drained
1 pitted ripe olive
½ green pepper
2 capers
Watercress (optional)

8609-01

A FALL HARVEST EXTRAVAGANZA!

Show off your fall harvest by serving fresh-from-the-garden vegetables with our delicious dilled-spinach dip. Follow our vegetable selection or choose your own favorites, but whatever you serve, be sure it is very fresh—preferably just picked. Plan to prepare the dip and slice all the vegetables ahead of time and store in the refrigerator. Then, just before dinner, arrange everything on a platter and serve. Delicious!

1 Remove spinach from package and thaw at room temperature or in microwave oven. Spoon into the center of a square of cheesecloth; wrap spinach tightly and twist with hands to remove excess moisture. Slice green onion, chop parsley to yield ½ cup each.

2 Put spinach, green onion, parsley, salt, dill, pepper, mayonnaise, and sour cream into a blender container. Cover and blend on high speed, stopping frequently to scrape down sides with a rubber spatula as needed, until mixture is smooth.

3 Taste spinach mixture and add more seasoning if necessary. Transfer mixture to a 2-cup serving bowl; cover and chill until serving time. This spinach dip may be prepared up to 2 days in advance. Be sure to stir it well just before serving.

4 Wash all vegetables thoroughly; dry with paper towels. Using a small, sharp knife, cut broccoli into florets. (Stalks can be reserved and used at another time to make broccoli puree, or peel, slice thinly, and use in a Chinese stir-fried vegetable dish.)

5 Using a small, sharp knife, cut cauliflower into florets. Trim ends from snow peas and green beans. Slice zucchini and cucumber thinly. Separate leaves of endive, and trim bottoms to make even. Wrap each kind of vegetable separately and store in the refrigerator.

6 Just before serving: Stir spinach mixture and sprinkle with parsley. Place on one end of serving platter and arrange vegetables decoratively in groupings as shown. Good served as an hors d'oeuvre before dinner. Makes 2 cups sauce, 24 servings.

HARVEST VEGETABLES WITH SOUR-CREAM DIP FLORENTINE

1 pkg (10 oz) frozen chopped spinach	¼ teaspoon pepper	¼ lb snow peas
1 bunch green onions or scallions	1 cup mayonnaise	¼ lb small green beans
Fresh parsley	1 cup sour cream	1 small zucchini squash
1 teaspoon salt	1 small bunch fresh broccoli	1 small cucumber
½ teaspoon dried dill	1 small head fresh cauliflower	2 endive
		Chopped parsley (for garnish)

8620-01   Gordon E. Smith

ARTICHOKES WITH HOLLANDAISE

Artichokes, which came to us via the French, are among the fanciest finger foods around. They make a very nice first course or substitute for salad. Here, we show you how to prepare them by trimming them, cooking them in seasoned water and then taking out the "choke" (thistle portion). Serve with hollandaise sauce, as shown, or with a vinaigrette. For directions, see the next page.

1 Wash artichokes under cold running water; drain. Cut off stem at base of each artichoke. Remove small bottom leaves. Trim sharp tips from leaves with scissors. Cut a 1-inch slice across top. In bottom of kettle, stand artichokes upright, resting on the base.

2 Add boiling water to measure 3 inches deep. Add olive oil, lemon slices, bay leaf, garlic, salt and peppercorns; bring to boiling. Reduce heat; simmer, covered, 30 to 45 minutes, or until base is pierced easily with fork. (Add more boiling water as needed.)

3 Using a slotted utensil, lift out cooked artichokes. Turn upside down to drain. To remove choke: Gently spread leaves apart. Using a metal spoon, remove choke (thistle portion) from center. Serve hot with hollandaise sauce, or serve chilled with mayonnaise.

4 While artichokes cook, make hollandaise: In top of double boiler, with wire whisk, beat egg yolks just to blend. Cook over hot, not boiling, water, stirring with whisk, until yolks start to thicken—1 minute. With whisk, beat in butter, 1 tablespoon (1 piece) at a time.

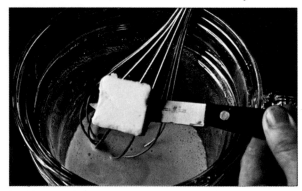

5 Beat until each piece of butter melts before adding more—takes 5 minutes in all. (Water in double-boiler base should not touch bottom of pan above. Water should not boil. Sauce will curdle over high heat.) Remove double-boiler top from hot water.

6 Using wire whisk, slowly beat in lemon juice, then salt, beating just until sauce becomes as thick as mayonnaise. To keep warm, replace sauce, covered, over lukewarm water, not heat. Serve in artichokes or in individual bowls with each. Makes 4 servings.

ARTICHOKES WITH HOLLANDAISE SAUCE

4 large artichokes
1 tablespoon olive oil
3 lemon slices
1 bay leaf
1 clove garlic, split

1 teaspoon salt
6 peppercorns

HOLLANDAISE SAUCE
3 egg yolks

½ cup (1 stick) butter,
cut into 8 pieces
2 tablespoons lemon juice
⅛ teaspoon salt

Many Germans are partial to ground meats, and one of the most famous ground-beef dishes they serve is Steak Tartare. Traditionally, the beef for this unusual dish is chopped or ground very fine and served as soon as possible thereafter. It is shaped into a loaf, a well is pressed into the center, and an egg yolk is carefully dropped into the well. The meat is surrounded with capers, onions, parsley, and anchovy fillets; salt and pepper are on the side. The beef is then combined with all the condiments at the table in front of the guests, and is served with plenty of dark bread, butter, and frosty cold steins of dark beer. Our version is just as good but is prepared before your guests arrive and molded into a decorative ring shape. Be sure to use only the finest beef—prime, if available!

GERMAN STEAK TARTARE

1 Lightly oil the inside of a 5-cup ring mold. Drain oil off anchovy fillets; separate and drain each on paper towels. Chop 4 of the fillets very finely and leave remaining whole; set aside. Chop onion very finely—you should have ½ cup.

2 Put chopped anchovy, chopped onion, ground beef, capers, egg yolks, salt, pepper, and parsley in a large bowl. Using a wooden spoon, toss and mix until very well combined. Taste, and if necessary, add more seasonings. Mixture should be highly seasoned.

3 Spoon meat mixture into the prepared ring mold, pressing down firmly with the back of a wooden spoon to pack tightly and remove all air holes. Cover meat-filled mold tightly with plastic wrap and chill for 2 to 3 hours or until ready to serve.

4 To unmold: Uncover ring mold. Using a small knife, loosen meat mixture from edges of mold. Place a serving dish upside down on top of mold; invert mold and serving dish. Shake firmly to release meat mixture; remove mold.

5 To garnish and serve: Arrange anchovies on top of meat mixture in a crisscross fashion as shown in photo; garnish with red-pepper cubes. Drain olives; mound in center of ring mold. Arrange watercress around edge of meat.

6 Be sure to keep the Steak Tartare refrigerated until ready to serve. It is especially good served on unsalted saltine crackers, English water biscuits, or small rounds of rye bread. Makes 24 hors d'oeuvre-sized servings.

STEAK TARTARE

2 cans (1 oz each) flat anchovy fillets
1 small onion
2 lb ground round beef
½ cup capers, drained

2 egg yolks
1 teaspoon salt
1½ teaspoons fresh-cracked pepper
¼ cup chopped parsley

12 pieces red pepper in ¼-inch cubes
2 cans (1 lb each) pitted ripe black olives
Watercress sprigs

Gordon E. Smith

8630-01

A FESTIVE PARTY PINEAPPLE

The next time you're having a large crowd for cocktails, remember this recipe for Cheddar-Cheese Pineapple. It's a decorative and delicious centerpiece—a spicy mixture of cheeses and German-style mustard that is accented by the sharp flavor of pimiento-stuffed green olives. Serve it with assorted crackers and party breads and complete the hors d'oeuvre table by adding an antipasto platter, herring in sour cream topped with chives, ham or veal pâté, and a big bowl of assorted nuts.

1 Put cream cheese and mustard in the large bowl of an electric mixer. Set on medium speed and beat until mixture is smooth and creamy, stopping frequently to scrape sides down with a rubber spatula. At low speed gradually beat in grated cheese until thoroughly combined.

2 Turn mixture out onto a wooden board and knead with hands until smooth and pliable. Using hands, mold cheese mixture into a pineapple-shaped cylinder about 6 inches high, 15½ inches in circumference at the widest part and 10½ inches at the narrowest part.

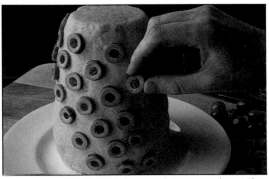

3 Put pineapple-shaped cheese mixture on a decorative serving platter. Using a small sharp knife, cut green olives crosswise into ¼-inch-thick slices. Carefully place olive slices on cheese pineapple in straight diagonal rows. (See photograph.)

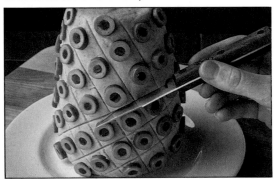

4 Using a wooden pick or the tip of a pointed knife, make diagonal lines, ⅛-inch deep, between rows of olive slices. Olives should resemble the eyes on a pineapple and the lines make the diamond-shaped cross-hatching characteristic of fresh pineapples.

5 Cover cheese with plastic wrap and refrigerate until serving time (overnight, if desired). To serve: Place fresh pineapple frond on top of cheese. Surround with small assorted crackers and party breads for spreading. Good served with fresh fruit.

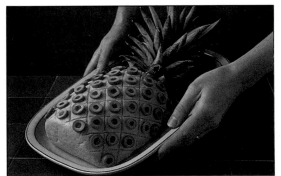

6 Let stand at room temperature for 30 minutes to soften before serving. If desired, select a long, oval-shaped platter and mold cheese mixture into a half-pineapple. Decorate as directed in steps 3 and 4; top with frond. Makes enough spread for 180 crackers.

CHEDDAR-CHEESE PINEAPPLE

1½ pkg (8-oz size) cream cheese, softened
⅓ cup prepared dark-brown mustard

2½ lb natural sharp Cheddar cheese, grated
1 jar (2 oz) small pimiento-stuffed green olives, drained

1 fresh green pineapple frond
Assorted crackers and party breads

Gordon E. Smith

8636-01

This Ham Pâté en Croûte is not nearly so difficult to make as it might appear. Simply hollow out a loaf of French bread and stuff with a ground-ham mixture that is highly

PICNIC PARTY LOAF

seasoned with onion, garlic, mustard, chives and Worcestershire sauce. It is perfect to pack and take on picnics and can be made well ahead of time.

1 Put butter in the small bowl of an electric mixer and beat at high speed until very light and fluffy. While mixer is running, gradually add ground ham, a little at a time. Beat thoroughly after each addition and scrape side of bowl with a rubber spatula as necessary.

2 When ham-butter mixture is thoroughly combined, add onion, garlic, heavy cream, prepared mustard and dry mustard, parsley, snipped chives, pepper and Worcestershire sauce. Beat again, scraping side of bowl as necessary, until mixture is well combined and almost smooth.

3 Remove bowl from mixer and scrape off beaters. Cover bowl tightly with plastic wrap and place in the refrigerator until it is firm enough to spread. This should take several hours. (If desired, this much can be completed 1 day in advance.)

4 Using a large bread knife, cut the ends off the loaf of French bread; reserve. Using a long slender knife, cut out and remove soft insides of bread, leaving a shell that is about ¼ inch thick. (Soft insides can be dried and used later for bread crumbs.)

5 Stand bread upright on one end. Using a spoon, gently push ham mixture into hollow crust, packing it firmly and filling it completely. Replace ends of bread and wrap in aluminum foil; refrigerate for several hours or until bread is cold and can be sliced easily.

6 Bread can be stuffed with ham mixture up to 24 hours before you plan to serve it. To serve: Cut bread into slices about ¼ inch thick. One loaf will make about 30 ¼-inch-thick slices and will serve about 6 people as a main course.

HAM PÂTÉ EN CROÛTE

¼ lb butter or margarine, softened
2 cups ground cooked (smoked or boiled) ham
1 tablespoon grated onion
1 teaspoon crushed garlic

3 tablespoons heavy cream
2 teaspoons strong prepared mustard
1 teaspoon dry mustard
2 tablespoons chopped parsley
2 tablespoons chopped chives

¼ teaspoon black pepper
2 teaspoons Worcestershire sauce
1 loaf French bread (about 8 inches long and 3 inches diameter)

Gordon E. Smith

8640-01

FAR EASTERN KEBABS

Tender, bite-size bits of beef, pork and chicken laced on wooden skewers, marinated in a soy sauce-and-ginger mixture and then barbecued over an open fire: This is *satay*, one of the traditional foods in the Indonesian islands of Bali, Sumatra and Java. You can duplicate this delicious appetizer in your own kitchen by following our easy directions. For a truly authentic flavor, twirl the cooked kebabs in very finely chopped peanuts and serve with chutney and toasted coconut.

1 Using a sharp knife, cut beef and pork tenderloins and the chicken cutlet into silver-dollar-size medallions, each about ¼ inch thick. Place each piece between two sheets of waxed paper. Put on a wooden board; pound with a meat pounder or the flat side of a skillet until very thin.

2 Thread 2 medallions of the same kind of meat onto a thin wooden skewer, keeping the meat as flat as possible. Arrange satays in a shallow glass baking dish in a single layer with skewers resting on edge of dish.

3 Mix soy sauce, ginger, garlic, pepper, water and sugar; pour over meat. Cover dish and refrigerate for at least 3 hours; turn satays occasionally. During this time the marinade will soak into the meat, giving it a rich, oriental-style flavor. This much can be done up to 24 hours ahead.

4 Meanwhile, wash and trim the green onions. Using a small, very sharp knife, make several lengthwise cuts through the dark green ends. Place in a small bowl of ice water. Cover and refrigerate. During chilling, the green onion tops will crisp and curl.

5 Cook satays under a broiler or over hot charcoal: Preheat broiler; arrange satays on broiler pan, with skewers all on one side. Cover skewers (not meat) with foil. Broil 3 inches from heat source for 3 minutes; turn and broil until done (about 2 minutes longer).

6 If using charcoal, be sure coals are glowing hot before you begin to cook. Place a strip of aluminum foil on grill; arrange satays so wooden skewers are on foil and meat is over fire; cook until done. Serve on platter garnished with green onions or scallions. Makes 12 cocktail servings.

INDONESIAN SATAYS*

½ **lb beef tenderloin**
½ **lb pork tenderloin**
½ **lb chicken cutlet (boneless, skinless chicken breast)**

½ **cup soy sauce**
1 **tablespoon grated fresh ginger root**
1 **tablespoon pressed garlic**
Dash pepper

¼ **cup water**
1 **teaspoon sugar**
1 **bunch green onions or scallions**

*Recipe contributed to McCall's by Executive Chef Edward Fitzpatrick, Hyatt Regency Waikiki, Honolulu, Hawaii.

8645-01   David Viens

These Swedish Meatballs are famous for their delicate flavor and dilled cream sauce. Next time you have a party, serve these meatballs on a smörgåsbord with pickled or creamed herring, smoked salmon, a selection of cheeses such as blue cheese, gouda, an herb-flavored cream or Neufchatel cheese, and a homemade liver pâté such as our Pâté Maison (Recipage—Appetizers 2). Serve with assorted crackers and breads and have several bottles of red and white wine on hand so that guests can choose their favorites.

SMÖRGÅSBORD APPETIZERS

1 Put bread crumbs and ¼ cup milk in a small bowl. Stir with a fork and let stand at room temperature for 5 minutes so that the bread can absorb the milk. Put ground beef, veal and pork in a large bowl. Add egg, onion, salt, pepper, allspice and soaked bread crumbs.

2 Toss meat mixture gently with a fork until thoroughly combined. Shape meat mixture into a loaf about 5-by-6-by-1 inch. Cut meat mixture into 30 equal-size pieces. Press together and shape each piece into round meatballs.

3 Put butter in a large skillet and heat over moderate heat. Add meatballs, about 15 at a time, and cook 10 minutes, turning frequently, until meatballs are browned on all sides and are cooked through. Remove meatballs as they are done and put in large bowl.

4 When all meatballs are browned and cooked, remove skillet from heat. Add flour all at once to the drippings in the skillet, and stir with a wooden spoon until smooth. Add bouillon cube and ¾ cup boiling water, stirring constantly as you add.

5 Return skillet to medium heat and bring flour mixture to a boil, stirring until bouillon cube dissolves and mixture is smooth. Add cream and ½ cup milk; bring to a simmer, stirring constantly, and cook 3 minutes longer or until sauce is thick and smooth.

6 Add meatballs to sauce in skillet; toss gently to coat well. Remove from heat. If desired, recipe can be made up to this point and refrigerated overnight. To serve, reheat over medium heat. Transfer meatballs to serving dish; top with sauce and garnish with dill. Serves 4 to 6.

SWEDISH MEATBALLS

½ **cup fresh white bread crumbs**
¾ **cup milk**
½ **lb ground beef**
¼ **lb ground veal**
¼ **lb ground pork**
1 egg (slightly beaten)

3 tablespoons chopped onion
1½ teaspoons salt
¼ **teaspoon white pepper**
¼ **teaspoon ground allspice**
2 tablespoons butter or margarine

2 tablespoons all-purpose flour
1 beef bouillon cube
Boiling water
½ **cup dairy half-and-half**
1 tablespoon snipped fresh dill or 2 teaspoons dried dillweed

8649-01   David Viens

BEAUTIFUL BREAKFAST BUNS

Sweet, moist Philadelphia sticky buns—a Pennsylvania Dutch treat—are wonderful any time, but especially at breakfast. The secret of their golden topping: It goes in the pan first; the buns are turned over for serving. Instructions on next page.

1 In small pan, heat milk just until bubbles form around edge of pan; remove from heat. Add granulated sugar, salt and ¼ cup butter; stir to melt butter. Cool to lukewarm (drop on wrist is not warm). Check temperature of warm water with thermometer.

2 Sprinkle yeast over water in large bowl; stir to dissolve. Stir in lukewarm milk mixture. Add the egg and 2 cups of the flour; beat with electric mixer until smooth. Add the remaining ½ cup flour; mix with hand until dough is smooth and leaves side of bowl.

3 Turn out dough onto lightly floured pastry cloth. Knead until dough is smooth and blisters appear. Place in lightly greased large bowl; turn to bring up greased side. Cover with towel; let rise in warm place (85F), free from drafts, until double—1 to 1½ hours.

4 Meanwhile, make filling: In small bowl, with wooden spoon, cream ¼ cup butter with ¼ cup light-brown sugar. Spread on bottom and sides of 9-by-9-by-2-inch square baking pan. Sprinkle with pecans. Roll dough on lightly floured pastry cloth or surface.

5 Roll dough into a 16-by-12-inch rectangle. Spread with ¼ cup soft butter; sprinkle with ½ cup brown sugar, the raisins and cinnamon. Roll up from long side, jelly-roll fashion; pinch edge to seal. Cut crosswise into 12 pieces; place, cut side down, in pan.

6 Let rise, covered, in warm place (85F), free from drafts—1 to 1½ hours, until doubled (rises to top of pan). Meanwhile, preheat oven to 375F. Bake 25 to 30 minutes, or until golden. Invert on board; let stand 1 minute; remove pan. Serve warm. Makes 12.

PHILADELPHIA STICKY BUNS

YEAST DOUGH
⅓ cup milk
¼ cup granulated sugar
½ teaspoon salt
¼ cup butter or margarine

¼ cup warm water
(105 to 115F)
1 pkg active dry yeast
1 egg
2½ cups unsifted all-purpose flour

FILLING
Butter or margarine, softened
Light-brown sugar
½ cup pecan or walnut halves
½ cup chopped raisins
½ teaspoon ground cinnamon

8602-1

There is no more tantalizing aroma than the smell of bread baking. The secret of this particular bread's moistness is in the addition of a cup of mashed potato. Cinnamon, sugar and raisins are swirled through the dough, and a light sprinkling of sugar goes on top. This bread tastes especially good when toasted for breakfast. For step-by-step directions, see next page.

CINNAMON-RAISIN SWIRL BREAD

1 In small saucepan, heat milk until bubbles form around edge of pan; remove from heat. Add ¼ cup sugar, the salt and ½ cup butter; stir until butter melts; add mashed potato; cool to lukewarm. If possible, check temperature of water with thermometer.

2 Sprinkle yeast over water in large mixer bowl; stir to dissolve. Add milk mixture and 3½ cups flour; beat with electric mixer until smooth—2 minutes. Stir in raisins. Gradually add remaining flour; mix in last by hand until dough is stiff and leaves side of bowl.

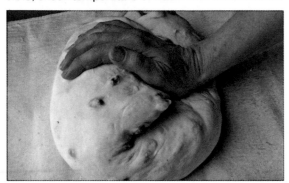

3 Turn dough onto lightly floured pastry cloth or board. Knead until smooth and elastic—10 minutes. Place in greased large bowl; turn dough to bring up greased side. Cover with towel; let rise in warm place (85F), free from drafts, until doubled—1½ hours.

4 Mix ½ cup sugar and cinnamon. Turn dough on lightly floured pastry cloth. Roll one half into 16-by-8-inch rectangle. Sprinkle with half of cinnamon-sugar. From narrow side, roll up, jelly-roll fashion. Pinch edges and ends together. Tuck ends under.

5 Place, seam side down, in greased 9-by-5-by-2¾-inch loaf pan. Brush with 1 tablespoon butter. Cover with towel. Repeat with other half of dough. Let rise in warm place, free from drafts, until sides come to top of pans and tops are rounded—1 hour.

6 Place oven rack in middle of oven. Preheat oven to 375F. Brush each loaf with rest of butter. Bake 35 to 40 minutes—tops should be well browned. Remove from pan at once; cool slightly on rack, away from drafts. Sprinkle with sugar. Serve warm. Makes 2.

CINNAMON RAISIN BREAD

1½ cups milk
¼ cup sugar
2 teaspoons salt
½ cup butter
1 cup unseasoned mashed potato

½ cup very warm water
(110 to 115F)
2 pkg active dry yeast
7½ cups unsifted all-purpose flour
1½ cups raisins

½ cup sugar
2 teaspoons ground cinnamon
¼ cup butter or regular
margarine, melted
Granulated sugar

HEARTY WHEAT BREAD

There's something special about a fragrant loaf of homemade bread fresh from the oven— especially when it's a beautifully shaped, wholesome loaf like this one. Made with 100-percent whole-wheat flour, it's a healthy treat the whole family will love. See recipe, next page.

1 In saucepan, heat milk till bubbles form around edge of pan; remove from heat. Add sugar, salt and ¼ cup butter; stir until butter melts; cool to luke-warm. If possible, check temperature of water with thermometer. Sprinkle yeast over water in large bowl.

2 Stir to dissolve yeast; stir in the lukewarm milk mixture. Add 4 cups whole-wheat flour; beat vigor-ously with wooden spoon until smooth. Gradually add rest of whole-wheat flour; mix in last of it with hand until dough is stiff enough to leave side of bowl.

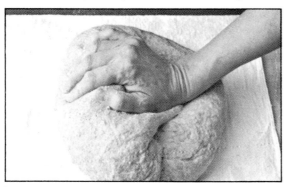

3 Turn dough out on lightly floured pastry cloth. Knead until dough is smooth and elastic—5 minutes. Place in lightly greased large bowl; turn dough to bring up greased side. Cover with towel; let rise in warm place (85F), draft free, until doubled—1 hour.

4 Again, turn dough on cloth. Halve; let rest, cov-ered, 10 minutes. Cut each half into two. With palms, roll each part into a 12-inch strip. Twist two strips together three times; press ends even; pinch ends to seal. Place in greased 9-by-5-by-2¾-inch pan.

5 Brush surface with a little melted butter. Repeat with other half. Let loaves rise in warm place, free from drafts, until sides come to top of pans and tops are rounded—1 hour. Place rack in middle of oven. Preheat oven to 400F. Bake 35 to 40 minutes.

6 Crust will be a deep golden-brown and loaves will sound hollow when tapped. (If crust is too brown after baking 25 minutes, cover with foil or brown paper.) Turn out of pans onto racks; brush tops with melted butter. Serve warm or cold. Makes 2 loaves.

100-PERCENT WHOLE WHEAT BREAD

2 cups milk
½ cup light-brown sugar, packed
1 tablespoon salt

¼ cup butter or regular margarine
1 cup warm water (105 to 115F)
2 pkg active dry yeast

8 cups unsifted whole-wheat flour
All-purpose white flour
3 tablespoons butter, melted

8605-01

OLD-FASHIONED BUTTERMILK BISCUITS

These delicate dinner rolls are a cross between baking powder biscuits and fluffy yeast rolls—and combine the best features of both. They are made in the traditional Southern manner, with plenty of buttermilk, and taste best fresh from the oven. For complete directions, please turn the page.

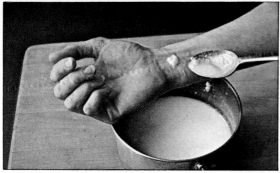

1 In small pan, slowly heat buttermilk until bubbles form around edge. Buttermilk will curdle. Cool to lukewarm (a drop sprinkled on wrist will not feel warm). Grease two large cookie sheets. Sift the flour with baking powder and salt into a large bowl.

2 Sprinkle yeast over warm water (first, check temperature with thermometer) in small bowl; add sugar; stir to dissolve completely. Stir in the lukewarm buttermilk. Cut shortening into flour mixture with a pastry blender or two knives (used scissors fashion).

3 Mixture will resemble coarse cornmeal. Make a well in the center. Pour in buttermilk mixture all at once. Stir around bowl with fork to mix well. Dough will be stiff. Turn out onto a lightly floured pastry cloth. To knead: Gently pick up dough from far side.

4 Fold dough over toward you; press out lightly with palm of hand. Give dough a quarter turn. Continue to knead until smooth—about 5 minutes. Using a stockinette-covered rolling pin, gently roll out the dough from center all around, to ½-inch thickness.

5 With floured 2-inch cutter, cut straight into dough. Do not twist. Reroll trimmings; cut more biscuits. Place on prepared cookie sheet 1 inch apart. Prick tops with fork. Cover loosely with towel; let rise in warm place (85F), free from drafts, a half hour.

6 Let rise until double in bulk—about 1 inch high. Meanwhile, preheat oven to 400F. Before baking, lightly brush tops with melted butter. Bake biscuits 10 to 12 minutes, or until golden-brown. Serve them, while still warm, with butter. Makes about 30 biscuits.

SOUTHERN RAISED BISCUITS

1 cup buttermilk	1 teaspoon salt	2 tablespoons sugar
4 cups sifted all-purpose	1 pkg active dry yeast	⅓ cup shortening
flour (sift before measuring)	½ cup warm water	2 tablespoons butter or
2 teaspoons baking powder	(105 to 115F)*	margarine, melted

*Water that is too hot will kill yeast; water that is too cold will retard action of yeast.

VIENNESE BREAKFAST CAKE

Next time you think of serving coffee cake, try our Viennese brioche instead. It's made with buttery yeast dough and filled with a sweet mixture of brown sugar, butter and finely chopped walnuts. For the complete recipe, turn the page.

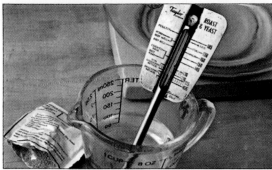

1 Day ahead, make dough: If possible, check temperature of warm water with thermometer. Sprinkle yeast over water in large bowl of electric mixer; stir until dissolved. Add granulated sugar, salt, grated lemon peel, 1 cup butter, 6 eggs and 3 cups flour.

2 At medium speed, beat 4 minutes. Add remaining flour; at low speed, beat until smooth—about 2 minutes. Cover bowl with waxed paper, then with a damp towel; let rise in warm place (85F), free from drafts, until double in bulk—about 1½ to 2 hours.

3 Refrigerate, covered, overnight. Next day, make filling: In medium bowl, with wooden spoon, mix 3 tablespoons butter, brown sugar and yolks. Stir in milk and vanilla; blend in nuts. Grease two 9-by-5-by-3-inch pans. Remove dough from refrigerator.

4 Stir down dough with wooden spoon. Dough will be soft. Turn out onto a lightly floured board; divide in half. Return half to bowl, and place in refrigerator. On lightly floured pastry cloth or surface, roll half of the dough into a rectangle, 14 by 9 inches.

5 Brush with 1 tablespoon melted butter. Spread with half of filling, to ½ inch from edge. From each end, roll up dough lengthwise, jelly-roll fashion, toward center. Turn loaf over; place in prepared pan, smooth side up. Lightly brush with melted butter.

6 Repeat with rest of dough. Let rise in warm place, covered with towel, free from drafts, until double in bulk—1½ hours. Preheat oven to 350F. Bake 35 minutes, or until golden-brown. Remove from pan to rack. Sprinkle with confectioners' sugar. Makes 2.

VIENNA BRIOCHE LOAF

½ cup warm water (105 to 115F)
1 pkg active dry yeast
¼ cup granulated sugar
1 teaspoon salt
1 teaspoon grated lemon peel
1 cup butter or regular
margarine, softened
6 eggs

4½ cups sifted all-purpose
flour (sift before measuring)

FILLING
3 tablespoons butter or
margarine, softened
⅔ cup light-brown sugar, packed
2 egg yolks

2 tablespoons milk
¼ teaspoon vanilla extract
2 cups finely chopped walnuts
or pecans

¼ cup butter or margarine,
melted
Confectioners' sugar

We've simplified the making of Europe's favorite breakfast rolls: Croissants that are crisp and flaky outside, buttery moist within. It takes patience to repeatedly roll and chill the dough—but the rewards are rich when the croissants are smeared with jam or marmalade and served with steaming coffee. For the recipe, see the next page.

CRISP AND FLAKY CROISSANTS

1 With spoon, beat butter, ¼ cup flour till smooth. Spread on waxed paper (on wet cookie sheet) in a rectangle 12 by 6 inches. Refrigerate. Heat milk; stir in sugar, salt to dissolve. Cool to lukewarm. With thermometer, check temperature of water.

2 Sprinkle with yeast; stir to dissolve. With spoon, beat in milk mixture and 3 cups flour until smooth. Turn on lightly floured pastry cloth; knead until smooth. Let rise, covered, in warm place, 85F, free from draft until double—1 hour. Refrigerate ½ hour.

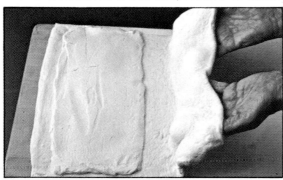

3 On lightly floured pastry cloth, with stockinette–covered rolling pin, roll into 14 by 14 inch rectangle. Place butter mixture on half of dough; remove paper. Fold other half over butter; pinch edges to seal. With fold at right, roll from center to 20 by 8 inches.

4 From short side, fold dough in thirds, making three layers; seal edges; chill 1 hour wrapped in foil. With fold at left, roll to 20 by 8 inches; fold; chill ½ hour. Repeat. Chill overnight. Next day, roll; fold twice; chill ½ hour between. Then chill 1 hour longer.

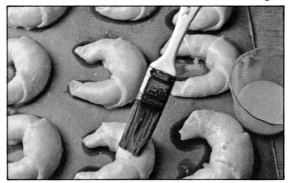

5 To shape: Cut dough into 4 parts. On lightly floured pastry cloth, roll each into a 12-inch circle. Cut each circle into 6 wedges. Roll up beginning at wide end. Form into crescent. Place point side down, 2 inches apart on brown paper on cookie sheet.

6 Cover; let rise in warm place, 85F, free from draft until double—1 hour. Heat oven to 425F. Brush with yolk beaten with milk. Bake 5 minutes; reduce oven to 375F; bake 10 minutes, until croissants are puffed and brown. Cool on rack 10 minutes. Makes 24.

CROISSANTS

1½ cups butter or regular margarine, softened
¼ cup unsifted all-purpose flour
¾ cup milk

2 tablespoons granulated sugar
1 teaspoon salt
½ cup very warm water (105 to 115F)

2 pkg active dry yeast
3 cups unsifted all purpose flour

1 egg yolk
1 tablespoon milk

8609-02

BAKING UP A BABKA

This round loaf made of slightly sweetened yeast dough is called a babka — and its substantial goodness has been enjoyed by Polish families for generations. Its ancestor is the baba, a sweet cake named by a Polish king in honor of his favorite fictional character, Ali Baba. Over the years other babas have been based on the recipe: baba au rhum, a dessert cake soaked in rum syrup, as well as the coffee-cake babka you see here, studded with raisins and crusted with sugar and cinnamon. Directions for making it are on the next page.

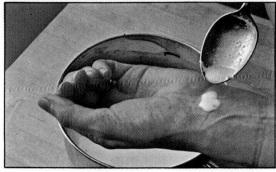

1 In small saucepan, heat milk until bubbles form around edge. Remove from heat; cool to lukewarm (a drop on wrist will not feel warm). Pour warm water into large bowl, first rinsed in hot water. If possible, check temperature of warm water with thermometer.

2 The temperature should be no less than 105F and no more than 115F. Water that is too hot will kill yeast; water that is too cold will slow down yeast action and bread will not be as light. Sprinkle yeast evenly over the surface of warm water, stirring until dissolved.

3 Add lukewarm milk, ½ cup sugar, salt, ½ cup butter, eggs, egg yolk and 3 cups flour. With mixer at medium speed, beat until smooth and blended. With wooden spoon, stir in 1½ cups flour; beat vigorously 2 minutes, or until dough leaves side of bowl.

4 Mix in raisins. Cover with towel; let rise in warm place (85F), free from drafts, until double in bulk—about 1 hour. Grease and flour 9-inch springform pan. Fold 30-inch strip of foil lengthwise around top, extending over rim 2 inches. Turn dough into pan.

5 Cover loosely with towel; let rise in warm place (85F), free from drafts, until dough is ¾ inch from top of foil—about 1 hour. Meanwhile, preheat oven to 350F. Make topping: Using a fork, beat egg white with 1 tablespoon water; use to brush top of the babka.

6 Mix flour, sugar, cinnamon and butter; sprinkle on babka. Bake 1 hour, or until cake tester inserted in center comes out clean. Cool in pan on wire rack 15 minutes. To serve: Remove side and bottom of the pan. Cut in wedges. Serve warm. Makes 16 servings.

BABKA

		TOPPING
1 cup milk	**½ cup butter**	**1 egg white**
¼ cup warm water	**4 eggs**	**2 tablespoons flour**
(105 to 115F)	**1 egg yolk**	**2 tablespoons sugar**
2 pkg active dry yeast	**4½ cups unsifted**	**¼ teaspoon cinnamon**
½ cup sugar	**all-purpose flour**	**2 tablespoons butter**
1 teaspoon salt	**½ cup seedless raisins**	

McCALL'S
COOKING
SCHOOL

PIPING-HOT POTATO ROLLS

In this era of convenience foods, an entire generation might have grown up without ever tasting the delights of homemade rolls. Yet they're not hard to make, and it's easy to serve them piping hot for dinner if you prepare the dough in advance and have it waiting in the refrigerator. These rolls are especially delicious because they're made with mashed potato, which gives them extra moistness and a subtly different flavor. The same basic dough can be used to make all the shapes pictured here.

1 Prepare mashed potato as package label directs for ½ cup, omitting salt and butter. Pour warm water into a large bowl. (First rinse bowl in hot water.) If possible, check temperature of hot water with thermometer. The temperature should be no less than 105F and no more than 115F. Water

2 that is too hot will kill yeast; water that is too cold will slow down yeast action and rolls will not be as light. Sprinkle the yeast over water; add sugar and salt, stirring with wooden spoon until completely dissolved. Let stand a few minutes; the mixture will start to bubble slightly.

3 Add 2 eggs, the soft butter, warm mashed potato and 3 cups flour. With portable electric mixer at high speed, beat just until smooth. Add 2 cups flour, beating with wooden spoon until flour is incorporated in dough. Add remaining 1½ cups flour, mixing with hands until the dough is

4 smooth and stiff enough to leave side of bowl. (This takes place of kneading to develop the gluten in the flour.) Brush top of dough with 1 tablespoon melted butter; cover with waxed paper and dish towel. Let rise in refrigerator 2 hours, or until double in bulk. Remove from the refrigerator.

5 Punch down with fist. Cover; refrigerate. Dough can be refrigerated from one to three days, but punch it down once a day. About 2 hours before serving, remove dough from refrigerator; shape. For crescents (picture 7): Remove one third of dough from refrigerator. On lightly floured pastry

6 cloth, divide dough in half. With rolling pin covered with lightly floured stockinette, roll each half into a 10-inch circle. Brush with 1 tablespoon melted butter. Cut into 6 wedges. Starting at wide end, roll up each wedge toward the point. Place on a greased cookie sheet, 2 inches

7 apart, point side down. Curl ends inward slightly. For figure eights and snails (picture 8): Remove one third of dough from refrigerator. On lightly floured surface, with palms, roll into a 12-inch rope. Divide into 12; roll each into a 12-inch strip. On greased cookie sheet, pinch ends together and twist

8 once into an 8. Snails: Press one end of a strip to greased cookie sheet; wind strip around itself; tuck other end underneath. Fan-tans (picture 9): Roll one third of dough into 15-by-8-inch rectangle. Spread with butter. With sharp knife, cut dough lengthwise into 5 (1½-inch) strips.

9 Stack strips; cut into 12. Place cut side up in greased, 2½-inch muffin-pan cups. To bake: Cover with towel; let rise in warm place (85F) until double in bulk—1 hour. Preheat oven to 400F. Brush with butter or with egg and seeds. Bake 12 minutes, or until golden. Serve warm. Makes 36.

REFRIGERATOR POTATO ROLLS

½ cup unseasoned warm mashed potato or packaged instant mashed potato	½ cup sugar	6½ cups unsifted all-purpose flour
1½ cups warm water (105 to 115F)	1 tablespoon salt	Melted butter, or 1 egg, beaten with 2 tablespoons water
2 pkg active dry yeast	2 eggs	Poppy or sesame seed
	½ cup butter or regular margarine, softened	

A fragrant loaf of homemade bread, hot from the oven, is a welcome addition to any meal. Our giant double ring of braided sesame-seed bread is spectacular enough to be the center of attention. Serve with lots of sweet butter and a hearty soup, followed by fruit and cheese for dessert. The important part of bread baking is getting the dough just right. Start by checking the date on the yeast package to be sure

BRAID A RING OF BREAD

the yeast is still active. For best results, measure the temperature of the water in which you dissolve the yeast. It should be between 105 and 115 degrees Fahrenheit. If it's too hot, it will kill the yeast organism; if it's too cold, the yeast will take too long to work. Yeast dough needs lots of kneading and a warm, draft-free place to rise—place it over a bowl of warm water or in a cupboard or an oven with the pilot light on.

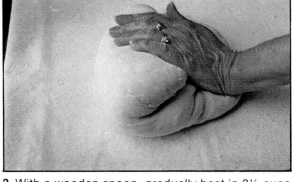

1 Into hot milk, stir sugar, salt, ½ cup butter. Cool to lukewarm. Sprinkle yeast over warm water (check temperature with thermometer) in electric-mixer bowl. Stir to dissolve. Stir in lukewarm milk mixture. Add 2 eggs, 3 cups flour; beat, at high speed, 2 minutes.

2 With a wooden spoon, gradually beat in 3½ cups flour; mix with hand until dough is stiff enough to leave side of bowl. Turn out on lightly-floured pastry cloth. Knead: Fold over; push away with palm of hand until smooth and elastic—about 10 minutes.

3 Place dough in a lightly-greased, large bowl. Turn the dough over to bring up greased side. Cover with towel; let dough rise in a warm place (85F), free from drafts, for about 1½ hours, or until the dough is double in bulk. Turn out on a lightly floured pastry cloth.

4 Divide dough in half; cut each half into thirds. Using palms of hands, roll each third into a 26-inch-long strip. Braid three strips; pinch ends together. On large, greased cookie sheet, form the braid into a ring (the center should be six inches in diameter).

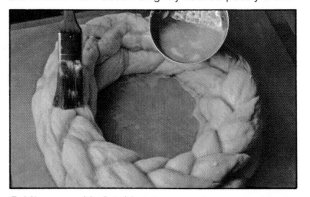

5 Mix egg with 2 tablespoons water; use some to brush top of ring. Braid remaining strips; form into ring on top of first ring. Brush with 2 tablespoons melted butter. Cover with towel. Let rise in warm place, free from drafts, until double in bulk—about 1 hour.

6 Place rack in middle of oven. Preheat oven to 375F. Brush top of braid with rest of the egg mixture. Sprinkle with sesame seed. Bake 45 minutes, or until golden-brown. (If it's too brown after 25 minutes, cover loosely with foil.) Cool slightly on rack.

BRAIDED SESAME-SEED BREAD

1½ cups hot milk	2 pkg active dry yeast	1 egg
¼ cup sugar	½ cup warm water (105 to 115F)	2 tablespoons butter or
1 tablespoon salt	2 eggs	margarine, melted
½ cup butter or regular margarine	6½ cups unsifted all-purpose flour	2 tablespoons sesame or poppy seeds

REAL OLD-FASHIONED JELLY DOUGHNUTS

You haven't tasted real doughnuts until you've tried the old-fashioned homemade kind with strawberry- or currant-jam centers and the incredible lightness that comes only from yeast-raised dough. Getting them just right requires care. The water in which you dissolve the yeast and the fat in which you fry the doughnuts must be exactly the right temperature—always use a thermometer. Take one bite and you'll know they're worth the trouble. Step-by-step directions, next page.

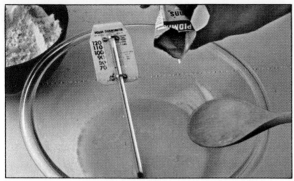

1 Heat milk in small pan until bubbles form around edge of pan; remove from heat. Add ⅓ cup sugar, salt and butter; stir to melt. Cool to lukewarm. In large bowl, sprinkle yeast over warm water (if possible, check temperature of water with a thermometer).

2 Stir yeast until dissolved. Add milk mixture, egg yolks and 2 cups flour. With portable electric mixer, at medium speed, beat until smooth—about 2 minutes. With wooden spoon, beat in remaining flour; beat until smooth. Dough will be soft.

3 Cover with towel; let rise in warm place (85F), free from drafts, until double in bulk—about 1½ hours. Punch down dough. Turn out onto lightly floured pastry cloth; turn over to coat with flour. Knead ten times, or until dough is smooth. Divide dough in half.

4 Roll out half of dough to ¼-inch thickness. Cut into 12 (3-inch size) rounds. Place 1 teaspoon jam in center of half of rounds; brush edge with egg white. Top with rest of rounds; press edges to seal. Place on floured cookie sheet. Repeat with rest of dough.

5 Cover with towel; let rise until double in bulk—about 1 hour. Meanwhile, in deep-fat fryer or heavy skillet, slowly heat oil (2 inches deep) to 350F on deep-frying thermometer. Gently drop the doughnuts, top side down, three at a time, into the hot oil.

6 Fry, turning as they rise to surface, turning again, until golden-brown—4 minutes in all. (Open one to test doneness; fry longer if needed.) Lift out with slotted utensil, draining slightly. Place on paper towels to drain. Dust with sugar while warm. Makes 14.

JELLY DOUGHNUTS

½ cup milk	½ cup warm water	Raspberry, currant or
⅓ cup sugar	(105 to 115F)	strawberry jam or jelly
1 teaspoon salt	3 egg yolks	Egg white
⅓ cup butter	3¾ cups sifted* all-purpose flour	Salad oil for deep-frying
2 pkg active dry yeast	*Sift before measuring.	Sugar

8619-02

APRICOT-AND-PRUNE COFFEECAKE

Whether served for brunch or brought forth at dessert or teatime, this apricot-prune coffeecake will be a moist, melt-in-your-mouth favorite. The rich sour-cream batter is studded with luscious bits of dried fruit, and a brown-sugar struesel is swirled through it all. Directions start on the next page.

1 Make streusel mixture: In small bowl, combine light-brown sugar, 2 tablespoons butter, 2 tablespoons flour and the cinnamon; mix with fork until crumbly. Makes 1 cup. Set aside. With sharp knife, coarsely chop apricots and prunes; toss to combine.

2 Grease well and lightly flour a 10-inch tube pan. Preheat oven to 350F. Make coffeecake batter: On a sheet of waxed paper, sift together 3 cups flour, the baking powder, baking soda and salt; set aside. Turn ¾ cup butter into the large bowl of electric mixer.

3 At medium speed, beat until fluffy. Gradually beat in granulated sugar, then eggs, one at a time. Beat until very light and fluffy—about 3 minutes, occasionally scraping the bowl with a rubber scraper. Add vanilla extract. Divide flour mixture into four parts.

4 At low speed, beat in flour mixture (in fourths) alternately with sour cream (in thirds), beginning and ending with flour mixture. Beat just until smooth—about 1 minute. With rubber scraper, gently fold in the prunes and apricots just until combined.

5 Turn one third of batter into prepared pan, spreading evenly. Sprinkle with one third of streusel mixture. Repeat layering of remaining batter and streusel mixture twice. Bake 55 to 60 minutes, until cake tester inserted in center comes out clean.

6 Let cool in pan on wire rack about 20 minutes. With spatula, carefully loosen edge of coffeecake from side of pan. Remove from pan to platter. Sift confectioners' sugar over top of coffeecake. Serve warm. Makes 10 servings. (This freezes very well.)

APRICOT-PRUNE COFFEECAKE

STREUSEL MIXTURE
½ cup light-brown sugar, packed
2 tablespoons butter or regular margarine, softened
2 tablespoons flour
1 teaspoon ground cinnamon

BATTER
¾ cup dried apricots
¾ cup pitted dried prunes
3 cups unsifted all-purpose flour
1½ teaspoons baking powder
¾ teaspoon baking soda
¼ teaspoon salt

¾ cup butter or regular margarine, softened
1½ cups sugar
4 eggs
1½ teaspoons vanilla extract
1 cup sour cream
2 tablespoons confectioners' sugar

8620-02

There's something deeply satisfying about a fragrant loaf of homemade bread, warm from the oven. Ours is a very special bread—a nutritious combination of white and whole-wheat flour, eggs, milk and golden honey. It's also a good yeast bread for beginners—most of the ingredients

HONEY WHEAT BREAD

are beaten together in an electric mixer, and no kneading is required. Instead of shaping the dough into a loaf, it is simply turned into a buttered casserole, allowed to rise, and baked into a giant glowing round. And you can make it ahead of time and freeze until needed.

1 In small saucepan, heat milk until bubbles form around edge of pan; remove from heat. Add shortening, honey and salt, stirring until shortening is melted. Let cool to lukewarm or tepid. If possible, check temperature of warm water with thermometer.

2 Sprinkle yeast over warm water in large bowl; stir until yeast is dissolved. Stir in milk mixture and the eggs. Combine all-purpose and whole-wheat flours. Add two thirds of flour mixture to yeast mixture; then, with electric mixer at low speed, beat until blended.

3 Then beat at medium speed until smooth—about 2 minutes. With wooden spoon, gradually beat in remaining flour mixture. Mix with hand, squeezing dough between fingers 20 to 30 times, to develop gluten. Cover the bowl with waxed paper and towel.

4 Let rise in warm place (85F), free from drafts, until batter is above rim of bowl—1 hour. Punch down dough; beat with spoon until smooth—about 30 seconds. Lightly grease a 3-quart casserole or heat-proof bowl. Turn dough into casserole; pat evenly.

5 Cover and let rise until double in bulk—40 to 50 minutes. Dough should rise slightly above casserole. Preheat oven to 375F. With a sharp knife, cut a 4-inch cross about ½ inch deep in top of dough. Bake 45 to 50 minutes, or until bread is browned.

6 Bread should sound hollow when rapped with knuckle. Remove to wire rack. Rub butter over top. Serve warm, cut in wedges. Makes 1 loaf. *To freeze:* Cool; wrap in foil; freeze. To serve: Thaw at room temperature several hours. Reheat, at 325F, ½ hour.

HONEY WHOLE-WHEAT BREAD

1 cup milk	¾ cup warm water	4½ cups unsifted all-purpose
¾ cup shortening	(105 to 115F)	flour
½ cup honey	2 pkg active dry yeast	1½ cups whole-wheat flour
2 teaspoons salt	3 eggs, slightly beaten	1 teaspoon soft butter

8623-01

The pride of a Budapest bakery, this festive yeast bread can be your culinary specialty, too! The soft, rich dough with a sugarplum filling—poppy seeds and candied fruit—is fashioned into a horseshoe-shape jelly roll. Scrumptious during the holidays and all year round.
For directions, turn the page.

HUNGARIAN POPPY-SEED BREAD

1 In small saucepan, heat milk until bubbles form around edge. Pour over ¼ cup butter, the sugar and salt in medium bowl; stir to melt butter. Cool to 105 to 115F. Sprinkle yeast over warm water (check temperature with thermometer); stir to dissolve; add to milk mixture.

2 Stir in 2 eggs and 2½ cups flour. Blend; then beat with wooden spoon until smooth. Add rest of flour, adding last by hand. Mix until dough leaves side of bowl. Turn out on floured pastry cloth. Roll over to coat with flour. Start kneading by folding dough toward you.

3 Then push down and away from you with heel of hand. Knead until smooth—5 minutes. Place in lightly greased medium-size bowl; turn greased side up. Cover with towel, and let rise in warm place (85F), free from drafts, until double in bulk—45 to 50 minutes.

4 Make filling: Cover poppy seed with boiling water; soak 30 minutes; drain. Place in small saucepan; add cream, honey, butter. Stir over medium heat until thick—10 minutes; remove from heat. Add nuts, fruit, cinnamon and vanilla. Cool 10 minutes; beat in 1 egg.

5 To shape: Turn dough out onto lightly floured pastry cloth. Grease a large cookie sheet. Roll dough into an 18-by-12-inch rectangle. Spread filling to 1 inch from edge. Roll up lengthwise; pinch edges. Place, seam side down, on cookie sheet. Shape into horseshoe.

6 Cover with towel; let rise in warm place (85F), free from drafts, until double in bulk—about 1 hour. Preheat oven to 375F. Brush surface with beaten egg; sprinkle with poppy seed. Bake 25 to 30 minutes, or until golden. Remove from cookie sheet to wire rack. Serve warm.

HUNGARIAN POPPY-SEED BREAD

½ cup milk
¼ cup butter or margarine
¼ cup sugar
½ teaspoon salt
1 pkg active dry yeast
¼ cup warm water (105 to 115F)
2 eggs
3 cups unsifted all-purpose flour

FILLING
1 cup poppy seed
2 cups boiling water
½ cup light cream
½ cup honey
2 tablespoons butter or margarine
½ cup chopped walnuts

½ cup mixed candied fruit, chopped
½ teaspoon ground cinnamon
1 teaspoon vanilla extract
1 egg, beaten

1 egg beaten with 1 tablespoon cold water
2 tablespoons poppy seed

8624-01

DOUGHNUTS WITH A FRENCH TWIST

French crullers and beignets (which are simply crullers made in round balls instead of ring shapes) might be described as doughnuts with a French connection. They're made with "pâte à chou"—the sweet pastry that is used to make cream puffs. When fried in hot deep fat (the temperature is important; use a thermometer) they expand to become light, airy and golden. They're at their best when freshly made; just serve plain, with a sprinkling of sugar, along with coffee. Or they can make a spectacular dessert with apricot sauce and whipped cream.

1 Make crullers: With shortening, grease one side of foil circles very well. In heavy, 2½-quart saucepan, combine sugar, salt, butter and 1 cup water. Bring to boiling; butter will melt. Remove from heat. Quickly add flour all at once; beat with wooden spoon until

2 flour is moistened. Cook over medium heat, beating vigorously until dough forms ball and leaves side of pan. Remove from heat. Add eggs, one at a time, beating with electric mixer at medium speed after each addition. Continue beating until the mixture is

3 smooth, shiny and satiny and forms strands that break apart. It should hold its shape when beater is slowly raised. Beat in vanilla. To make crullers, turn mixture into a large pastry bag with a number-6 star tip. Press mixture onto greased foil to form circles

4 about 3¼ inches in diameter, overlapping ends of circles slightly. Let stand 20 minutes. In electric skillet or large, heavy skillet, slowly heat oil (1½ to 2 inches) to 350F on deep-frying thermometer. Place crullers, including the foil, in hot oil, four at a time.

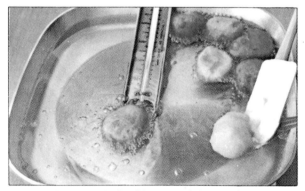

5 Turn each as it rises to top. Lift out foil. Fry about 10 minutes, or until golden, turning several times. Lift out with slotted spoon. Drain on paper towels; remove to wire rack. Serve warm, sprinkled with confectioners' sugar. Makes 14. For beignets, drop

6 batter by rounded tablespoonfuls into hot oil, six at a time. Fry about 7 minutes, or until golden, turning several times. Lift out; drain. Keep warm in oven. Melt preserves with lemon juice; strain; add kirsch. Serve with warm beignets and cream. Makes 24.

FRENCH CRULLERS AND BEIGNETS

Shortening **14 (3½-inch) foil circles**	**1¼ cups sifted** **all-purpose flour** **4 eggs**	**APRICOT SAUCE** **1 jar (12 oz) apricot preserves** **2 tablespoons lemon juice**
2 tablespoons granulated sugar **½ teaspoon salt** **¼ cup butter or regular margarine**	**1 teaspoon vanilla extract** **Salad oil or shortening for frying** **Confectioners' sugar**	**½ tablespoon kirsch** **Sweetened whipped cream**

HOMEMADE SWEDISH RYE BREAD

This homemade limpa bread is easy to make if you follow our step-by-step directions. It is a traditional bread of Sweden—laced with brown sugar, molasses, caraway seeds, and orange peel. Try it toasted with lots of sweet butter or sprinkle it with grated Cheddar cheese and broil until cheese is melted and browned. It's also good for a simple ham-and-cheese sandwich!

1 In large bowl, combine sugar, molasses, ¼ cup butter, the salt, anise and orange peel. Add 1 cup boiling water; stir until sugar dissolves and butter melts. Add 1 cup cold water. Cool to lukewarm. Check temperature of warm water with thermometer.

2 Sprinkle yeast over water in measuring cup; stir until dissolved. Add to molasses mixture; mix well. Gradually add 4½ cups all-purpose flour and 1 cup rye flour; beat vigorously until smooth and dough leaves side of bowl. Gradually add 3 cups rye flour.

3 Mix in last of flour with hand until dough leaves side of bowl. (Dough is stiff.) Turn out onto lightly floured pastry cloth or board. Knead until smooth and elastic—10 minutes. Place in lightly greased large bowl; turn dough to bring up the greased side.

4 Cover with towel; let rise in warm place (85F), free from drafts, until double in bulk—about 1½ hours. Grease a large cookie sheet, and sprinkle lightly with cornmeal. Punch down dough, and turn out onto lightly floured pastry cloth or board. Cut in half.

5 Shape each half into an oval. With palms of hands, on lightly floured surface, roll each half into a loaf, 12 inches long, tapering ends. Place on prepared cookie sheet, 5 inches apart. With sharp knife, make four diagonal slashes in top of loaf, ¼ inch deep.

6 Cover with towel; let rise in warm place, free from drafts, until double in bulk—1 to 1¼ hours. Preheat oven to 375F. Bake on middle shelf 35 minutes; cover with foil last 10 minutes, if necessary. Brush with butter. Serve warm, or cool on rack. Makes two.

SWEDISH LIMPA BREAD

½ cup light-brown sugar, packed	2 tablespoons grated orange peel	4½ cups unsifted all-purpose flour
¼ cup light or dark molasses	1 cup boiling water	4 cups unsifted rye flour
¼ cup butter or margarine	1 cup cold water	Cornmeal
1 tablespoon salt	½ cup warm water (105 to 115F)	2 tablespoons butter or margarine, melted
1 teaspoon anise or caraway seed	2 pkg active dry yeast	

BRIOCHE
À TÊTE

Brioche, a cakelike bread rich in butter and eggs, is said to have originated centuries ago in Brie and to have been flavored with the cheese for which this district of France is so famous. It can be shaped in many ways, but the most traditional is the Brioche à Tête—a large ball of dough topped by a small topknot baked in a fluted pan with sloping sides. Be sure to start this bread one day before you plan to serve it, because it requires a very slow rising time—overnight!

1 Day ahead: If possible, check temperature of water with thermometer, or test by dropping a little water on inside of wrist; it should feel warm, not hot. Sprinkle yeast over water in large electric-mixer bowl; stir to dissolve. Add sugar and salt.

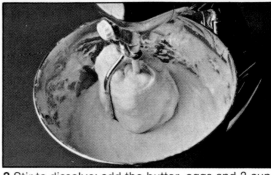

2 Stir to dissolve; add the butter, eggs and 2 cups flour. Beat at medium speed 4 minutes, occasionally scraping bowl and beaters with rubber scraper. Add remaining cup of flour. Beat at low speed 1 minute, or until smooth (dough will be soft).

3 Let rise in warm place (85F), covered with towel, free from drafts, until double in bulk—2 to 2½ hours. With rubber scraper, beat down dough. Refrigerate, covered with waxed paper and damp towel, overnight. Next day, grease 1½-quart brioche pan.

4 Cut off one sixth dough for cap. On lightly floured surface, form into ball, coating with flour. Turn out rest of dough onto lightly floured surface. Knead** dough until smooth—about 1 minute; shape into 5-inch round. Fit evenly into prepared pan.

5 Make 1½-inch-wide indentation in center. Insert ball of dough. Let rise in warm place (85F), covered with towel, free from drafts, until dough rises to top of pan—takes about 2½ hours. Preheat oven to 375F. Beat the egg yolk with 2 teaspoons water.

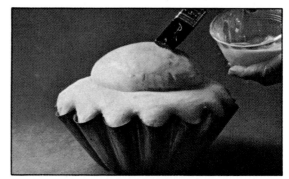

6 Gently brush surface of dough (do not let egg run between brioche and cap). Bake 20 minutes. Cover loosely with foil; bake 40 minutes, or until cake tester comes out clean. Cool 15 minutes. With small spatula, loosen from pan. Remove. Serve warm.

BRIOCHE

⅓ cup warm* water
(105 to 115F)
1 pkg active dry yeast
3 tablespoons sugar

1¼ teaspoons salt
⅔ cup butter, softened
4 large eggs, at room
temperature

3 cups sifted all-purpose
flour (sift flour
before measuring)
1 egg yolk

*Water that is too hot will kill yeast; water too cold will retard action of yeast.
**To knead: With floured hands, fold dough toward you; then push it down and away from you with back of hand. Give dough a quarter turn; repeat as in Step 4.

8629-01

A EUROPEAN DELICACY

This traditional Yugoslavian nut roll is more commonly known in Europe as "Potica." The rich, sweetened egg bread is filled with a mixture of ground walnuts, brown sugar, butter, vanilla, and cinnamon. All rolled together, jelly-roll style, and formed into the traditional ring shape, this beautiful bread is perfect to serve with morning coffee or for brunch.

1 Stir sugar, salt and ¼ cup butter into hot milk. Cool to lukewarm. (A drop sprinkled on wrist will not feel hot.) Sprinkle yeast over warm water (check temperature with thermometer) in large bowl. Stir to dissolve. Stir in lukewarm milk mixture.

2 Add 2 eggs and 2½ cups flour; beat at high speed with electric mixer 2 minutes. With wooden spoon, gradually beat in remaining 2 cups flour; knead with hand until the dough is stiff enough to leave side of bowl. Place dough in lightly greased large bowl.

3 Turn the dough over to bring up greased side. Cover with a towel. Let rise in warm place (85F), free from drafts, until double in bulk — about 1 hour. Make filling: In medium bowl, beat eggs slightly. Add nuts, brown sugar, ⅓ cup butter, the cinnamon and vanilla.

4 Stir filling to blend well. Shape dough: Punch down dough. On lightly floured surface, turn out dough; cover with bowl; allow to rest for 10 minutes. Roll out to a rectangle 30 inches long and 20 inches wide. Spread with filling, to 1 inch from edge.

5 Starting from wide side, roll up tightly, as for a jelly roll. Seal by pinching edges to dough with fingers. With palms of hands, roll back and forth so that roll is even all over. On large greased cookie sheet, form roll into a large coil, as shown, seam side down.

6 Let rise in warm place (85F), cover with towel, free from drafts, until double in bulk — 1 hour. Preheat oven to 350F. Brush with 2 tablespoons butter. Bake 35 to 40 minutes, until golden. Cool on wire rack. Slice crosswise ¼ inch thick. Makes 4-pound loaf.

POTICA

½ cup granulated sugar
1 teaspoon salt
¼ cup butter or regular margarine
1 cup hot milk
2 pkg active dry yeast
¼ cup warm water (105 to 115F)

2 eggs
4½ cups unsifted all-purpose flour

FILLING
3 eggs
4 cups (1lb) walnuts, ground or finely chopped

1 cup light-brown sugar, packed
⅓ cup butter or regular margarine, melted
1½ teaspoons cinnamon
1 teaspoon vanilla extract

2 tablespoons butter, melted

A SWEET BREAD FROM GENOA, ITALY

Genoa, Italy, is famous for its good food—especially its sweet bread called *Pandolce.* Our recipe follows Italian tradition and is flavored with orange-flower water, fennel seed and aniseed and is studded with raisins soaked in Marsala wine, pine nuts, pistachio nuts and candied fruits. It is traditionally served during the holidays, but you will find it is perfect for any occasion. Don't be alarmed by the long list of ingredients—it is really a very easy bread to make and well worth the effort.

1 In a small saucepan, heat milk just until bubbles form around edge of pan. Remove from heat; add sugar, salt and butter, stirring until butter is melted and sugar dissolves. Cool to lukewarm (a drop sprinkled on your wrist will not feel warm).

2 If possible, check temperature of water with a thermometer. It should be 105 to 115F. Sprinkle yeast over warm water in a large bowl, stirring until yeast is completely dissolved. Stir in lukewarm milk mixture and orange-flower water.

3 Add 4 cups of the flour; beat with a wooden spoon until batter is smooth—about 2 minutes. Gradually add remaining flour, working with hands until dough is stiff enough to leave sides of bowl. Turn out onto lightly floured board and knead 5 minutes until smooth and elastic.

4 Wash, dry and grease bowl; return dough to bowl and turn to bring greased side up. Cover with waxed paper, then a dish towel. Put in a warm place, free from drafts, for 1 to 1½ hours or until doubled in bulk. In a small bowl soak raisins in Marsala wine for 1 hour.

5 On a floured surface, roll dough to a 14-inch square; sprinkle with raisins, nuts, fennel seed, aniseed, lemon peel, citron and orange peel. Roll dough up jelly-roll-style. Roll to a 13-inch square; roll up jelly-roll-style again. Form into an 8-inch-round loaf.

6 Place loaf in greased cookie sheet; cover with towel, and let rise 1 to 1¼ hours until doubled in bulk. Heat oven to 350F. Slash top of loaf to make a triangular cut; brush with butter and bake 65 to 70 minutes; cool on wire rack. Makes one 5-pound loaf.

PANDOLCE

1¾ cups milk
¾ cup sugar
1 teaspoon salt
½ cup butter or margarine
½ cup warm water (105 to 115F)
2 pkg active dry yeast
¼ cup orange-flower water
7 cups unsifted all-purpose flour

1½ cups raisins
3 tablespoons Marsala or dry sherry wine
⅓ cup pine nuts
½ cup pistachio nuts
2 teaspoons crushed (see Note) fennel seed

1 teaspoon crushed (see Note) aniseed
⅓ cup chopped candied lemon peel
⅓ cup chopped candied citron
3 tablespoons grated orange peel
2 tablespoons butter or margarine, melted

Note: Crush with rolling pin.

Nothing adds to a good home-cooked meal like bread, warm from the oven. You don't need to be an expert baker, either. It's easy to make this Brown-Sugar Oatmeal Bread if you follow our simple step-by-step directions carefully. This recipe has very few ingredients—probably all are on your pantry shelf right now. So why don't you try it and see how easy and good homemade bread really is. Serve it warm from the oven or cool; toast thick slices and serve with butter and cinnamon-sugar. It's delicious!

BREAD LIKE GRANDMA USED TO MAKE

1 In a medium-sized saucepan bring 2 cups water to a boil. Gradually stir in oats, mixing until smooth. Cook, stirring until thick—about 1 minute. Remove from heat. Add margarine, brown sugar and salt. Stir until margarine is melted. Let cool to lukewarm.

2 In a large mixing bowl sprinkle yeast over warm water; stir until dissolved. Add lukewarm oats and 3 cups flour; beat with wooden spoon until smooth—about 2 minutes. Using hand, gradually mix in 2 more cups of flour; turn dough out onto lightly floured surface.

3 Knead in remaining ½ cup flour (dough will be stiff). Knead 10 minutes longer. Place in greased large bowl; turn, to bring greased side up. Cover with waxed paper and then with towel; let rise in warm place (85F) free from drafts until double in bulk—about 1 hour.

4 Lightly grease two 9-by-5-by-2¾-inch loaf pans. Turn dough out onto floured surface; divide in half. Roll out one half to a 12-by-8-inch rectangle; roll up, starting at narrow end. Press ends even; pinch to seal; tuck under loaf.

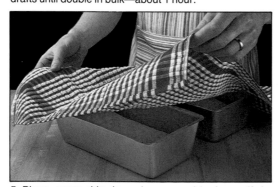

5 Place, seam side down, in prepared loaf pan. If desired, brush surface lightly with extra melted butter and sprinkle with more oats. Repeat with other half of dough. Cover with towel and let rise about 1½ hours or until sides of dough come to top of pan.

6 Preheat oven to 375F. Bake loaves of bread on center rack of oven for 50 to 55 minutes or until crust is deep golden brown and loaves sound hollow when tapped on the bottom. Turn bread out of pans onto wire racks; let cool completely. Makes 2 loaves.

BROWN-SUGAR OATMEAL BREAD

2 cups water	½ cup light-brown sugar, packed	1 cup warm water (105 to 115F)
2 cups quick-cooking oats	1 tablespoon salt	5½ cups unsifted all-purpose
¼ cup margarine	2 pkg active dry yeast	flour

8634-01   Gordon E. Smith

A DELICIOUS BREAKFAST BREAD

Corn bread is traditionally served with hearty Southern breakfasts. Either sweetened with sugar or made plain, it is always served with plenty of sweet creamery butter. Try our version, sweetened slightly with sugar and served with whipped butter lightly flavored with honey. It's easy to make and will quickly become a family favorite.

1 Prepare Corn Bread: Heat oven to 350F. Put 2 tablespoons butter or shortening in a 9-by-5-by-2¾-inch loaf pan; place in oven to let butter melt. Meanwhile, sift together into a large bowl the cornmeal, flour, sugar, salt, baking powder and baking soda.

2 Add buttermilk and egg to cornmeal-flour mixture. Remove loaf pan from oven and pour hot melted butter into cornmeal mixture. Set loaf pan aside to cool. Using a wooden spoon, mix corn-bread batter only until all dry ingredients are moistened.

3 Thoroughly grease the inside of the cooled loaf pan with solid vegetable shortening. This corn bread can stick to the pan, so be sure you grease the pan very heavily. If possible, use a pan with a nonstick finish.

4 Pour bread batter into prepared pan and put it on the center rack of the preheated oven. Bake for 1 hour or until a cake tester or wooden pick inserted in center of bread comes out clean. Bread should be a very light golden brown.

5 Remove pan from oven and immediately turn bread out onto a breadboard. Let cool about 5 minutes and cut into thick slices. Serve with plenty of sweet creamy butter, or, if desired, serve with Whipped Honey Butter. Makes 1 loaf of bread.

6 To make Whipped Honey Butter: Beat 1 cup butter with an electric mixer at high speed until smooth and creamy. Gradually add honey while beating constantly. Serve at room temperature on hot corn bread, toasted if desired. Makes about 1½ cups whipped butter.

TENNESSEE CORN BREAD WITH WHIPPED HONEY BUTTER

CORN BREAD
2 tablespoons butter or solid vegetable shortening
2 cups white cornmeal
½ cup all-purpose flour (sifted before measuring)

½ cup sugar
½ teaspoon salt
1 teaspoon baking powder
½ teaspoon baking soda
2 cups buttermilk

1 egg, beaten

WHIPPED HONEY BUTTER
1 cup butter, at room temperature
½ cup honey

Cicero/Fimage Inc.

8636-02

Quick breads have a cakelike texture and, unlike yeast breads that use yeast for leavening and take several hours to rise, quick breads are leavened with baking soda and/or baking powder and rise in the oven during baking. They are easy and quick to make since all the ingredients are mixed together into a batter and then poured into a pan to be baked immediately. Because of their fragile texture, be sure to let quick breads cool for 10 minutes in the pan before turning out and cooling completely on a wire rack. After baking you will notice a crack down the middle of the loaf—it is characteristic of quick breads and should not be considered a flaw! Try this Holiday Fruit-Nut Bread studded with apricots, raisins, candied cherries and walnuts and moistened with crushed pineapple. It's perfect to make any time of the year or to give as a holiday gift.

A FRUIT-AND-NUT QUICK BREAD

1 Preheat oven to 350F. Use solid vegetable shortening to grease the inside of a 9-by-5-by-3-inch loaf pan. Sprinkle with a little extra flour to coat thoroughly. Sift 2¾ cups flour with baking powder, soda and salt over a large piece of waxed paper. Set aside.

2 In the large bowl of an electric mixer, put sugar, butter and egg. Beat at medium speed for about 3 or 4 minutes, until mixture is smooth and fluffy. Use a rubber spatula if necessary to guide sugar-butter mixture in toward beaters.

3 Using a wooden spoon, gradually stir milk into the sugar-butter mixture in bowl. When thoroughly blended, stir in the pineapple, dried apricots, raisins and the chopped candied red and green cherries. Mix well with spoon to blend thoroughly.

4 Add flour mixture to sugar-butter mixture, beating just until all dry ingredients are moistened. Stir in chopped nuts and spoon batter into the prepared pan. Spread batter evenly with the back of the wooden spoon or rubber spatula.

5 Place loaf pan on the center rack in preheated oven. Bake for 60 minutes or until cake tester or a wooden pick inserted in center of bread comes out clean. The actual baking time will depend on the accuracy of your oven. Do not underbake.

6 Remove pan from oven and let cool 10 minutes. Remove bread from pan and let cool completely on a wire rack. Before serving, spread top of cake with corn syrup. Decorate as pictured, using candied red and green cherries and walnut halves. Makes 1 loaf.

HOLIDAY FRUIT-NUT BREAD

BREAD
2¾ cups sifted all-purpose flour
(sift before measuring)
1 tablespoon baking powder
¼ teaspoon baking soda
¼ teaspoon salt
¾ cup sugar
⅓ cup butter, softened

1 egg
⅓ cup milk
1 can (8¼ oz) crushed pineapple,
undrained
⅓ cup chopped dried apricots
¼ cup light or dark raisins
2 tablespoons chopped candied

green and red cherries
1 cup chopped walnuts

GARNISH
1 tablespoon light corn syrup
Candied red and green cherries
Walnut halves

Gordon E. Smith

8637-01

GREEK
HOLIDAY
BREAD

This sweet, light-and-airy yeast bread, called *Vasilopita*, is traditionally served in Greece to usher in the New Year. A lucky coin is usually inserted in the bread dough before baking. In Greece this coin can be a gold lira or small drachma, and legend says that luck will come to the person who finds the coin! While the bread bakes, a wonderful sweet aroma fills the air, the crust turns a deep chestnut color, and the bread becomes light and almost cakelike in texture.

1 In a small saucepan, heat milk over moderate heat until bubbles form around the edge of pan; remove from heat. Add butter, sugar and salt; stir until butter melts and sugar dissolves. Set aside and let cool to lukewarm (about 105 to 115F).

2 If possible, check temperature of warm water with a thermometer. Sprinkle yeast over warm water in a large bowl; stir until yeast dissolves. Add lukewarm milk mixture to yeast mixture. Beat eggs thoroughly and add to milk-yeast mixture. Stir to combine.

3 Using a large wooden spoon, gradually beat half of the flour into the yeast mixture, beating for about 2 minutes or until smooth and no lumps of flour remain. Add lemon and orange peels. Gradually beat in remaining flour, mixing in the last part with your hands.

4 Turn dough out onto a lightly floured pastry cloth or surface and knead for 5 minutes. Put dough in a large greased bowl; turn to bring greased side up. Cover with a towel; let rise in a warm place (85F), free from drafts, until double in bulk—about 1½ hours.

5 Grease a 12-inch-round by 2-inch-deep baking pan. Turn raised dough out onto a lightly floured surface and knead until smooth (several minutes). Shape dough into a 10-inch-diameter circle and place in the prepared pan. Cover with towel and let rise 1½ hours.

6 Preheat oven to 350F. Beat egg yolk with 1 tablespoon water and brush over the surface of the dough. Arrange almonds on top as shown and sprinkle with sesame seeds. Bake for 45 to 50 minutes or until golden brown. Remove from pan and let cool on rack. Makes one 4½-lb loaf.

VASILOPITA

½ **cup milk**	½ **cup warm water (105 to 115F)**	2 **teaspoons grated orange peel**
⅔ **cup butter or margarine**	3 **eggs**	1 **egg yolk**
¾ **cup sugar**	5½ **cups unsifted all-purpose**	1 **tablespoon water**
½ **teaspoon salt**	**flour**	**Whole blanched almonds**
2 **pkg active dry yeast**	2 **teaspoons grated lemon peel**	**Sesame seeds**

8639-01 Gordon E. Smith

◆ *IRISH SODA BREADS PART I* ◆

A TRADITIONAL BREAD

Soda breads are quick to make because instead of using yeast for leavening, they use soda powder. Soda, when combined with an acid (in this case it's buttermilk), forms carbon dioxide gas bubbles that make the bread dough rise during baking. In Ireland, this bread (which they call "cake") is made from soft Irish wheat and baked in an oven over a peat fire. It is well known for its unsurpassed flavor. Now you can make it in your own kitchen, from start to finish, in only about 50 minutes!

1 Preheat oven to 375F. Using solid vegetable shortening, lightly grease the surface of a small baking sheet. Set aside until bread is shaped. Assemble all ingredients for Irish Soda Bread. (Make bread the same day you plan to serve it.)

2 Put flour, sugar, baking powder, baking soda and salt in a sifter; sift over a large bowl. Add softened butter and cut into flour mixture, using a pastry blender or fork until mixture looks like fine crumbs. Add raisins and toss thoroughly.

3 Pour buttermilk into flour mixture all at once. Gently toss mixture together with a fork until all dry ingredients are just moistened. Do not overmix. Using hands, gently gather flour mixture together and press firmly into a ball.

4 Put dough on a lightly floured pastry cloth or board. Knead gently with the palms of your hands until dough is smooth (about 1 minute). Shape into a smooth round ball and place on the prepared baking sheet.

5 Using hands, flatten dough into a circle that is about 7 inches in diameter. (Dough will be about 1½ inches thick.) Press a large floured knife into center of loaf, halfway through dough. Repeat, at right angle, to divide loaf into quarters.

6 Bake bread for 30 to 40 minutes, or until top is golden brown and loaf sounds hollow when tapped on the bottom and sides with a wooden spoon. Remove to a wire rack to cool. Brush top with melted butter and later, dust with flour. Makes 1 loaf.

IRISH SODA BREAD

2 cups unsifted all-purpose flour
2 tablespoons sugar
1 teaspoon baking powder
1 teaspoon baking soda

½ teaspoon salt
3 tablespoons butter or margarine, softened
½ cup dark seedless raisins

1 cup buttermilk
1 tablespoon butter or margarine, melted

Gordon E. Smith

8640-02

◆ *IRISH SODA BREADS PART II* ◆

WHOLE-WHEAT IRISH SODA BREAD

Soda-bread doughs are handled just the opposite of yeast doughs: High speed and quick baking is the key rather than hours of patience while the dough slowly rises and is kneaded and reshaped. Before you begin, be sure to gather together all the ingredients needed, prepare the baking sheet and preheat the oven. This Whole-Wheat Irish Soda Bread is heartier than the traditional Irish Soda Bread but it is just as good. Its whole-wheat flavor is delicious when the bread is served with lots of butter and wild honey.

1 Preheat oven to 375F. Using solid vegetable shortening, lightly grease the surface of a small baking sheet. Set aside until bread is shaped. Assemble all ingredients for Whole-Wheat Irish Soda Bread. Bake bread the same day you plan to serve it.

2 Put all-purpose flour, baking powder, baking soda, salt and sugar in a sifter; sift into a large bowl. Add whole-wheat flour and, using two forks, toss the flour mixture together until very well combined.

3 Pour buttermilk into flour mixture all at once. Gently toss mixture together with a fork until all dry ingredients are just moistened. Do not overmix. Using hands, gently gather flour mixture together and press firmly into a ball.

4 Put dough onto a lightly floured pastry cloth or board. Knead gently with the palms of your hands until dough is smooth (about 1 minute). Shape into a smooth round ball and place on the prepared baking sheet.

5 Using hands, flatten dough into a circle that is about 7 inches in diameter. (Dough will be about 1½ inches thick.) Press a large floured knife into center of loaf, halfway through the dough. Repeat, at right angle, to divide loaf into quarters.

6 Bake bread for 40 minutes or until top is golden brown and loaf sounds hollow when tapped on the bottom and sides with a wooden spoon. Remove to a wire rack to cool. Brush top with melted butter. Slice when cool and enjoy the same day. Makes 1 loaf of bread.

WHOLE-WHEAT IRISH SODA BREAD

1 cup unsifted all-purpose flour	1 teaspoon salt	1½ cups buttermilk
1 teaspoon baking powder	2 tablespoons sugar	1 tablespoon butter or
1 teaspoon baking soda	2 cups whole-wheat flour	margarine, melted

A CINNAMON-LACED COFFEE CAKE

Next weekend surprise your family and let them wake up to the aroma of a home-baked cinnamon-flavored streusel coffee cake. Nothing can tease the appetite so much! Serve it warm with plenty of sweet butter and hot coffee. For the children serve it with hot chocolate!

1 Preheat oven to 375F. Using solid vegetable shortening, lightly grease the inside of an 8-by-8-by-2-inch square baking pan or a 9-by-1½-inch round layer-cake pan. Assemble all ingredients needed for cake before you begin the streusel mixture and batter.

2 Prepare Streusel Mixture: In a small bowl, combine brown sugar, 2 tablespoons soft butter, 2 tablespoons all-purpose flour, ground cinnamon and nuts. Mix with a fork until flour mixture is crumbly and ingredients are thoroughly combined. Set aside.

3 Make Batter: Sift flour with baking powder and salt over a piece of waxed paper and set aside. In a medium-sized bowl, beat egg with a mixer until frothy. Add sugar and butter and beat until thoroughly blended. Add milk and vanilla; stir in flour mixture.

4 Spoon half of the batter into the prepared pan you have selected. Sprinkle half of the streusel mixture evenly over the batter. Spread remaining batter on top of the streusel layer; sprinkle batter again with remaining streusel mixture.

5 Put pan on center rack in oven and bake for 25 to 30 minutes or until a cake tester or wooden pick inserted in the center of cake comes out clean. If cake is not done, return to oven and bake for a few minutes longer. Top of cake should be a light golden brown.

6 When cake is done, remove from oven and put pan on wire rack; let cool for 15 to 25 minutes. Cut warm coffee cake into squares or wedges and arrange in a napkin-lined basket to keep warm. Serve immediately with sweet butter. Makes 1 cake, 9 servings.

STREUSEL-LAYERED COFFEE CAKE

STREUSEL MIXTURE
½ cup light brown sugar, firmly packed to measure
2 tablespoons butter or margarine, softened
2 tablespoons all-purpose flour
1 teaspoon ground cinnamon

½ cup coarsely chopped walnuts

BATTER
1½ cups sifted all-purpose flour (sift before measuring)
2½ teaspoons baking powder

½ teaspoon salt
1 egg
¾ cup granulated sugar
⅓ cup butter or margarine, melted
½ cup milk
1 teaspoon vanilla extract

Cicero/Fimage Inc.

8643-01

A SPICY NUT BREAD

Of all the nut breads we can think of, this one is probably the easiest to make. In a matter of only 25 minutes it can be ready to pop into the oven, and then, just one hour later, out it comes: moist, flavorful, spicy! It keeps well too — make it up to two days before serving and keep it fresh by wrapping tightly in aluminum foil.

1 Preheat oven to 350F. This is a pumpkin quick bread and should be mixed and baked immediately. Be sure you assemble all ingredients and utensils before you begin to mix the batter. Lightly grease a loaf pan that measures 9 by 5 by 3 inches.

2 Put a large piece of waxed paper on a flat surface. Put flour, baking powder, baking soda, cinnamon, nutmeg and salt into a sifter; sift over paper to lighten and combine thoroughly. Set aside until you are ready to add mixture to the bread batter.

3 Put pumpkin, granulated sugar, milk, eggs and softened butter in a large bowl. Beat with a wooden spoon until thoroughly combined. Add flour-spice mixture all at once, beating with the spoon only until all dry ingredients are moistened and the batter is smooth.

4 Add nuts to pumpkin batter and stir just until combined. Do not overmix. Pour batter into prepared baking pan and spread evenly with a rubber spatula. Put pan on center rack in preheated oven and bake for 50 to 60 minutes.

5 Bread is done when a cake tester inserted into the center of the bread comes out clean. If cake tester comes out with batter clinging to it, the bread is not done. Return it to the oven and bake a few minutes longer until tests done.

6 Remove pan from oven and place on a wire rack to cool for 10 minutes. Remove bread from pan and return to wire rack to cool completely. Before serving, sprinkle with confectioners' sugar, as shown. Cut into thin slices and serve. Makes 1 loaf.

PUMPKIN-NUT BREAD

2 cups unsifted all-purpose flour
2 teaspoons baking powder
½ teaspoon baking soda
1 teaspoon ground cinnamon
½ teaspoon ground nutmeg

½ teaspoon salt
1 cup canned pumpkin
1 cup granulated sugar
½ cup milk
2 eggs

¼ cup butter or margarine (softened)
½ cup chopped nuts (pecans or walnuts)
Confectioners' sugar

8645-02   David Viens

This Italian bread is spicy with cracked black peppercorns and crunchy with cracklin' bits (crumbled crisp-fried bacon). It goes well with baked ham and sliced tomatoes and packs well for a picnic. Make it in either the loaf or the crescent shape, or make one of each!

CRACKLIN' BREAD

1 In a small saucepan, heat milk just until bubbles form around edge of pan; remove from heat. Add sugar, basil, salt and butter; stir until butter melts; cool to lukewarm. Sprinkle yeast over warm water in large bowl; stir until yeast is dissolved. Stir in lukewarm milk mixture.

2 Add 3 cups flour and egg to yeast mixture; beat 2 minutes with a wooden spoon until batter is smooth. Gradually add remaining flour and 1½ teaspoons pepper, mixing with hands if necessary. Knead dough on a lightly floured board for 10 minutes or until smooth and elastic.

3 Place dough in greased large bowl; turn over to bring greased side up. Cover and let rise in warm place (85F), free from drafts, until double in bulk (1 hour). Meanwhile, fry bacon until crisp; drain on paper towels. Grease a large baking sheet and a 9-by-5-by-3-inch loaf pan.

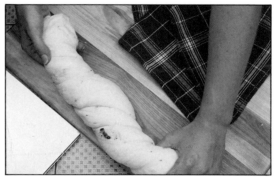

4 Punch dough down; knead in bacon; divide in half. For crescent shape: Cut one half into 3 parts; roll each to make a 20-inch strip, tapering ends. Twist strips together; pinch ends to seal. Shape into crescent on baking sheet. Cut slashes in top of loaf with knife, 2 inches apart.

5 For loaf: Cut remaining dough into 3 parts. Roll each part to make a 12-inch strip; braid; pinch ends to seal. Place in loaf pan. Cover crescent and loaf with towel; let rise in warm place (85F), free from drafts, until double in bulk (about 1 hour). Preheat oven to 375F.

6 Brush surface of breads lightly with egg-yolk mixture. Lightly sprinkle each loaf with cracked peppercorns. Bake 30 to 35 minutes, or until nicely browned. Remove from pans to wire racks to cool. Serve cool or slightly warm with softened butter. Makes 2 loaves of bread.

BLACK-PEPPER BREAD

1½ cups milk	2 pkg active dry yeast	1½ teaspoons pepper
3 tablespoons sugar	¾ cup warm water (105 to 115F)	4 strips bacon (cut up)
½ teaspoon dried basil leaves	7 cups unsifted all-purpose flour	1 egg yolk beaten with 2
1 tablespoon salt	1 egg	teaspoons water
¼ cup butter or margarine		Cracked black peppercorns

8646-01 David Viens

CHEDDAR-CHEESE BREAD

This quick bread is flavored with lots of grated Cheddar cheese, grated onion and dill-weed and is delicious served warm while the cheese is still soft and partially melted. Or toast thick slices under the broiler and serve with a chef's salad that is topped with sticks of smoked ham.

1 Preheat oven to 350F. This is a cheese quick bread and should be mixed and baked quickly. Be sure you assemble all ingredients and utensils before you begin to mix the batter. Lightly grease a loaf pan that measures 9 by 5 by 3 inches.

2 Put flour, baking powder, sugar and salt into a sifter; sift over a large mixing bowl. Cut butter into small pieces and add to flour mixture. Using 2 knives or a pastry blender, cut butter into flour until mixture resembles coarse crumbs.

3 Coarsely grate cheese. Add cheese, onion and dried dillweed to the flour-butter mixture in bowl. Toss well with 2 forks until the cheese and onion are well coated with flour and the cheese does not stick together in lumps.

4 Put milk and egg in a small bowl and beat with a fork or a rotary hand beater until thoroughly combined. Add to flour mixture all at once; stir quickly with a fork until all dry ingredients are moistened. Do not overmix.

5 Pour batter into prepared baking pan and spread evenly with a rubber spatula. Put pan on center rack in preheated oven and bake for 40 to 45 minutes or until a cake tester inserted in center of bread comes out clean.

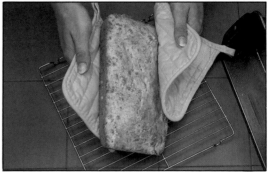

6 Remove pan from oven and place on a wire rack to cool for 10 minutes. Remove bread from pan and return to wire rack to finish cooling. Serve Brethren's Cheese Bread slightly warm or let it cool completely. Makes 1 loaf of bread.

BRETHREN'S CHEESE BREAD

2 cups sifted all-purpose flour
(sift before measuring)
2 teaspoons baking powder
1 tablespoon sugar

½ teaspoon salt
¼ cup butter or
margarine
¼ lb sharp natural
Cheddar cheese

1 tablespoon grated onion
1½ teaspoons dried dillweed
¾ cup milk
1 egg

8648-01   David Viens

BRITISH ISLES BREAKFAST BREAD

Scones are dear to the
hearts of the Scots and the
English and are frequently served
for breakfast. They can be baked in the
oven or, as the Scots prefer, baked on a "girdle,"
more commonly known as a *griddle!* Our baked version is
studded with currants and topped with a creamy cinnamon-
sugar glaze. They are best when eaten immediately after baking.

1 Scones are best when prepared and baked just before eating for breakfast. The night before you plan to serve the scones, measure and assemble all dry ingredients and utensils so that in the morning, preparation will be quick and easy.

2 Prepare Scones: In a medium-sized bowl, put biscuit mix, 2 tablespoons sugar and currants or dark seedless raisins. Toss with a fork until all ingredients are thoroughly combined. Lightly grease a baking sheet with solid vegetable shortening. Heat oven to 425F.

3 Add milk to dry ingredients, all at one time, and stir with a fork until ingredients are moistened and the dough clings together and is soft. (Be very careful that you do not overmix the dough or the scones will be tough.)

4 Using a large spoon, drop scone dough onto prepared baking sheet, 1 heaping tablespoon at a time, to make a total of 15 scones. Place scones at least 1 inch apart on the baking sheet to allow for expansion during baking. Bake scones for 15 minutes.

5 Prepare Glaze: Combine 3 tablespoons sugar with the ground cinnamon, butter and cream to make a paste. Remove baked scones from oven and brush with glaze. Return to oven and bake for 2 minutes longer or until scones are lightly browned.

6 Remove scones from baking sheet and place in a napkin-lined basket to keep warm. Serve scones with whipped sweet butter, clotted cream (available at specialty food markets) or strawberry preserves. Makes 15 scones.

BREAKFAST SCONES

SCONES
3 cups packaged biscuit mix
2 tablespoons sugar
½ cup currants or chopped dark seedless raisins

1 cup milk

GLAZE
3 tablespoons sugar

¼ teaspoon ground cinnamon
1 tablespoon butter or margarine, melted
1 tablespoon heavy cream

AN ENGLISH TEA-CAKE BREAD

This very light bread is named for the woman who invented it: Sally Lunn. Tradition says that Sally, a resident of Bath, England, made small tea cakes for Beau Brummell, the early 19th-century English dandy. These cakes were rich with cream and butter and quickly became a local favorite for breakfast and tea. Since small tea cakes are tedious to make, we suggest making one large bread. To retain its lightness, split the warm bread apart with two forks, or, after cooling, serve the bread sliced, toasted and buttered.

1 Put milk in a small saucepan and heat over medium heat until bubbles form around edge of pan; remove from heat. Add 2 tablespoons sugar, salt and ⅓ cup butter, stirring until butter is melted. Let cool at room temperature until lukewarm.

2 If possible, check temperature of warm water with a thermometer to make sure it is not too hot (too much heat kills yeast). Put water in a large bowl of an electric mixer and sprinkle with yeast. Let stand about 5 minutes and stir to dissolve yeast.

3 When yeast is dissolved, add milk mixture, eggs and all of the flour. Beat at medium speed for about 2 minutes or until batter is smooth and no lumps of flour remain. Cover bowl with waxed paper and then a damp kitchen towel.

4 Let batter rise in a warm place (85F), free from drafts, for about 1 hour or until double in bulk. The batter should be bubbly. Meanwhile, grease a 10-by-4½-inch tube pan *without* a removable bottom with solid vegetable shortening.

5 Beat yeast batter vigorously for ½ minute, using a wooden spoon. Pour batter into the prepared pan; cover with waxed paper and a towel; let rise in a warm place (85F), free from drafts, until double in bulk (about 45 minutes). Preheat oven to 350F.

6 Bake cake for 35 to 40 minutes or until golden brown. Remove from pan to a wire rack; brush with 1 tablespoon melted butter. Serve warm. This cake should not be cut with a knife, instead split into pieces with two forks. Makes 1 cake.

VIRGINIA SALLY LUNN

1 cup milk	⅓ cup butter or margarine	4 cups sifted all-purpose flour
2 tablespoons sugar	½ cup warm water (105 to 115F)	(sifted before measuring)
1 teaspoon salt	1 pkg active dry yeast	1 tablespoon melted butter
	3 eggs	

AN EASTER TREASURE

This Austrian Easter Braid is a rich twist of sweet yeast
dough studded with almonds and raisins—and a real egg! It
is truly festive and will be a beautiful addition to your next
Easter brunch. And you can make the bread in half the
usual time because you use quick-rising yeast!

1 In small saucepan, heat milk just until bubbles form around edge of pan. Remove from heat; add sugar, salt and butter, stirring until butter melts. Cool to lukewarm. Sprinkle yeast over warm water in large bowl of electric mixer; stir until dissolved. Add milk mixture.

2 Beat 3 egg yolks and 1 whole egg with fork; add to milk mixture. Add lemon peel and 2½ cups of flour; beat with electric mixer until smooth (about 2 minutes). Gradually add 2 cups flour; mix with hands until dough is stiff enough to leave bowl; mix in remaining ¼ cup flour if needed.

3 Turn dough out onto a lightly floured pastry cloth or board. Knead until smooth and elastic (about 10 minutes). Knead in raisins and chopped almonds. Place in a lightly greased large bowl; turn over to bring greased side up. Cover with a towel.

4 Place bowl of dough in a warm place (85F), free from drafts, and let rise for about 45 minutes or until double in bulk. Turn dough out onto a lightly floured pastry cloth or board; divide into three equal parts. Using palms of hands, roll each piece into a 24-inch-long strip.

5 Braid dough strips; press ends together to seal. Place braid on large, greased cookie sheet. Put whole egg (still in shell) in center of the middle strip. Cover with a towel and let rise about 25 to 30 minutes or until double in bulk. Preheat oven to 375F.

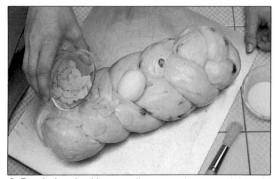

6 Brush dough with egg yolk-water mixture; sprinkle with sliced almonds. Bake 35 to 40 minutes or until a rich golden brown. (If crust seems too brown after 25 minutes of baking, cover with aluminum foil.) Let cool on wire rack; serve warm. Makes 1 braid.

AUSTRIAN EASTER BRAID

¾ cup milk
½ cup sugar
1 teaspoon salt
½ cup butter or margarine
2 pkg quick-rise active dry yeast
½ cup warm water
(105 to 115F)

3 egg yolks
1 whole egg
1 tablespoon grated lemon peel
4¾ cups unsifted all-purpose flour
½ cup raisins

¼ cup chopped blanched almonds
1 whole egg
1 egg yolk beaten with 1 tablespoon water
2 tablespoons sliced blanched almonds

David Viens

9801-01

Cakes, Cookies 4

THE PERFECT CHOCOLATE CAKE

We're going to come right out and say it: This is the most delicious chocolate cake you ever tasted! Moist, light, sinfully rich, made with cocoa, lots of chocolate, and whipped cream, it can't be found in a bakery or made from a cake mix. Follow our recipe exactly—accurate measurements, no substitutions, the right pan size—and you'll have a perfect dessert that you (and we) can really be proud of. Turn the page for step-by-step directions.

1 In medium bowl, combine cocoa with boiling water, mixing with wire whisk until smooth. Cool completely. Sift flour with soda, salt, and baking powder. Preheat oven to 350F. Grease well and lightly flour three 9-by-1½-inch layer-cake pans.

2 In large bowl of electric mixer, at high speed, beat butter, sugar, eggs, and vanilla, scraping bowl occasionally, until light—about 5 minutes. At low speed, beat in flour mixture (in fourths), alternately with cocoa mixture (in thirds), beginning

3 and ending with flour mixture. Do not overbeat. Divide evenly into pans; smooth top. Bake 25 to 30 minutes, or until surface springs back when gently pressed with fingertip. Cool in pans 10 minutes. Carefully loosen sides with spatula; remove

4 from pans; cool on racks. Frosting: In medium saucepan, combine chocolate pieces, cream, butter; stir over medium heat until smooth. Remove from heat. With whisk, blend in 2½ cups confectioners' sugar. In bowl set over ice, beat until it

5 holds shape. Filling: Whip cream with sugar and vanilla; refrigerate. To assemble cake: On plate, place a layer, top side down; spread with half of cream. Place second layer, top side down; spread with rest of cream. Place third layer, top side

6 up. To frost: With spatula, frost sides first, covering whipped cream; use rest of frosting on top, swirling decoratively. Refrigerate at least 1 hour before serving. To cut, use a thin-edged sharp knife; slice with a sawing motion. Serves 10 to 12.

PERFECT CHOCOLATE CAKE

CAKE
1 cup unsifted unsweetened
  cocoa
2 cups boiling water
2¾ cups sifted
  all-purpose flour
2 teaspoons baking soda
½ teaspoon salt
½ teaspoon baking powder

1 cup butter or regular
  margarine, softened
2½ cups granulated sugar
4 eggs
1½ teaspoons vanilla extract
FROSTING
1 pkg (6 oz) semisweet
  chocolate pieces
½ cup light cream

1 cup butter or regular
  margarine
2½ cups unsifted
  confectioners' sugar
FILLING
1 cup heavy cream, chilled
¼ cup unsifted confectioners'
  sugar
1 teaspoon vanilla extract

8602-2

This sumptuous-looking cake is delicious any way you slice it, but is even better if made a day ahead and refrigerated. The fluffiest of butter

A CREAMY COCONUT CAKE

cakes layered with a fresh lemon-and-lime filling, it is frosted with whipped cream, covered with grated coconut. Directions, next page.

1 Preheat oven to 350F. Grease and flour three (9-by-1½-inch) round pans. Sift flour with baking powder and ½ teaspoon salt. In large bowl of mixer, at high speed, beat butter and 2 cups sugar until light. Add 4 eggs, one at a time; beat after each addition.

2 Continue beating, occasionally scraping bowl with rubber scraper, until fluffy—2 minutes. At low speed, beat in flour mixture (in fourths) alternately with milk (in thirds), beginning and ending with flour. Add vanilla. Beat just until smooth—about 1 minute.

3 Pour into prepared pans; bake 25 to 30 minutes, or until surface springs back when gently pressed with finger. Cool in pans on wire racks 10 minutes. Remove from pans; cool on racks. Filling: In small saucepan, mix 1 cup sugar with cornstarch and salt.

4 Gradually stir in orange, lemon and lime juices and the water. Bring to boiling over medium heat, stirring. Remove from heat. Add egg yolks, one at a time, beating well after each addition. Bring to boiling, stirring; boil 1 minute. Remove the pan from heat.

5 Stir in lemon and lime peels and a few drops color. Turn into bowl; cool over ice water. Make frosting: In medium bowl, combine cream and confectioners' sugar. Refrigerate ½ hour. Beat until stiff. Measure 1 cup whipped cream, and, with whisk, fold into filling.

6 Place one cake layer, top side down, on large cake plate. Spread with half of filling almost to outer edge. Repeat with second layer and rest of filling; place top layer right side up. Frost with rest of whipped cream; decorate with coconut and lime. Refrigerate.

COCONUT-CREAM CAKE WITH LEMON-AND-LIME FILLING

CAKE
2½ cups sifted (sift before measuring) all-purpose flour
2½ teaspoons baking powder
½ teaspoon salt
1 cup butter or regular margarine, softened
2 cups granulated sugar
4 eggs
1 cup milk

1 teaspoon vanilla extract

FILLING
1 cup granulated sugar
3 tablespoons cornstarch
½ teaspoon salt
½ cup orange juice
2 tablespoons lemon juice
2 tablespoons lime juice
¼ cup water

3 egg yolks
1 tablespoon grated lemon peel
1 tablespoon grated lime peel
Green food color (optional)

FROSTING
2 cups heavy cream, chilled
½ cup sifted confectioners' sugar
1 can (4 oz) flaked coconut
3 thin slices lime, halved

M-M-MOCHA CAKE

For a dessert that's as special as your celebration: mocha cream cake. In a wonderful marriage of flavor and texture, the chocolaty layers are joined with mocha frosting; the top is ringed with chocolate-dipped almonds. See next page for the step-by-step recipe.

1 In double-boiler top, combine chocolate and hot water. Stir constantly over hot, not boiling, water, to melt chocolate. Add ½ cup granulated sugar; cook, stirring, 2 minutes, to dissolve. Remove from hot water. Cool to lukewarm. Sift flour with soda and salt.

2 Preheat oven to 350F. Grease and lightly flour two 9-by-1½-inch round layer-cake pans. In large mixer bowl, at medium speed, beat butter until fluffy. Gradually beat in 1¼ cups granulated sugar, beating until very light and fluffy—5 minutes. Add vanilla.

3 Add eggs, one at a time; beat well after each addition, scraping down side of bowl and beaters. At low speed, add flour mixture (in fourths) alternately with milk (in thirds); begin and end with flour. Beat just to blend. With scraper, blend in chocolate.

4 Turn into pans. Bake 25 minutes, or until surface springs back when gently pressed with finger. Do not overbake. Cool 10 minutes. Loosen sides with spatula. Remove layers; cool on racks. In medium bowl, combine cream, sugar, cocoa, salt and coffee.

5 Refrigerate, covered, ½ hour. Beat with rotary beater until stiff. Refrigerate. With long, thin-bladed knife, split layers in half to make four. Place layer, cut side up, on plate. Spread with ⅔ cup mocha filling. Repeat twice. Top with last layer, cut side down.

6 Turn 1¼ cups mocha into pastry bag with number-2 star tip. With metal spatula, frost top and side of cake smoothly with remaining mocha. With pastry bag, make ruching around top and base, as pictured. Dip almonds in chocolate. Arrange on cake. Serves 10.

MOCHA CREAM CAKE

CAKE LAYERS
4 squares unsweetened chocolate
½ cup hot water
½ cup granulated sugar
2 cups sifted (sift before measuring) cake flour
1 teaspoon baking soda
1 teaspoon salt

½ cup butter or regular margarine, softened
1¼ cups granulated sugar
1 teaspoon vanilla extract
3 eggs
⅔ cup milk

MOCHA FROSTING AND FILLING
3 cups heavy cream, chilled

1½ cups sifted confectioners' sugar
½ cup sifted unsweetened cocoa
⅛ teaspoon salt
2 teaspoons instant coffee

½ square semisweet chocolate, melted
14 whole unblanched almonds

8605-02

SENSATIONAL STRAWBERRY CAKE

Sweet ripe strawberries and meringue turn a simple layer cake into a spectacular dessert. The cake rounds are baked first, returned briefly to the oven topped with meringue, and then—when cool—layered with fruit and whipped cream. The recipe, next page.

1 Sift flour with baking powder and salt three times; set aside. Preheat oven to 375F. Grease well and lightly flour two 9-by-1½-inch layer pans. In large bowl of mixer, at medium speed, cream butter until light. Gradually beat in sugar until light and fluffy.

2 Beat in egg yolks, half at a time; beat until very light. At low speed, beat in flour mixture (in fourths) alternately with milk (in thirds), beginning and ending with flour mixture. Beat just until combined. Add vanilla. Divide evenly into cake pans; smooth tops.

3 Bake 20 to 25 minutes, until tops spring back when gently pressed with finger. Do not overbake. Meanwhile, in small bowl of mixer, let whites warm to room temperature—1 hour. Cool layers in pans on racks 5 minutes. Loosen edges with sharp knife.

4 Invert on cake racks to cool. Place cooled layers on cookie sheets. Preheat oven to 350F. At high speed, beat whites just until soft peaks form when beater is slowly raised. Beat in ½ cup sugar, 2 tablespoons at a time, beating after each addition.

5 Beat until stiff peaks form when beaters are slowly raised. Spread meringue lightly on layers. Bake 10 to 15 minutes, until meringue is golden. Let cool on racks. Reserve half of berries for top of cake. Slice rest into bowl. Sprinkle with ½ cup sugar; chill.

6 To serve: Place one layer on cake plate. Top with sliced berries. Spread with whipped cream. Place second layer on top. Halve reserved berries; arrange on cake; brush with jelly. Serve at once or within several hours. Do not refrigerate. Serves 10.

STRAWBERRY MERINGUE CAKE

2 cups sifted cake flour
(sift before measuring)
2 teaspoons baking powder
⅛ teaspoon salt
½ cup butter, softened
1 cup sugar

4 egg yolks, slightly beaten
¾ cup milk
1 teaspoon vanilla extract

MERINGUE
4 egg whites

Sugar
1 quart strawberries,
washed and hulled
1 cup heavy cream, whipped
¼ cup currant jelly,
melted

8606-02

Our light and lemony daffodil cake is really two cakes in one—a golden, rich spongecake and a delicate angel-food cake. The batters are made separately and swirled together into marble cake right in the baking pan. What's more, it's

A LIGHT AND LEMONY CAKE

one of the least expensive cakes you can bake. The basic ingredients are flour, sugar and eggs—and the absence of butter makes this recipe a boon for dieters. The cake will stay fresh and moist for days. Instructions, next page.

1 Make white batter: In large bowl, let whites warm to room temperature 1 hour. Sift 1¼ cups flour with ½ cup sugar; resift three times. With electric mixer at high speed, beat whites with salt and cream of tartar until soft peaks form when beater is slowly raised.

2 Beat in 1 cup sugar, ¼ cup at a time, beating well after each addition. Beat until stiff peaks form when beater is slowly raised. With wire whisk, fold vanilla into egg whites until combined. Sift flour mixture, one fourth at a time, over egg whites.

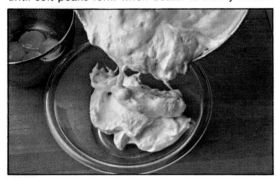

3 With wire whisk, using an under-and-over motion, gently fold in each addition with 15 strokes, rotating bowl a quarter of a turn after each addition. Fold ten more strokes, to blend completely. Turn one third batter into medium bowl. Preheat oven to 375F.

4 Make yellow batter: In small bowl, combine yolks, cake flour and sugar. With mixer at high speed, beat until very thick. Add lemon peel. With wire whisk, using an under-and-over motion, fold yolk mixture into reserved one third batter with 15 strokes.

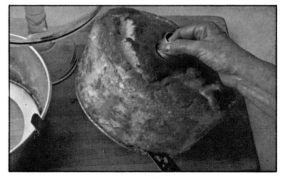

5 For marbling, spoon batters alternately into an ungreased 10-inch tube pan, ending with white batter on top. With knife, cut through batter twice. With rubber scraper, gently spread batter in pan until it is smooth on top and touches side of pan all around.

6 Bake on lower oven rack 35 to 40 minutes, or until cake springs back when pressed with fingertip. Invert pan over neck of bottle to cool 2 hours. With spatula, loosen cake from pan; remove. Sprinkle with confectioners' sugar, if desired. Serves 10.

McCALL'S BEST DAFFODIL CAKE

WHITE BATTER
1¾ cups egg whites (12 to 14)
1¼ cups sifted cake flour
(sift before measuring)
1½ cups sugar
½ teaspoon salt

1½ teaspoons cream of tartar
1½ teaspoons vanilla extract

YELLOW BATTER
5 egg yolks
2 tablespoons cake flour

2 tablespoons sugar
2 tablespoons grated lemon peel

Confectioners' sugar

Note: To get good volume, let egg whites warm to room temperature before beating them. Be sure to use cake (not all-purpose) flour in this recipe. If you are baking the cake a day ahead, leave it in the pan overnight, and remove it just before serving. Cut cake with a knife with a serrated edge, using a light, sawing motion. Nice served with ice cream.

Stiffly beaten egg whites are the secret of a chiffon cake that's as light as angel food—and its center is filled with devilishly rich chocolate cream. Give in to temptation and turn the page for the complete step-by-step recipe.

CHOCOLATE~LOVERS' CHIFFON CAKE

1 Make cake: In large electric mixer bowl, let whites warm to room temperature—1 hour. Into cocoa in small bowl, stir boiling water; stir until smooth; let cool ½ hour. Preheat oven to 325F. Sift flour with sugar, soda and salt in large bowl. Make a well in center.

2 Pour in oil, yolks, vanilla and cocoa. With wooden spoon, beat just until smooth. Sprinkle cream of tartar over whites. With mixer at high speed, beat until very stiff peaks form when beater is slowly raised. Do not underbeat. Pour batter over whites.

3 With whisk, and an under-and-over motion, gently fold to combine. Turn into ungreased 10-inch tube pan. Bake 60 to 65 minutes, until top springs back when pressed with finger. Invert over neck of bottle; cool 1½ hours. With spatula, loosen cake; remove.

4 Cool on rack. Make chocolate filling: In large bowl, combine cream, sugar, cocoa, vanilla, salt; refrigerate 1 hour. With mixer, beat until stiff; refrigerate. Sprinkle gelatine over 2 tablespoons cold water to soften. Heat, stirring, over hot water to dissolve; cool.

5 Prepare cake: Cut 1-inch slice crosswise from top of cake; set aside. With sharp knife, outline a cavity in cake, leaving 1-inch-thick walls around center, side and bottom. With spoon carefully remove cake from this area. Reserve 1½ cups crumbled cake.

6 Measure 2½ cups chocolate filling into small bowl; fold in gelatine. Use to fill cavity. Replace top. Mix ½ cup filling with reserved crumbled cake. Use to fill center hole. Frost top and side of cake with remaining filling. Refrigerate until serving. Serves 12.

CHOCOLATE MOUSSE CAKE

CHOCOLATE CHIFFON CAKE
1 cup egg whites (7 or 8)
½ cup sifted* unsweetened cocoa
¾ cup boiling water
1¾ cups sifted* cake flour

*sift before measuring

1¾ cups sugar
1½ teaspoons baking soda
1 teaspoon salt
½ cup salad oil
7 egg yolks
2 teaspoons vanilla extract
½ teaspoon cream of tartar

CHOCOLATE FILLING
3 cups heavy cream
1½ cups sifted* confectioners' sugar
¾ cup sifted* unsweetened cocoa
2 teaspoons vanilla extract
¼ teaspoon salt
1 teaspoon unflavored gelatine

Make any occasion special by crowning it with a dessert that's as wholesome
as it is delicious. Our carrot-walnut cake is rich with nuts and raisins and is covered
with a snowy cream-cheese glaze. And it's moist enough to last for days.
Step-by-step instructions on the next page.

THE RICHEST CARROT CAKE EVER

1 Lightly grease and flour a 10-by-4-inch tube pan. Sift flour with baking powder, soda, cinnamon and salt; set aside. Wash and pare carrots; grate on medium grater, or use coarse blade of food processor. Should measure 4 cups. Preheat oven to 350F.

2 In large bowl of mixer, at high speed, beat butter and brown and granulated sugars, occasionally scraping side of bowl with rubber scraper, until light and fluffy—about 4 minutes. Add eggs, one at a time; beat well after each addition until smooth and light.

3 In measuring cup, combine lemon and orange peels and juices. At low speed, beat in flour mixture (in fourths), alternately with lemon-orange mixture (in thirds), beginning and ending with flour mixture. Beat just until smooth—about 1 minute.

4 With wooden spoon, stir in grated carrot, nuts and raisins; mix well. Turn into the prepared tube pan; spread evenly. Bake 60 minutes, or until a cake tester inserted in center of the cake comes out clean. Cool in pan on wire rack 20 minutes, to cool slightly.

5 Meanwhile, make cream-cheese glaze: In medium bowl, combine cream cheese, lemon juice, lemon peel and confectioners' sugar. With portable electric mixer at medium speed, beat mixture until smooth. Set aside. Gently loosen edge of cake with a spatula.

6 Turn out of pan onto rack. Spread glaze over top of the warm cake, letting it run down side of cake. Carefully remove cake to cake platter. Sprinkle chopped walnuts around top edge of cake. Serves 12. (Keeps well stored in a tightly covered cake tin.)

CARROT-WALNUT CAKE

3 cups unsifted all-purpose flour
2 teaspoons baking powder
1 teaspoon baking soda
1 teaspoon ground cinnamon
½ teaspoon salt
1 lb carrots
1 cup butter or regular margarine, softened

1 cup light-brown sugar, packed
1 cup granulated sugar
4 eggs
2 tablespoons grated lemon peel
2 tablespoons grated orange peel
2 tablespoons lemon juice
2 tablespoons orange juice
1 cup coarsely chopped walnuts

1 cup seedless raisins

CREAM-CHEESE GLAZE
1 pkg (8 oz) cream cheese, softened
1 tablespoon lemon juice
1 teaspoon grated lemon peel
1½ cups confectioners' sugar
½ cup coarsely chopped walnuts

A RICH, CREAMY CHOCOLATE CAKE

This chocolate cake would be downright sinful if it didn't taste so divine. We've made it irresistibly rich by layering it with a filling of dates, raisins and nuts, spread with whipped cream, and then lavishing on a silky sour-cream icing. Directions begin on the next page.

1 Preheat oven to 350F. Sift flour with soda into large bowl. Grease well and flour two 8-by-8-by-2-inch-square cake pans. In small saucepan, combine butter, oil and chocolate; stir over low heat to melt the chocolate. Add 1 cup water. Cool 15 minutes.

2 To flour mixture, add 2 cups sugar, the eggs, sour milk and 1 teaspoon vanilla; mix with wooden spoon. Stir in cooled chocolate just to combine. Quickly turn into prepared pans; bake 30 to 35 minutes, till surface springs back when pressed with finger.

3 Cool in pans 5 minutes. Carefully loosen sides with spatula. Turn out on racks; cool. Make filling: In small saucepan, combine milk, sugar and ¼ cup water. Cook over medium heat, stirring to dissolve sugar. Add raisins and dates. Stir with wooden spoon.

4 Cook, stirring, until mixture is thickened—about 5 minutes. Add vanilla and nuts. Cool completely. In small bowl, beat cream with rotary beater just until stiff. On plate, place layer, top side down; spread with filling, then whipped cream. Top with second layer.

5 Make frosting: Melt chocolate pieces in top of double boiler over hot water. Remove top of double boiler from hot water. Stir in sour cream and salt. With wooden spoon, beat until smooth. Cool 5 minutes, until frosting is of spreading consistency.

6 With spatula, frost top of cake, swirling decoratively; use rest of frosting to cover sides. Refrigerate one hour before serving. To serve: With sharp thin knife, mark top of cake into four quarters; then cut each quarter into four slices. Makes 16 servings.

CREOLE CHOCOLATE CAKE

CAKE
2 cups unsifted all-purpose flour
1 teaspoon baking soda
½ cup butter or regular margarine
½ cup salad oil
3 squares unsweetened chocolate
2 cups sugar
2 eggs, beaten

½ cup sour milk
(place 1½ teaspoons vinegar in a 1-cup measure; fill with milk to measure ½ cup)
1 teaspoon vanilla extract

FILLING
1 can (5.3 oz) evaporated milk
¾ cup sugar
¼ cup chopped seedless raisins

½ cup chopped dates
1 teaspoon vanilla extract
½ cup chopped walnuts or pecans
½ cup chilled heavy cream

FROSTING
1 pkg (6 oz) semisweet-chocolate pieces
½ cup sour cream
Dash salt

DIETER'S DELIGHT

Fluffy, light-as-a-feather angel-food cake is sheer heaven for dieters. It's by far the lowest in calories of all cakes—since the main ingredient is egg whites beaten to a froth. Whether you're dieting or not, serve it often—either plain, or with ice cream, sherbet or with fresh fruit.

1 Separate eggs while still cold from the refrigerator. Measure whites; pour into large bowl of electric mixer to warm to room temperature—about 1 hour. Sift flour; measure, then sift with ¾ cup sugar; resift three times. Preheat the oven to 375F.

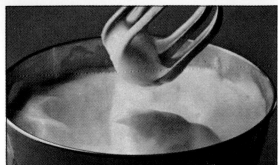

2 At medium speed, beat whites with salt and cream of tartar just until soft peaks form when beater is slowly raised. Do not overbeat. (Bowl, beaters, wire whisk and rubber scraper must be free of any grease as it retards beating of egg whites.)

3 At high speed, gradually beat in 1 cup sugar, ¼ cup at a time, beating well after each addition. Continue beating until stiff peaks form when beater is slowly raised. With wire whisk or rubber scraper, gently fold extracts into whites to combine.

4 Sprinkle one fourth of flour mixture over whites. With wire whisk, using an under-and-over motion, gently fold flour mixture into whites (about 15 strokes), rotating bowl a quarter turn after each stroke, folding just until flour mixture disappears.

5 Continue folding in flour mixture, one fourth at a time, as in step 4. With rubber scraper, gently push batter into an ungreased 10-inch tube pan. With knife, cut through batter twice to remove any large air bubbles. Spread evenly, to smooth the top.

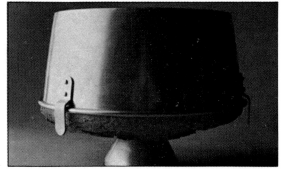

6 Bake on lowest rack in oven 30 to 35 minutes, or until top springs back when gently pressed with finger. Invert pan over neck of bottle to cool completely—2 hours. With knife, loosen cake from side of pan; turn out. Serve right side up. Serves 12.

ANGEL-FOOD CAKE

1¾ cups egg whites (12 to 14 whites, depending on size of the eggs)	1¼ cups sifted cake flour (sift before measuring) 1¾ cups granulated sugar ½ teaspoon salt	1½ teaspoons cream of tartar 1 teaspoon vanilla extract ½ teaspoon almond extract

Note: To get good volume, let egg whites warm to room temperature before beating them. Be sure to use cake (not all-purpose) flour in this recipe. If you are baking the cake a day ahead, leave it in the pan and remove it just before serving. Cut cake with a knife with a serrated edge, using a light sawing motion.

POUNDCAKE: PENNY-WISE AND POUND-WISE, TOO

In the old days, a poundcake was literally a "pound cake"—it took a pound of butter, a pound of eggs, a pound of sugar, a pound of flour, and considerable culinary skill to make one. Consequently, poundcake was a special treat, to be saved for special occasions.

A perfect poundcake is still a special treat, but the old rule of thumb has given way to a more scientific blend of ingredients, and a perfect cake depends more on a good recipe than great culinary skill. Here is our best poundcake recipe.

1 With a little shortening, lightly grease bottom and side of a 10-inch tube pan. Sprinkle with a little flour. Rotate to coat inside of pan evenly; shake out excess flour.

2 Sift flour on waxed paper. Gently spoon into a 1-cup measure; level off. Measure 3 cups flour in all. Turn back into sifter, along with baking powder and ¼ teaspoon salt.

3 Sift all together onto waxed paper; set aside. With mixer at high speed, beat egg whites with ¼ teaspoon salt till foamy throughout. Beat in 1 cup sugar, ¼ cup at a time,

POUNDCAKE

CAKE
- 8 egg whites (1 cup)
- 3 cups sifted all-purpose flour
- 1 teaspoon baking powder
- salt
- 2 cups granulated sugar
- 8 egg yolks
- 2 cups butter or regular margarine (4 sticks)
- 1 tablespoon grated orange peel
- 2 tablespoons grated lemon peel
- 2 tablespoons lemon juice

First, separate eggs, turning yolks into one large bowl and whites into another. Let egg whites warm to room temperature—about 1 hour. Preheat oven to 350F.

GLAZE
- 1 tablespoon butter
- 1 package (1 pound) confectioners' sugar
- 1 teaspoon grated lemon peel
- ⅓ cup lemon juice

4 beating well after each addition. Beat until soft peaks form when beater is slowly raised. On foil or waxed paper, grate orange and lemon peels on fine grater; measure.

5 In large bowl, at high speed, with same beater (don't wash), beat butter with remaining cup of sugar until light and fluffy—5 minutes. Beat in yolks until light and fluffy.

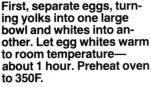

6 At high speed, beat in peels, lemon juice, and 2 tablespoons water until smooth. Divide flour mixture into thirds; at low speed, blend in, ⅓ at a time, just until combined—

7 takes about 1 minute. At low speed, blend in egg whites, half at a time, just until blended, scraping bowl and guiding batter into the beater. (Be sure not to overmix.)

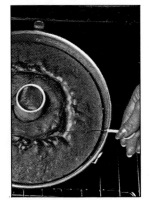

8 Turn batter into prepared pan, cleaning bowl with rubber scraper. Bake, in middle of oven, 60 minutes, or until cake tester inserted in center of cake comes out clean.

9 Cool on rack 15 minutes. Gently loosen sides with spatula; turn out; cool. To glaze: Blend butter, sugar, lemon juice, peel until smooth. Then drizzle over cake.

A LOVELY LAYER CAKE

This chocolate cake looks like such a professional creation your guests will hardly believe it's homemade. Only you know how easy to make: three buttermilk layers—top and bottom with cocoa mixture, center with pistachio nuts—are baked and assembled with whipped cream. All, frosted with chocolate icing, decorated with more pistachio nuts.

1 Cake layers: In small bowl, mix cocoa with boiling water. Cool completely. Preheat oven to 350F. Grease and flour three 8-by-1½-inch layer-cake pans. Sift flour, baking powder, soda and salt. In large bowl of electric mixer, combine the butter, sugar, eggs and vanilla.

2 Beat at high speed until fluffy—about 5 minutes, occasionally scraping side of bowl and guiding mixture into beaters with rubber scraper. At low speed, blend in flour mixture (in fourths), alternately with buttermilk: Begin and end with flour mixture; beat just until smooth.

3 Measure 1⅔ cups batter into a small bowl. Stir in ½ cup chopped nuts; pour into a prepared pan. Add cocoa mixture to remaining batter; mix until smooth; divide evenly between other pans. Bake 30 to 35 minutes, until cake tester inserted in center of cake comes out clean.

4 Cool 10 minutes on rack; remove from pans; cool completely. Whip heavy cream until stiff; refrigerate. Frosting: In saucepan, heat cream until bubbles form; remove from heat. Add the hot cream to butter, cocoa, 1½ cups confectioners' sugar, corn syrup and vanilla.

5 With portable mixer or wooden spoon, beat frosting until smooth. Add remaining confectioners' sugar, beating until smooth and thick enough to spread. To assemble cake: Place one chocolate layer on cake plate, right side down; spread with half of the whipped cream.

6 Place the nut cake layer on next; spread with rest of whipped cream. Top with remaining chocolate layer, right side up. With spatula, spread frosting on the side and top; garnish top edge of cake with the coarsely chopped nuts. Refrigerate. Makes 12 servings.

COCOA-NUT LAYER CAKE

CAKE LAYERS
½ cup unsweetened cocoa
½ cup boiling water
1¾ cups unsifted all-purpose flour
1 teaspoon baking powder
1 teaspoon baking soda
⅛ teaspoon salt
½ cup butter or regular margarine, softened

2 cups granulated sugar
2 eggs
1 teaspoon vanilla extract
1⅓ cups buttermilk
½ cup finely chopped pistachio nuts or walnuts
1 cup heavy cream

CHOCOLATE FROSTING
⅓ cup light cream

⅓ cup butter or regular margarine
⅔ cup unsweetened cocoa
2⅔ cups sifted confectioners' sugar
1 teaspoon light corn syrup
1 teaspoon vanilla extract
¼ cup coarsely chopped pistachio nuts or walnuts

Pineapple upside-down cake probably brings back memories of your childhood when your mother made this simple dessert for a perfect end to a Sunday dinner. And you can make it in a matter of about 20 minutes from ingredients you probably have on hand! The juice from the

AN UPSIDE-DOWN DELIGHT

tart-but-sweet pineapple combines with the brown-sugar caramel to create a delicious sauce that slowly soaks into the light, fluffy cake. It's a wonderful and easy dessert that can be topped off with whipped cream or ice cream. Why don't you try it right now?

1 Preheat oven to 350F. Drain pineapple slices, reserving 2 tablespoons of the syrup. In a very heavy or iron, 10-inch skillet with heat-resistant handle, melt butter over medium heat. Add brown sugar, stirring until sugar is melted. Remove from heat.

2 Arrange 8 pineapple slices on sugar mixture, overlapping slices slightly around edge of pan. Put one slice in center. Fill centers with pecan halves. Halve three remaining pineapple slices. Arrange around inside edge of skillet. Put pecans in centers.

3 Into medium bowl, sift flour with granulated sugar, baking powder and salt. Add shortening and milk. With electric mixer at high speed, beat 2 minutes, or until mixture is smooth. Add egg and reserved 2 tablespoons pineapple syrup; beat 2 minutes longer.

4 Gently pour cake batter over pineapple in skillet, spreading evenly, being careful not to disarrange pineapple. On rack in center of oven, bake 40 to 45 minutes, or until golden in color and surface of cake springs back when it's gently pressed with fingertip.

5 Let skillet stand on wire rack 5 minutes to cool just slightly. With rotary beater, beat cream until stiff. With small spatula, loosen cake from edge of skillet all around. Place serving platter over the cake, and turn upside down; shake gently; lift off skillet.

6 Serve cake warm, with the whipped cream or ice cream. *Note:* The pineapple upside-down cake was traditionally baked in an iron skillet. If your skillet does not have an iron or heatproof handle, wrap handle in foil before placing in the oven. Serves 8.

OLD-FASHIONED PINEAPPLE UPSIDE-DOWN CAKE

3 cans (8¼-oz size) sliced pineapple in heavy syrup (12 slices)
¼ cup butter or margarine
⅔ cup light brown sugar, packed

⅓ cup pecan halves
1 cup unsifted all-purpose flour
¾ cup granulated sugar
1½ teaspoons baking powder
½ teaspoon salt

¼ cup shortening
½ cup milk
1 egg
1 cup heavy cream, chilled, or 1 pint vanilla ice cream

8626-03

The Swiss make these charming cookies to celebrate Christmas. They're called Biberli and are made with honey. Their outer shells

A HONEY OF A COOKIE

curl over a luscious filling flavored with apricot, lemon, and almond. They're so delicious, you'll want to treat your family with them year round!

1 Make dough: In small saucepan, combine 1 cup honey, ⅔ cup sugar and 2 tablespoons water. Heat, stirring with wooden spoon, until sugar dissolves—do not boil. Cool until lukewarm—about 20 minutes. Stir in 1½ teaspoons lemon peel and the brandy.

2 Into large bowl, sift flour with baking soda, anise, cinnamon, ginger, cloves and coriander. Add honey mixture; mix with wooden spoon to a stiff dough; then, with hands, knead in bowl until smooth. Shape into a ball. Refrigerate dough, covered, overnight.

3 Next day, make filling: In bowl, combine almonds, 1 cup sugar, the preserves, honey, lemon peel and juice and almond extract; mix well. Preheat oven to 350F. On lightly floured surface, roll half of dough into a rectangle 10 inches wide and 12 inches long.

4 Cut crosswise into four strips, 10 by 3 inches each. Place 5 tablespoons filling in a ¼-inch-wide mound down center of each strip. Bring edges of dough over filling, to overlap; press to seal. Turn rolls seam side down. Repeat with remaining dough and filling.

5 Cut rolls into 1-inch pieces, using moistened sharp knife. Place, seam side down, on lightly greased cookie sheets. Bake 20 minutes on high rack. Make glaze: In heavy saucepan, combine granulated sugar with ½ cup water. Bring to boil, stirring.

6 Boil 5 to 7 minutes, or until 2-inch thread forms from tip of spoon, or to 230F on candy thermometer. Remove from heat. Stir in confectioners' sugar; use at once. Brush warm cookies with glaze. Cool. Store in cookie tin to mellow two weeks. Makes 80.

SWISS BIBERLI

DOUGH
1 cup honey
⅔ cup granulated sugar
1½ teaspoons grated lemon peel
2 tablespoons brandy, rum or kirsch
4 cups unsifted all-purpose flour
2 teaspoons baking soda
1 teaspoon ground anise

¼ teaspoon ground cinnamon
¼ teaspoon ground ginger
¼ teaspoon ground cloves
¼ teaspoon ground coriander

FILLING
3 cups blanched almonds, finely ground
1 cup granulated sugar

½ cup apricot preserves
⅓ cup honey
1 tablespoon grated lemon peel
3 tablespoons lemon juice
1½ teaspoons almond extract

GLAZE
1½ cups granulated sugar
¾ cup sifted confectioners' sugar

8626-04

Some occasions call for a very special cake, and what could be more special than this spectacular confection? It's a strawberry cream cake, covered with whipped cream and strawberries glazed with melted currant jelly. Underneath, a delicate lemon spongecake baked in a tube pan and carefully cut into three layers—our toothpick method makes the job foolproof. For step-by-step illustrations, turn the page.

A STRAWBERRY SPECTACULAR

1 In large electric-mixer bowl, let egg whites warm to room temperature—1 hour. Sift flour with salt. With mixer at high speed, beat egg whites until foamy. Beat in ¾ cup of the granulated sugar, 2 tablespoons at a time, beating after each addition.

2 Beat until soft peaks form when beater is slowly raised. Preheat oven to 350F. In small mixer bowl, at high speed and with the same beater, beat yolks until very thick and lemon-colored. Gradually beat in remaining granulated sugar; beat 2 minutes.

3 At low speed, gradually beat in flour mixture. Add lemon juice, 2 tablespoons water and the lemon peel, beating just to combine—1 minute. With wire whisk, with an under-and-over motion, gently fold egg-yolk mixture into egg whites just to blend.

4 Pour batter into an ungreased 10-by-4-inch tube pan; bake 40 minutes, or until top springs back when gently pressed with fingertip. Invert pan over neck of bottle; let cake cool completely—1 hour. With spatula, carefully loosen cake from pan; remove cake.

5 Divide cake into thirds with toothpicks. With these as guide, split cake into three layers, using a long-bladed serrated knife. Place bottom layer, cut side up, on plate. Slice 1 pint berries. In medium bowl, beat cream with confectioners' sugar; add vanilla.

6 Spread bottom layer with ¾ cup cream and half of sliced berries. Repeat with second layer. Top with last layer, cut side down. Frost top and side with rest of whipped cream; toss 1 pint berries with jelly. Arrange on the cake. Refrigerate 1 hour. Serves 12.

STRAWBERRY CREAM CAKE

6 egg whites
1¾ cups sifted (sift before measuring) all-purpose flour
½ teaspoon salt
1½ cups granulated sugar

6 egg yolks
¼ cup fresh lemon juice
1 tablespoon grated lemon peel
2 pints strawberries, washed and hulled

2 cups heavy cream, chilled
½ cup confectioners' sugar
½ teaspoon vanilla extract
¼ cup currant jelly, melted

8627-02

FESTIVE OLD-COUNTRY COOKIES

Lebkuchen—spicy cookies studded with fruits and nuts—are a delicious alternative to fruitcake. Ours are made with molasses and chocolate, according to an old German family recipe, frosted and individually decorated with candied pineapple and cherry slices.

1 Preheat oven to 350F. Lightly grease a 15-by-10-by-1-inch jelly-roll pan. Line bottom with brown paper; then grease lightly. Coarsely chop dates and walnuts; chop citron finely. Turn into bowl; mix well. Sift flour with baking powder and the four spices.

2 In large bowl, with mixer at medium speed, beat butter and brown sugar until light. At high speed, beat in eggs, one at a time; beat until light and fluffy. Add chocolate and molasses; beat to blend well. At low speed, add flour mixture, beating until smooth.

3 With wooden spoon, stir in fruit-nut mixture. Gradually stir in bourbon to blend well. Stir in pineapple preserves. Pour batter into prepared pan, spreading evenly. Bake 45 to 50 minutes, or until cake tester inserted in the center comes out clean.

4 Cool in pan on wire rack. Wrap pan well in plastic film, then in foil; store in cool place, or refrigerate—keeps well several weeks. To serve, frost with snowy frosting: In small, heavy saucepan (1½-quart), combine granulated sugar, salt and ¼ cup water.

5 Over medium heat, bring to boiling; stir to dissolve sugar. Boil 5 minutes, without stirring, to 236F on candy thermometer, or until a little dropped from a spoon forms a 2-inch thread. Meanwhile, in small bowl, with mixer at medium speed, beat egg white.

6 Beat until stiff peaks form when beater is slowly raised. Pour syrup in continuous stream into egg white, beating constantly, until thick enough to spread. Frosting loses its gloss when set. Cut lebkuchen into bars; decorate as pictured. Makes 48.

NATHAN'S LEBKUCHEN

1 lb pitted dates
1½ cups walnuts or pecans
1 jar (4 oz) candied citron
1¼ cups unsifted all-purpose flour
¾ teaspoon baking powder
1½ teaspoons ground cinnamon
½ teaspoon ground cloves
½ teaspoon ground allspice

½ teaspoon nutmeg
½ cup butter or regular margarine, softened
¾ cup light-brown sugar, packed
3 eggs
1 square (1 oz) unsweetened chocolate, melted
¾ cup light or dark molasses

½ cup bourbon or other whisky
½ cup pineapple preserves

SNOWY FROSTING
1 cup granulated sugar
¼ teaspoon salt
1 egg white
Candied pineapple and cherries

Here's a sweet way of getting even the fussiest eater to eat zucchini — make a Chocolate Zucchini Cake! The shredded zucchini adds texture and moistness to the chocolate cake, not to mention all the vitamins and minerals. So let your children have their cake and rest assured that they are eating what they want and what you want, too!

A VITAMIN-PACKED CHOCOLATE CAKE

1 Generously grease a 10-inch fluted tube (Bundt) pan with vegetable shortening. Sprinkle with flour until well coated; invert pan and tap to remove excess flour. Preheat oven to 350F. Sift together flour, baking powder, baking soda, salt, cinnamon, and cocoa. Set aside.

2 Wash zucchini and dry with paper towels. Coarsely shred by hand or put through a food processor fitted with a shredding blade. Drain zucchini very well, squeezing with hands, if necessary, to remove all excess moisture. Discard accumulated liquid.

3 Put eggs in the large bowl of an electric mixer and beat on high speed for several minutes, scraping bowl as necessary until eggs are very light and fluffy. While beater is running, gradually add sugar and beat until eggs are pale and form ribbons when beater is lifted.

4 While beater is running, gradually add vegetable oil. Reduce mixer speed to low and add about one-third of the flour mixture and one-third of the buttermilk. Beat, scraping sides of bowl as necessary until mixture is smooth and no lumps of flour remain.

5 Add about half of the remaining flour and half of the buttermilk while beating batter constantly. Beat until there are no lumps of flour remaining, scraping bowl as necessary with rubber spatula. Repeat with remaining flour and buttermilk.

6 Fold zucchini, walnuts, raisins, and vanilla into batter. Turn into pan and bake 55 to 60 minutes or until cake tester comes out clean. Cool 10 minutes; turn out of pan and cool completely. Sprinkle with confectioners' sugar. Makes 12 servings.

CHOCOLATE ZUCCHINI CAKE

2 cups unsifted all-purpose flour	¼ cup unsweetened cocoa	¾ cup buttermilk
1 teaspoon baking powder	½ lb raw zucchini squash	1 cup coarsely chopped walnuts
1 teaspoon baking soda	3 eggs	½ cup dark seedless raisins
¼ teaspoon salt	1½ cups granulated sugar	1 teaspoon vanilla extract
1 teaspoon ground cinnamon	½ cup vegetable oil	Confectioners' sugar

Gordon E. Smith

8630-03

The next time you have guests over for dessert and coffee you'll want to serve them this impressive and delicious triple-layered Walnut-Raisin Spice Cake. Each layer is flavored with cinnamon, studded with raisins and walnuts, and frosted with a rich cream-cheese-and-butter frosting. Make it ahead of time and refrigerate it until your guests arrive. Then serve it with lots of hot coffee, or surprise everyone and make espresso or cappucino.

A GERMAN WALNUT-SPICE CAKE

1 Preheat oven to 350F. Grease and flour lightly three (8-by-1½-inch) layer-cake pans. Chop raisins and 1 cup walnuts fine; place in a medium bowl. Add baking soda; then stir in boiling water. Let mixture cool ½ hour. Sift flour with cinnamon and salt.

2 In large bowl, with electric mixer at medium speed, beat ¾ cup butter until creamy. Add sugar, a little at a time, beating until light and fluffy. Stop beater once or twice; scrape down side of bowl with rubber spatula. Add eggs and egg yolks, one at a time.

3 Beat after each addition; scrape side of bowl with rubber spatula. Beat until light and fluffy. Add lemon juice and 1½ teaspoons vanilla. With wooden spoon, beat in flour mixture, in fourths, alternately with nut mixture, in thirds; begin and end with flour mixture.

4 Pour batter into prepared pans. Place in oven, leaving space between pans. Bake 25 to 30 minutes, or until top springs back when lightly pressed with fingertip and cake pulls away from edge. Cool on wire rack 5 minutes. With small spatula, loosen edge.

5 Turn out on wire rack; turn top up; let cool completely—about 1 hour. Make frosting: In large bowl, with electric mixer at medium speed, beat cheese with butter and vanilla until creamy. Add the confectioners' sugar; beat until light and fluffy.

6 Using 1½ cups frosting, put layers together. Use rest of frosting to cover top and side of cake. With metal spatula, make decorative swirls in frosting; coarsely chop remaining walnuts; sprinkle around top. Refrigerate until serving. Makes 16 servings.

WALNUT-RAISIN SPICE CAKE

1½ cups seedless raisins
1½ cups walnuts
1½ teaspoons baking soda
1½ cups boiling water
2¼ cups sifted all-purpose flour
(sift before measuring)
1½ teaspoons cinnamon
¼ teaspoon salt

¾ cup butter or regular
margarine
1½ cups sugar
2 whole eggs
2 egg yolks
1½ teaspoons lemon juice
1½ teaspoons vanilla
extract

FROSTING
1 pkg (8 oz) cream cheese,
softened
⅔ cup butter or regular
margarine, softened
3 teaspoons vanilla
extract
1½ lb confectioners' sugar

8633-02

CREAM-CHEESE-FROSTED PUMPKIN CAKE

This pumpkin-spice cake is very moist and rich and the cream-cheese frosting keeps it that way for several days! In fact, the spice blend actually improves and mellows in flavor if the cake is made one day before serving. Re-member that the frosting is made with cheese and that the cake must be refrigerated to main-tain its freshness—especially during warm weather. But don't worry, this cake is so good that it won't be around very long!

1 Prepare Pumpkin Cake: Crack eggs into the large bowl of an electric mixer; cover and let stand 30 minutes until room temperature. Preheat oven to 350F. Meanwhile, sift flour with baking soda, salt, cloves, cinnamon, ginger and nutmeg.

2 With electric mixer at high speed, beat eggs thoroughly. Add sugar and continue to beat until eggs are lemony in color and the mixture is light and fluffy. Gradually add oil and pumpkin, beating well after each addition to blend thoroughly.

3 With electric mixer at low speed, beat in flour mixture, several spoonfuls at a time, beating only until flour is moistened. Pour into ungreased 10-inch tube pan without removable bottom. Bake about 1 hour, or until surface springs back when gently pressed with fingertips.

4 Remove cake from oven and cool completely in pan on wire rack. Meanwhile, prepare Cream-Cheese Frosting: In a small bowl, with electric mixer at medium speed, beat cream cheese with rum until smooth and soft. Gradually add confectioners' sugar, beating until light and fluffy.

5 Using a long, narrow metal spatula, carefully loosen cake from pan; remove. Place on cake plate and frost top and sides with cream-cheese frosting. Use the tip of the spatula to swirl the frosting in a spoke-like fashion in toward the center of the cake.

6 Arrange pecan or walnut halves decoratively around top edge of cake as shown in photo. Serve cake immediately or store, tightly covered, in refrigerator. Remove about 30 minutes before serving. Makes 12 servings.

PUMPKIN CAKE WITH CREAM-CHEESE FROSTING

CAKE
4 large eggs
2 cups all-purpose flour, sifted before measuring
2 teaspoons baking soda
½ teaspoon salt
1 teaspoon ground cloves
2 teaspoons ground cinnamon

½ teaspoon ground ginger
¼ teaspoon ground nutmeg
2 cups sugar
1 cup salad oil
1 can (1 lb) pumpkin

FROSTING
2 pkg (3 oz-size) cream cheese, softened
1 tablespoon rum *or* 1 teaspoon vanilla extract
3 cups confectioners' sugar
Pecan or walnut halves for garnish

Gordon E. Smith

8634-02

OLD-FASHIONED PLUM CAKE

This delicious cake will remind you of the ones Grandma made with fresh sour cream, eggs and just-picked plums. You can make it too—just wait for summer when sweet ripe plums are plentiful in the market. You'll love to serve it warm with whipped cream or vanilla ice cream. It's so good it's almost sinful!

1 Preheat oven to 350F. Thoroughly grease and flour a 9-inch springform pan. Sift flour with baking powder, baking soda and salt; set aside. In large bowl of an electric mixer, at high speed, beat butter, 1 cup sugar, eggs and vanilla until light and fluffy (about 5 minutes).

2 Reduce mixer speed to low. Alternately add about one-fourth of the flour mixture and one-third of the sour cream, beginning and ending with flour and beating thoroughly after each addition. After all has been added, scrape down sides of bowl and beat 1 minute longer.

3 Pour batter into prepared springform pan; spread evenly with rubber spatula. Put pan on center rack of oven and bake for about 50 minutes until cake is golden brown and a cake tester inserted in center of cake comes out clean.

4 Meanwhile, make Crumb Topping: Put sugar, flour, butter and cinnamon in a small bowl. Toss lightly with a pastry blender or two forks until mixture is crumbly and the butter is in fine pieces. Set aside.

5 Wash plums; dry well. Cut fresh plums in half, remove pits and discard. If using canned plums, drain thoroughly, cut in half and remove pits. Remove cake from oven and sprinkle with crumb topping. Arrange plums on top and bake 10 minutes longer.

6 Remove cake from oven and place on wire cake rack to cool for 10 minutes. Loosen cake from sides of pan, using a small knife or long metal spatula. Remove pan sides and brush plums with warm melted jam. Serve warm. Makes 10 servings.

SOUR-CREAM PLUM CAKE

2 cups unsifted all-purpose flour
1 teaspoon baking powder
½ teaspoon baking soda
¼ teaspoon salt
½ cup butter or margarine, softened
1 cup sugar

3 eggs
1 teaspoon vanilla extract
¾ cup sour cream

CRUMB TOPPING
¼ cup sugar
2 tablespoons all-purpose flour

1 tablespoon butter or margarine, softened
½ teaspoon ground cinnamon
9 fresh Italian plums or 9 canned purple plums
2 tablespoons plum jam or red currant jelly, melted

Cicero/Fimage Inc.

8636-03

LADY BALTIMORE CAKE

This spectacular showcase dessert can be a sumptuous finale to your next special dinner. It is made from delicate white layer cakes, joined by a brandied fruit-and-nut filling and surrounded with a white cloud of meringue frosting. Make the layer cakes and filling up to 1 day ahead, but for best results, assemble and frost the cake just an hour or two before serving.

1 Make Cake: Preheat oven to 375F. Grease and flour three 9-by-1½-inch round layer-cake pans. Sift flour with baking powder and salt. In large bowl, beat butter with electric mixer at high speed. Add vanilla and 1½ cups sugar; beat until very fluffy (about 2 minutes).

2 Gently fold flour mixture into butter mixture alternately with milk, beginning and ending with flour; set aside. With mixer at high speed, beat egg whites until soft peaks form when beaters are slowly raised. Gradually add remaining ½ cup sugar and beat until stiff peaks form.

3 Gently fold beaten egg whites into batter; do not over-mix. Spread into prepared pans and bake 25 to 30 minutes or until cake springs back when gently pressed with fingertip. Cool pans on wire racks for 10 minutes; turn out of pans and let cakes cool completely.

4 Make Filling: In medium bowl, mix dates, cherries, pecans, raisins and brandy; let stand at room temperature 1 hour. Make Frosting: In medium-sized saucepan, mix sugar, cream of tartar and water. Cook over medium heat, stirring until syrup registers 240F on a candy thermometer.

5 Meanwhile, beat egg whites at high speed with electric mixer until soft peaks form when beaters are slowly raised. Slowly pour hot syrup into egg whites while beating constantly with mixer at high speed. Add vanilla; beat until stiff. Mix 2 cups of this frosting with the fruit filling.

6 On serving plate put layers together, using half of the filling mixture on each of two layers. Frost top and sides of cake with remaining frosting. Decorate as pictured with dates, cherries and pecans. Refrigerate if keeping overnight. Makes 16 servings.

LADY BALTIMORE CAKE

CAKE
3½ cups sifted cake flour (sift before measuring)
4 teaspoons baking powder
1 teaspoon salt
1 cup butter or margarine, softened
2 teaspoons vanilla extract
2 cups sugar
1 cup milk

1 cup egg whites (7 or 8), at room temperature

FILLING
¾ cup chopped dates
½ cup chopped candied cherries
1 cup chopped pecans
½ cup chopped raisins
¼ cup brandy or bourbon

FROSTING
2¼ cups sugar
¾ teaspoon cream of tartar
½ cup water
¾ cup egg whites (5 or 6), at room temperature
¾ teaspoon vanilla extract
GARNISH
Date halves, candied red and green cherries, pecan halves

Cicero/Fimage Inc.

8637-02

A RUM-AND-SHERRY-SPIKED NUT CAKE

This nut-studded cake is rich and delicious and gets better with the passage of time! After baking, the cake is wrapped in sherry-soaked cheesecloth and aluminum foil and is stored for as little as 2 or 3 days or as long as several months—the longer it is mellowed, the better the flavor. At first glance it may seem to be an expensive cake to make, but the flavor is so rich that a very thin slice makes a satisfying serving. This 5¼-pound cake goes a long, long way!

1 Using solid vegetable shortening, lightly grease the inside of a 10-by-4½-inch tube pan *without* a removable bottom. Line the bottom of the pan with a piece of brown paper or waxed paper that has been cut to fit. Lightly grease paper with shortening.

2 Put nuts into a large mixing bowl. Sift flour, baking powder and salt over a piece of waxed paper and set aside. In a measuring cup, combine the milk with rum or brandy and set aside with other ingredients. Preheat oven to 275F.

3 Put butter and sugar into the large bowl of an electric mixer. Beat at medium speed, pushing mixture into center of bowl with a rubber spatula as necessary, until mixture is smooth and very light and fluffy. Add eggs, one at a time, beating thoroughly after each addition.

4 Reduce speed to low; beat in flour mixture (in fourths), alternately with milk mixture, beginning and ending with flour. Pour batter over nuts and mix well with a rubber spatula. Turn batter into prepared pan and spread evenly. Bake 2½ hours or until cake tests done.

5 Remove cake from oven and place pan on wire rack to cool for 30 minutes. Turn cake out of pan; remove and discard paper and place cake on wire rack to cool completely. To store: Wrap cake in cheesecloth that has been soaked in sherry wine; wrap cake in foil.

6 Store cake in a cool place for several days to mellow. (If storing for several weeks, keep in the refrigerator or freeze.) To serve: Sprinkle with confectioners' sugar. Cut cake into very thin slices and let warm to room temperature. Makes a 5¼-pound cake.

OLD-FASHIONED NUT CAKE

8 cups coarsely chopped walnuts or pecans
3½ cups sifted all-purpose flour, sift before measuring
2 teaspoons baking powder

½ teaspoon salt
¾ cup milk
¼ cup rum or brandy
1½ cups butter or margarine, softened

2 cups granulated sugar
6 eggs
Dry sherry wine
Confectioners' sugar

8639-02   Gordon E. Smith

Gingerbread, an old-fashioned spice-cake originally made from stale bread, is today made from flour spiced with ginger, cinnamon, nutmeg and molasses. Ours is dotted with raisins and is good served hot with whipped cream or sweet butter. A thin chocolate frosting can also dress up this tasty cake, or add some grated orange rind or a tablespoon of cocoa to the batter before baking. Be creative and use your imagination.

AN OLD-FASHIONED SPICECAKE

1 Preheat oven to 375F. Using solid vegetable shortening, grease a 13-by-9-by-2-inch baking pan. Lightly dust the inside with flour; tap out excess. Assemble all ingredients before you start, and bake the gingerbread the day you plan to serve it.

2 Put flour (remember to sift before measuring), baking soda, ginger, cinnamon, nutmeg or mace, and salt into a sifter. Sift over a piece of waxed paper and set aside until you are ready to add it to the gingerbread batter.

3 Put butter in the large bowl of an electric mixer. Beat at high speed until smooth, scraping sides down as necessary with rubber spatula. Add sugar and eggs and beat about 5 minutes longer or until mixture is very light and fluffy.

4 Reduce mixer speed to low and gradually beat in molasses and hot water. Add flour mixture, a small amount at a time, beating just until batter is smooth and all dry ingredients are moistened. Use a rubber spatula to stir in raisins.

5 Pour batter into prepared baking pan and smooth surface evenly. Place on the center rack of oven and bake 35 to 40 minutes or until a cake tester inserted in the center of the gingerbread comes out clean.

6 Place pan on a wire rack and cool for about 10 to 15 minutes. Sprinkle with confectioners' sugar, if desired, and cut cake into about 12 rectangles. Serve Raisin Gingerbread warm with whipped cream. Makes 12 servings.

RAISIN GINGERBREAD

2½ cups sifted all-purpose flour (sift before measuring)	¼ teaspoon salt	1 cup light molasses
1 teaspoon baking soda	1 cup butter or margarine, softened	¾ cup hot water
1½ teaspoons ground ginger	1 cup sugar	½ cup dark seedless raisins
1 teaspoon ground cinnamon	3 eggs	Confectioners' sugar (optional)
½ teaspoon ground nutmeg or mace		Whipped cream (optional)

Quick breads are just that: QUICK! This one is dotted with luscious blueberries and can be made, from start to finish, in only 35 minutes. For something a little different, stir ½ cup cubed cream cheese into the batter before spreading it in the pan. Then, for a quick frosting, mix 1 cup confectioners' sugar with 1 tablespoon softened butter and enough milk to make it spreadable. Spread gently over the top of the baked Blueberry Tea Cake and it's perfect for your next luncheon get-together.

A
BLUEBERRY
QUICK
BREAD

1 Preheat oven to 400F. Using solid vegetable shortening, lightly grease the inside of a shallow 1½-quart baking dish (about 11 by 7 by 1½ inches). Assemble all the ingredients and equipment you'll need before you begin to make the cake.

2 In a medium-sized bowl, beat egg with a wooden spoon. Gradually add the ⅔ cup sugar, beating thoroughly after each addition until mixture is smooth, light and fluffy. (Most of the sugar should be dissolved before you proceed to Step 3.)

3 Put flour, baking powder, cinnamon and salt in a sifter. Sift over a large bowl or a piece of waxed paper. Add sifted-flour mixture to sugar-egg mixture alternately with milk, beginning and ending with flour and beating thoroughly after each addition.

4 When batter is thoroughly blended and all dry ingredients are moistened, add melted butter and vanilla extract. Beat thoroughly. Add blueberries all at one time and gently fold into batter, being careful you don't break the blueberries.

5 Pour cake batter into the prepared pan and smooth top evenly with a rubber spatula. Sprinkle top of batter with 2 tablespoons sugar. Place in oven on center rack and bake for 25 minutes or until top springs back when lightly touched with fingertip.

6 Remove cake from oven and place pan on a wire rack to cool slightly. Serve cake while still warm and have lots of sweet butter on the side to spread on the warm cake. This is a good tea cake to serve for breakfast. Makes 8 servings.

BLUEBERRY TEA CAKE

1 egg
⅔ cup sugar
1½ cups sifted cake flour (sift before measuring)

2 teaspoons baking powder
½ teaspoon ground cinnamon
¾ teaspoon salt
⅓ cup milk
3 tablespoons butter or

margarine, melted
1 teaspoon vanilla extract
1 cup fresh blueberries
2 tablespoons sugar

Cicero/Fimage Inc.

8642-02

SUMMERTIME CHERRY COBBLER

This will remind you of your grandmother's kitchen: always filled with the aroma of something just baked. Back then, this Cherry Cobbler was a special summertime treat, made only when fresh tart cherries were available. Now you can have it anytime by using the canned sour cherries you find in the supermarket. The results will be just as delicious, and your own children and grandchildren will remember you forever!

1 Preheat oven to 350F. Make Cherry Sauce: Drain cherries thoroughly in a colander, reserving 1 cup of the cherry syrup. In a medium-sized saucepan, mix cornstarch with ¾ cup sugar, the food color and the reserved cherry liquid.

2 Bring cornstarch mixture to a boil over medium heat, stirring constantly. Boil 1 minute, remove from heat, and add butter, lemon peel, almond extract and reserved drained cherries. Stir with a wooden spoon until the butter melts and mixture is thoroughly blended.

3 Pour cherry sauce into a baking dish that measures about 10 by 6 inches; set aside while you prepare the Cake Topping. Sift flour, ¾ cup sugar, baking powder and salt into the large bowl of an electric mixer. Add milk, shortening and vanilla extract.

4 With electric mixer set at medium speed, beat flour mixture for about 2 minutes, occasionally scraping side of bowl with rubber spatula. All dry ingredients should be moistened. Add egg and beat 2 minutes longer, scraping bowl with spatula as necessary.

5 Using a large spoon, spread cake-topping batter evenly over the cherry mixture in dish. Place cobbler on center rack in oven and bake for 35 to 40 minutes or until cake topping springs back when gently pressed with fingertips.

6 Remove Cherry Cobbler from oven and place on wire rack. Cool for 15 to 20 minutes. To serve: Spoon warm Cherry Cobbler into individual serving dishes and top each with a scoop of vanilla ice cream. Serve immediately. Makes 6 servings.

CHERRY COBBLER À LA MODE

CHERRY SAUCE
2 cans (1-lb size) pitted sour red cherries, packed in water
3 tablespoons cornstarch
¾ cup sugar
½ teaspoon red food color
3 tablespoons butter or margarine

1 tablespoon grated lemon peel
¼ teaspoon almond extract

CAKE TOPPING
1 cup sifted all-purpose flour (sift before measuring)
¾ cup sugar

1 teaspoon baking powder
½ teaspoon salt
½ cup milk
¼ cup solid vegetable shortening
1 teaspoon vanilla extract
1 egg

Vanilla ice cream

A DRAMATIC CHOCOLATE MINT CAKE

Chocolate-coated mint triangles adorn our superrich Chocolate Crème-de-Menthe Cake. It is made with three chocolate cake layers, filled with a light green crème-de-menthe filling and frosted with a dark chocolate frosting. It just might be the best chocolate cake you've ever tasted!

1 Prepare Dark-Chocolate Cake Layers: In medium bowl, combine cocoa with boiling water, mixing with wire whisk until smooth. Cool completely. Sift flour with soda, salt, and baking powder. Preheat oven to 350F. Grease and lightly flour three 9-by-1½-inch layer-cake pans.

2 Beat butter, sugar, eggs and vanilla in large bowl with electric mixer at high speed until light (5 minutes). At low speed, beat in flour mixture in fourths, alternately with cocoa mixture (in thirds), beginning and ending with flour mixture. Do not overbeat. Pour evenly into pans.

3 Bake layers 25 to 30 minutes or until surface springs back when gently pressed with fingertip or until a cake tester inserted in center comes out clean. Remove from oven and cool in pans for 10 minutes. Remove cakes from pans and cool completely on wire racks.

4 Prepare Crème-de-Menthe Filling: In a small bowl, beat 6 tablespoons butter, sugar and 6 tablespoons crème-de-menthe with an electric mixer until smooth and fluffy. On cake stand, put cake layers together, dividing the Crème-de-Menthe Filling equally between layers.

5 Prepare Dark-Chocolate Frosting: In medium saucepan, combine chocolate pieces, cream and butter; stir over medium heat until smooth. Remove from heat. With wire whisk, blend in confectioners' sugar. Turn into bowl placed over ice; beat until frosting holds its shape.

6 With metal spatula, frost side of cake as pictured. Use rest of frosting over top, swirling decoratively. Cut mints in half diagonally and use to decorate cake as shown. Refrigerate cake until serving time. Makes 16 servings.

CRÈME-DE-MENTHE CHOCOLATE CAKE

DARK-CHOCOLATE CAKE LAYERS
1 cup unsifted unsweetened cocoa
2 cups boiling water
2¾ cups sifted all-purpose flour
(sift before measuring)
2 teaspoons baking soda
½ teaspoon salt
½ teaspoon baking powder

1 cup butter, softened
2½ cups sugar
4 eggs
1½ teaspoons vanilla extract

CRÈME-DE-MENTHE FILLING
6 tablespoons butter, softened
3½ cups unsifted confectioners' sugar

6 tablespoons green crème de menthe

DARK-CHOCOLATE FROSTING
1 pkg (6 oz) semisweet-chocolate pieces
½ cup light cream
1 cup butter
2½ cups unsifted confectioners' sugar
1 box (6 oz) chocolate-coated square mints

Make these Caramel-Walnut Bar Cookies when time is at a premium. They are much less time-consuming to make than drop cookies and can be cut into tiny pieces for afternoon tea or into large ones for packing in school lunch boxes. Save cleanup time by lining the baking pan with aluminum foil before adding the cookie mixture. Then, when cookies are done, simply remove the foil from pan and cut cookies into bars, using a large sharp knife.

A CRUNCHY WALNUT COOKIE

1 To make preparation easy, be sure to gather together all the ingredients and utensils you will need to complete these bar cookies. Preheat oven to 350F. Using solid vegetable shortening, lightly grease the inside of a 9-by-9-by-2-inch baking pan.

2 Place a piece of waxed paper on a flat surface. Sift flour and baking powder over paper to lighten and combine thoroughly; set aside. Put butter and granulated sugar in the large bowl of an electric mixer; beat at high speed until smooth.

3 Add egg yolks to creamed-butter mixture, one at a time, beating thoroughly after each addition until mixture is light and fluffy. Reduce mixer speed to low; alternately add flour and milk, beginning and ending with flour, beating until just combined.

4 Add vanilla extract and beat mixture again, making sure that all ingredients are thoroughly combined. Using a rubber spatula, scrape the cookie batter into the prepared pan, spreading evenly. Place on center rack in oven and bake for 20 minutes.

5 Meanwhile, beat egg whites in the small bowl of an electric mixer with mixer set at high speed. Beat until stiff peaks form when beaters are lifted. With electric mixer running, gradually add brown sugar, beating well after each addition.

6 Scrape meringue from beaters into bowl. Using a rubber spatula, gently fold nuts into brown-sugar meringue. Spread evenly over baked cookie crust; bake 20 minutes longer. Cut into 16 bars while warm; cool completely on wire rack. Makes 16 bar cookies.

CARAMEL-WALNUT BARS

1½ cups unsifted all-purpose flour	1 cup granulated sugar	2 egg whites
1 teaspoon baking powder	2 egg yolks	1 cup light brown sugar (packed to measure)
½ cup butter or margarine (softened)	2 tablespoons milk	1 cup coarsely chopped walnuts
	1 teaspoon vanilla extract	

CHOCOLATE BUTTERMILK CAKE WITH FRUIT-AND-NUT FILLING

This very impressive 2-layer chocolate cake is made in a jellyroll pan. After baking, the cake is cut in half and sandwiched with a rich date, raisin, fig and nut filling and enrobed in a satiny sour-cream-and-chocolate frosting. It's the ultimate!

1 Make Cake: Lightly grease a 15½-by-10½-by-1-inch jellyroll pan; line bottom with waxed paper; grease paper. Preheat oven to 325F. Put shortening in a large bowl and beat with an electric mixer or a large wooden spoon until fluffy, scraping side of bowl frequently.

2 Slowly add the sugar, salt and vanilla to the shortening, beating until mixture is smooth and no lumps remain. Add eggs, one at a time, beating well after each addition. Mix buttermilk and baking soda in a small bowl (mixture will foam).

3 Alternately add flour and buttermilk-soda mixture to egg mixture in bowl, beating well after each addition, beginning and ending with flour. Stir in melted chocolate and pour batter into prepared pan. Bake 35 minutes. Turn cake out onto a wire cake rack to cool; remove paper.

4 Make Fruit-Nut Filling: Pour evaporated milk, water and sugar in a small saucepan and cook, stirring frequently, until sugar dissolves. Add fruit and bring to a boil, stirring constantly, and cook until thick. Cool completely and stir in vanilla and chopped nuts.

5 Make Chocolate Icing: In the top of a double boiler, melt chocolate pieces and butter over hot water. Remove from heat and stir in sour cream, vanilla and salt. Gradually beat in confectioners' sugar until icing is of spreading consistency.

6 Flip cooled cake over and cut in half crosswise. Place one-half on a serving platter and top with fruit-nut filling, spreading evenly. Place remaining cake on top; frost top and sides of cake with chocolate icing. Makes 32 small servings.

MAYOR'S CHOCOLATE CAKE*

CAKE
¾ cup solid vegetable shortening
2 cups sugar (sifted before measuring)
Pinch of salt
1 teaspoon vanilla extract
5 eggs
1 cup buttermilk
1 teaspoon baking soda
2 cups all-purpose flour (sifted before measuring)

3 squares unsweetened chocolate (melted)

FRUIT-NUT FILLING
¾ cup evaporated milk
¼ cup water
¾ cup sugar
¼ cup chopped pitted dates
¼ cup chopped dark seedless raisins
¼ cup chopped dried figs (or more dates)

1 teaspoon vanilla extract
½ cup chopped nuts

CHOCOLATE ICING
1 pkg (6 oz) semisweet chocolate pieces
¼ cup butter
½ cup sour cream
1 teaspoon vanilla extract
¼ teaspoon salt
3 cups confectioners' sugar

*Recipe contributed to McCall's by Helen Exum, Chattanooga *News-Free Press*, Chattanooga, Tenn.

A CARAMEL-FROSTED BUTTERMILK-CLOVE CAKE

Cloves are the dried unopened buds of an evergreen plant in the myrtle family; they have a distinctively spicy and pungent flavor that is mellowed by cooking. This delicious spice cake is predominantly flavored with ground cloves and is complemented by the addition of ground cinnamon and a creamy caramel frosting. This is a very special cake that is worthy of a very special occasion!

1 Make Cake: Preheat oven to 350F. Lightly grease the inside of a 10-by-4½-inch tube pan without a removable bottom. Sift 2¾ cups of the flour with cloves, cinnamon, baking powder, baking soda and salt over a piece of waxed paper. Toss raisins with remaining flour.

2 In small bowl of electric mixer, beat eggs until light and fluffy; set aside. In large bowl of electric mixer, at medium speed, beat butter until creamy. Gradually add sugar, beating until mixture is light (about 5 minutes). Beat eggs into sugar mixture, scraping down sides as necessary.

3 Reduce mixer speed to low; alternately blend flour mixture and buttermilk into sugar-egg mixture, beginning and ending with flour. Beat only until blended; stir in raisins; pour batter into pan. Bake for 60 to 65 minutes or until a cake tester inserted in center of cake comes out clean.

4 Place pan on wire rack to cool for 20 minutes. Gently loosen with spatula; turn cake out onto wire rack; cool completely (1 hour). Make Caramel Frosting: Melt butter in small saucepan over low heat; remove from heat. Add brown sugar; stir until smooth.

5 Bring sugar mixture to a boil and cook 1 minute, stirring constantly; remove from heat. Add cream; return just to a boil over low heat; remove from heat and cool to 110F (lukewarm). Beat confectioners' sugar into warm butter mixture until frosting is thick; add vanilla or maple extract.

6 If frosting seems too thin, gradually beat in a little more confectioners' sugar. Set in bowl of ice water; beat until thick enough to spread (frosting should barely hold its shape). Frost cake immediately and decorate the sides with nuts. Makes 16 servings.

CLOVE CAKE WITH CARAMEL FROSTING

CAKE
3 cups all-purpose flour (sifted before measuring)
1 tablespoon ground cloves
1 tablespoon ground cinnamon
1 teaspoon baking powder
½ teaspoon baking soda
⅛ teaspoon salt

1 cup dark seedless raisins
5 eggs
1 cup butter or margarine, softened
2¼ cups sugar
1 cup buttermilk

CARAMEL FROSTING
½ cup butter or margarine

1 cup light-brown sugar (packed to measure)
⅓ cup dairy half-and-half cream or undiluted evaporated milk
2 cups unsifted confectioners' sugar
1 teaspoon vanilla extract or
½ teaspoon maple extract

1 cup coarsely chopped walnuts

These chocolate-chip-studded cookies are glazed with chocolate and bedecked with fruits, nuts and silver dragées. Bake the cookies early in the day and set aside to cool

IN HOLIDAY DRESS

at room temperature. When your children come home from school, the cookies will be ready to glaze and decorate: It's a project the whole family will enjoy!

1 Preheat oven to 375F. Make Cookies: Sift flour with salt and baking soda over a piece of waxed paper; set aside. In a large bowl, with a wooden spoon or an electric mixer set at medium speed, beat butter, light-brown and granulated sugars, eggs and vanilla until light and fluffy.

2 Gradually add the flour mixture into the beaten butter-sugar-and-egg mixture, stirring thoroughly until smooth and until ingredients are well combined. Add semisweet chocolate pieces and chopped nuts. Stir until chocolate pieces and nuts are evenly distributed.

3 Drop slightly rounded teaspoonfuls of dough 2 inches apart on ungreased cookie sheet. Bake for 10 to 12 minutes or until cookies are golden-brown. Transfer to a wire rack to cool. Repeat with remaining dough until all cookies are baked.

4 Make Chocolate Glaze: Put semisweet chocolate squares, 2 tablespoons butter and milk in the top of a double boiler. Heat over hot water, stirring occasionally, until butter and chocolate are melted and smooth. Remove from heat and let stand about 5 minutes.

5 Garnish Cookies: Drizzle or spread Chocolate Glaze over cookies. (If glaze becomes too stiff to drizzle, place over hot water again to thin.) Sprinkle glazed cookies with nuts, silver dragées or candied cherries. Makes about 6 dozen cookies.

6 Variation: If desired, instead of cookies, make bars. Pour the batter into a greased 15-by-10-by-1-inch baking pan. Bake at 375F for 20 minutes. Cool; garnish bars as in Step 5. Cut into 2-inch bars as shown. Makes about 3 dozen bars.

FESTIVE CHOCOLATE CHIP COOKIES

COOKIES
2¼ cups all-purpose flour (sifted before measuring)
¾ teaspoon salt
1 teaspoon baking soda
1 cup butter or margarine
¾ cup light-brown sugar (packed to measure)

¾ cup granulated sugar
2 eggs
1 teaspoon vanilla extract
1 pkg (12-oz size) semisweet chocolate pieces
1 cup chopped walnuts or pecans

CHOCOLATE GLAZE
2 squares semisweet chocolate

2 tablespoons butter or margarine
2 teaspoons milk

GARNISH
Chopped pistachio nuts
Silver dragées
Chopped red and green candied cherries

David Viens

8649-04

A PROTEIN-PACKED PEANUT-BUTTER CAKE

Here's a great way to have kids eat lots of protein for dessert! This cake not only tastes great but is also rich with protein-packed peanut butter. And when you add the other ingredients—eggs, flour, milk and chopped peanuts—you end up with about 21 grams of protein per serving. That's as much as you get in one 4-ounce hamburger! You'll never feel guilty about giving your family dessert again.

1 Make Cake: Preheat oven to 350F. Lightly grease and flour two 9-inch-round layer-cake pans. Over a large piece of waxed paper sift flour with baking powder and salt. In a large bowl, beat butter and sugar until light with electric mixer set at high speed.

2 Add eggs to butter mixture, one at a time, beating thoroughly after each addition. Beat in ½ cup peanut butter and the vanilla; continue beating, occasionally scraping sides of bowl with rubber spatula, until mixture is light and fluffy (about 2 minutes).

3 Reduce mixer speed to low and beat in flour mixture (in fourths), alternately with milk (in thirds), beginning and ending with flour mixture. Beat just until mixture is smooth (about 1 minute). Spread batter into prepared cake pans.

4 Place pans on center rack in preheated oven and bake for 30 to 35 minutes or until surface springs back when gently pressed with fingertip, or a cake tester inserted in center of cake comes out clean. Transfer to wire racks and let cool 10 minutes.

5 Remove cakes from pans and place them on wire racks. When cakes are completely cool, prepare Frosting: Put chocolate syrup and 1 cup peanut butter in a medium-sized bowl. Beat until smooth with an electric mixer set at medium speed.

6 Add corn syrup to chocolate mixture; beat until thick enough to spread. Put one cake layer on platter; spread with ¾ cup frosting and top with second cake layer. Frost sides and top of cake. Sprinkle top with chopped peanuts. Makes 1 cake, 8 to 10 servings.

PEANUT BUTTER CAKE

CAKE
3 cups sifted cake flour
2½ teaspoons baking powder
½ teaspoon salt
1 cup butter or margarine (softened)

2 cups sugar
4 large eggs
½ cup creamy peanut butter
1 teaspoon vanilla extract
1 cup milk

FROSTING
1 cup prepared chocolate-flavor syrup
1 cup creamy peanut butter
¼ cup light corn syrup

½ cup coarsely chopped peanuts

David Viens

9800-02

A GREEK COOKIE

Sampling these Greek Butter Cookies is like eating fine butter pastry: They are so buttery that they almost melt in your mouth! Flavored with ground walnuts and just a hint of clove, they will be a perfect addition to your cookie platter.

1 Preheat oven to 350F. Put butter, granulated sugar, egg yolks and the vanilla and almond extracts into the large bowl of an electric mixer. Beat, with mixer set at medium speed, until the mixture is smooth, light and fluffy.

2 Remove bowl from mixer; scrape butter mixture from beaters and return to bowl. Add flour and nuts to butter mixture all at once and mix, using your hands if necessary, until no traces of the flour remain.

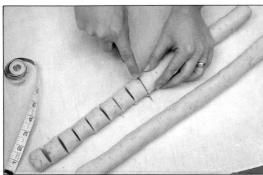

3 Turn dough out onto a lightly floured board or pastry cloth; divide dough in half. With your hands, shape each half into a roll that is 16 inches long. Cut each roll into 16 (1-inch size) pieces and then shape each piece into a ball.

4 Press a whole clove into each dough ball so that the end of the clove is visible. Place balls, clove side up, 1 inch apart on ungreased baking sheet. Place on center rack in oven and bake for 20 to 25 minutes or until cookies are set but not browned.

5 When cookies are done, transfer them to a wire rack. Sprinkle them lightly with confectioners' sugar while they are still warm. Let cool completely on the wire rack. Repeat until all the cookies have been baked and cooled.

6 Just before serving, sprinkle the Greek Butter Cookies with more confectioners' sugar so that they are well coated. (If desired, store cookies in a well-sealed tin box for up to 1 week.) Yields 32 Greek Butter Cookies.

GREEK BUTTER COOKIES (Kourabiedes)

1 cup butter or margarine (softened)
¼ cup granulated sugar
2 egg yolks

1 teaspoon vanilla extract
½ teaspoon almond extract
2½ cups unsifted all-purpose flour

½ cup finely chopped walnuts
32 whole cloves
Confectioners' sugar

9801-02   David Viens

ROAST CHICKEN WITH A DIFFERENCE

Our roast chicken is cooked in herbs and chicken broth and served with a flavorful gravy of vegetable puree. French chefs call this kind of preparation—using fresh herbs and spices and eliminating heavy fats—*la nouvelle cuisine*, but we think it's a delicious, sensible way to cook in any language. Turn page for recipe.

1 Preheat oven to 350F. Wash chicken and giblets; dry with paper towels. Remove any excess fat from chicken. Peel tomatoes: Dip each into boiling water 1 minute; lift out with slotted utensil; peel off skin. Cut one tomato in half; remove seeds; chop pulp.

2 In a heavy, 6-quart Dutch oven, combine giblets, carrot, onion, bay leaf and chopped tomato. Cook over medium heat 5 minutes, stirring occasionally. In small bowl, combine salt, rosemary or thyme and pepper. Use this to sprinkle chicken inside and out.

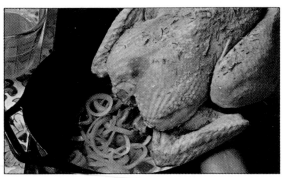

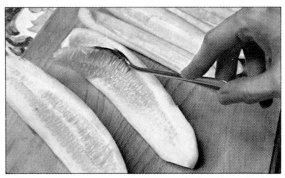

3 Tie chicken legs together with twine. Place chicken, breast side up, on top of sautéed vegetables. Pour 1 can chicken broth over vegetables. Roast chicken, uncovered, 1¾ hours. Every 15 minutes during first hour, baste the chicken with pan liquid.

4 Meanwhile, pare cucumbers; halve lengthwise; remove and discard seeds. Cut each cucumber half into two strips. In medium saucepan, bring to boiling remaining can of chicken broth. Add cucumber; simmer, uncovered, 10 to 15 minutes, or until tender.

5 Drain cucumber; reserve ½ cup broth. Remove chicken to warm serving platter. Discard bay leaf. Skim fat from drippings. Make sauce: Turn pan drippings, vegetables and reserved chicken broth into blender or food processor; blend until smooth.

6 To serve: Remove twine from chicken legs. Cut remaining tomatoes into sixths. Arrange tomato and cucumber around chicken. Pour ½ cup sauce over chicken breast; sprinkle with chopped parsley. Serve remaining sauce with chicken. Makes 8 servings.

ROAST CHICKEN NOUVELLE CUISINE

4-lb ready-to-cook roasting chicken
3 medium-size tomatoes (1 lb)
Boiling water
2 medium carrots (½ lb),
pared and thinly sliced

2 medium onions (½ lb),
peeled and thinly sliced
1 bay leaf
1 teaspoon salt
½ teaspoon dried rosemary or
thyme leaves

⅛ teaspoon pepper
2 cans (10¾-oz size)
condensed chicken broth,
undiluted
3 medium cucumbers
Chopped parsley

Each guest gets an individual bird, stuffed with tarragon and garlic, basted in buttery wine sauce. The luscious hens that are shown here are nestled on a bed of cracked-wheat pilaf. How-to-do-it steps start on the next page.

PLUMP, MEATY CORNISH GAME HENS

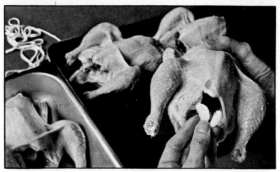

1 If Cornish hens are frozen, let thaw overnight in refrigerator. Wash hens inside and out under cold water; drain. Dry well with paper towels. Wash giblets. Make basting sauce: Melt ¾ cup butter in small saucepan; stir in wine and 1 tablespoon tarragon.

2 Preheat oven to 450F. Sprinkle inside of each hen with ¼ teaspoon salt, ⅛ teaspoon pepper and 1 tablespoon dried tarragon leaves. Place one clove of garlic, halved, inside each. Sprinkle outside of each hen liberally with garlic salt; tie the legs together.

3 Place close together, in shallow roasting pan without rack. Roast, basting often with sauce, 1 hour, until browned and tender. Meanwhile, place giblets (reserve liver) in large saucepan. Add 1 can broth, celery, onion, carrot, 1 teaspoon salt, peppercorns.

4 Bring to boiling; reduce heat; simmer, covered, 45 minutes, or until tender. Add liver; simmer 10 minutes. Also, make pilaf: In medium saucepan, combine cracked wheat and chicken broth. Cover; bring to boiling. Reduce heat, and simmer 20 minutes.

5 Remove from heat. Let stand 10 minutes, or until all liquid is absorbed. Add butter; toss gently to combine. Mound pilaf in center of heated platter; arrange hens around edge. Keep warm while making gravy. Strain giblets and liver; chop; reserve broth.

6 Combine flour and ¼ cup water; mix until smooth. Stir into drippings in roasting pan with 1 cup reserved broth and chopped giblets. Bring to boiling, stirring until thickened. Turn into heated gravy boat. Garnish serving platter with watercress. Serves 6.

ROAST CORNISH HENS

6 Cornish hens, about 1¼ lb each

BASTING SAUCE
¾ cup butter or margarine
¾ cup dry white wine
1 tablespoon dried tarragon leaves

Salt
Pepper

6 tablespoons dried tarragon leaves
6 cloves garlic, peeled
Garlic salt
1 can (13 ¾ oz) chicken broth
1 celery stalk, cut up
1 medium onion, peeled and quartered
1 medium carrot, pared and cut up

4 whole black peppercorns

PILAF
2 cups cracked wheat
2 cans (13¾-oz size) chicken broth
¼ cup butter or margarine

2 tablespoons flour
Watercress

8604-4

For an Easter dinner that's an exciting change, try this classic duckling à l'orange. Our version of the famous French dish is stuffed with orange, onion—and just a hint of garlic. To make it all the more flavorful, it's served with a brandy laced orange sauce. We carve it a special way, removing the wishbone and slicing diagonally, so that one duckling will feed four people generously.

DELICIOUS DUCK À L'ORANGE

1 Remove giblets and neck from duckling and reserve. Wash duckling under running water; drain; dry with paper towels. Turn breast side down; using sharp scissors and knife, carefully cut out wishbone from breast for easier carving. Preheat oven to 425F.

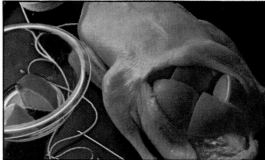

2 Sprinkle inside with ½ teaspoon salt. Tuck onion inside neck; bring skin of neck over back. Fasten with poultry pins. Stuff body cavity with garlic, black peppers and oranges. Close cavity with poultry pins. Tie legs together; bend wing tips under body.

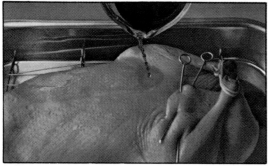

3 Place on rack in shallow roasting pan. Pour ½ cup Burgundy over duckling. Roast, uncovered, 30 minutes. Reduce oven to 375F; roast 1½ hours. Bring giblets to boiling in 2 cups water and ½ teaspoon salt; reduce heat; simmer, covered, 1 hour. Strain.

4 Sauce: In 2 tablespoons butter in skillet, brown liver. Remove from heat. Heat brandy slightly. Ignite; pour over liver. Remove liver; chop. In same skillet, in rest of butter, sauté orange peel and garlic 3 minutes. Stir in flour, catsup, bouillon cube and pepper.

5 Gradually add giblet broth, Burgundy, ¼ cup marmalade and the orange juice; mix well. Bring to boiling; reduce heat; simmer, stirring, 15 minutes. Add liver and orange sections; heat. Spread duckling with ½ cup marmalade; roast 10 minutes longer.

6 Remove pins and twine. Place on heated platter. Using sharp knife, cut each side of breast into diagonal slices, ½ inch wide, starting at leg. Then run knife down center of breast to separate two sides; run knife around outer edge to cut skin. Pass sauce.

DUCKLING À L'ORANGE

5-lb ready-to-cook duckling (if frozen, thaw completely)	**ORANGE SAUCE**	1 chicken-bouillon cube
1 teaspoon salt	3 tablespoons butter or margarine	Dash pepper
1 large onion, peeled	Liver from duckling	1¼ cups broth from giblets
1 clove garlic, chopped	3 tablespoons brandy	⅓ cup Burgundy
3 whole black peppers	2 tablespoons grated orange peel	¼ cup orange marmalade
2 unpeeled oranges, quartered	¾ teaspoon chopped garlic	¼ cup orange juice
½ cup Burgundy	2 tablespoons flour	1 cup orange sections
	2 teaspoons catsup	
		½ cup orange marmalade

Note: If desired, roast 2 ducklings at same time, leaving sauce recipe as is. Nice served with white rice combined with sautéed sliced mushrooms.

CHICKEN IN WINE — A FRENCH CLASSIC

Coq au Vin—it's an American favorite that's right from the heart of French cuisine. Tender pieces of chicken are sautéed and flamed with brandy, then simmered in a silky mixture of wines, herbs, garlic and nutmeg. This elegant but easy-to-do dish can be made ahead—and is even better when re-warmed. See next page.

1 Wash chicken under cold water; drain. Dry on paper towels. In 6-quart Dutch oven, over medium heat, sauté bacon until crisp; lift out with slotted spoon and drain. In bacon fat, sauté onions over medium heat 5 minutes; stir occasionally. Lift out.

3 When vapor rises, ignite Cognac; pour over chicken. Remove chicken. To Dutch oven, add shallot, mushrooms, garlic, bouquet garni, salt, pepper, sugar and nutmeg; mix well. Over low heat, simmer, covered, 5 minutes. Stir in the red and white wines.

5 Cut rounds in half. In ¼ cup hot butter in skillet, sauté until golden on both sides; place on paper. In small bowl, mix softened butter with flour until smooth; stir into liquid in Dutch oven. Bring to boiling, stirring, until thickened. Remove bouquet garni.

2 Add 2 tablespoons butter to drippings; heat. In hot fat, over medium heat, brown chicken, a third at a time, turning with tongs until golden all over—about ½ hour in all; remove as it browns. Return chicken to Dutch oven. In pan or ladle, heat Cognac slightly.

4 Return chicken to Dutch oven; bring to boiling; reduce heat; simmer, covered, ½ hour. Add onions; cook 25 minutes longer, until chicken and onions are tender. Meanwhile, make croûtes: With 3-inch round biscuit cutter, cut out centers from 4 bread slices.

6 Turn into serving dish. Sprinkle with bacon and parsley. Garnish with croûtes. Serves 8. *Note:* For bouquet garni, tie large parsley sprig, 3 sprigs fresh thyme and a bay leaf together. (If using dried thyme, tie 1 teaspoon leaves in a small cheesecloth bag.)

COQ AU VIN

2 (2-to-2½-lb size) broiler-fryers, quartered
¼ lb bacon, in ½-inch pieces
15 small white onions
(1¼ lb), peeled
2 tablespoons butter or margarine
¼ cup Cognac or brandy
4 shallots, peeled and coarsely chopped

½ lb small whole fresh mushrooms, washed and sliced
½ inch thick
1 clove garlic, crushed
Bouquet garni (see Note, Step 6)
1½ teaspoons salt
½ teaspoon freshly ground pepper
1 teaspoon sugar
¼ teaspoon nutmeg
2 cups dry red wine

1 cup dry white wine

CROÛTES
4 slices white bread
¼ cup butter

2 tablespoons butter or margarine, softened
3 tablespoons flour
2 tablespoons chopped parsley

If you took a poll to discover everybody's favorite one-dish meal, this one would probably win. It's old-fashioned chicken-and-vegetable pot pie, baked in a deep-dish casserole. The basic ingredients of this native American dish are chicken, a creamy gravy, onions and carrots, but it's made a little differently in different parts of the country. In New England, for example, it's often made with two crusts. Ours, prepared the Southern way, uses a single layer of golden-brown pastry on top, with a pattern of vents to let out the steam. We've also added something of our own—a savory bit of thyme to the crust dough. Serve with a crisp, green salad. Step-by-step instructions, next page.

REAL OLD SOUTHERN POT PIE

1 Prepare chicken and vegetables: Wash chicken and giblets under cold water. Place in large kettle with quartered onion, celery, parsley, 2½ teaspoons salt, the black peppers, bay leaf and 2 cups water. Bring to boiling. Reduce heat; simmer, covered.

2 Simmer gently 1½ hours, or until chicken is tender. Remove chicken; cool. Chop giblets fine. Remove chicken from bones in large pieces; meat should measure 5 cups. Strain stock; measure. Skim off fat. Add water to make 4 cups, if necessary.

3 In 4 cups stock in medium saucepan, cook carrots and onions, covered, 20 minutes, or until tender. Strain; liquid should measure 3 cups. In small bowl, combine flour, salt and pepper. Stir in milk until smooth. Add to stock in pan; bring to boil, stirring.

4 Reduce heat; simmer, 8 minutes, or until sauce is thick. Add chicken, vegetables and giblets. Turn into a round 3-quart casserole. Preheat oven to 400F. Prepare the piecrust as package label directs, adding ¾ teaspoon dried thyme leaves to flour mixture.

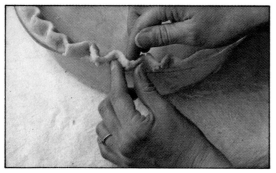

5 Form pastry into a ball. On lightly floured pastry cloth or surface, roll out pastry to form a circle ½ inch larger all around than top of casserole. Place the pastry on top of casserole, turning edge under; crimp decoratively; press to rim of casserole to seal.

6 With serrated knife, make five or six slits for air vents, evenly dispersed in top of pastry. Brush surface of pastry evenly with melted butter. Bake 35 to 40 minutes, or until crust is golden and the mixture bubbles through slits. Makes 8 to 10 servings.

CHICKEN POT PIE

CHICKEN AND VEGETABLES
5-lb roasting chicken, cut up
1 large onion, peeled and quartered
3 celery tops
3 parsley sprigs
2½ teaspoons salt
10 whole black peppers

1 bay leaf
8 small carrots, pared and halved crosswise (1 lb)
12 small white onions, peeled (1 lb)
½ cup unsifted all-purpose flour
1 teaspoon salt

⅛ teaspoon pepper
½ cup milk

PASTRY
1 pkg (11 oz) piecrust mix
¾ teaspoon dried thyme leaves
2 tablespoons butter or margarine, melted

MARVELOUS CHICKEN MARENGO

Napoleon's chef cooked it after the battle of Marengo— and to this day it's a fantastic way to make chicken special. Sauté it in oil with garlic and herbs, and then simmer it with tomatoes and wine. A special touch here: heart-shape bits of toast topped with a spread of chicken livers. Step-by-step instructions begin on the next page.

1 Wash chicken under cold water; dry well on paper towels. On sheet of waxed paper, combine flour, salt and pepper; mix well. Roll chicken pieces in flour mixture, coating evenly. In a 5-quart Dutch oven, slowly heat the olive oil and 2 tablespoons butter.

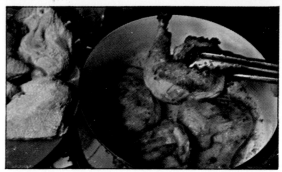

2 Add chicken pieces to hot fat in a single layer; sauté on all sides, turning with tongs, until nicely browned—10 minutes. Remove chicken as it browns. Brown rest of chicken; remove and set aside. Add the garlic, thyme, basil and parsley to Dutch oven.

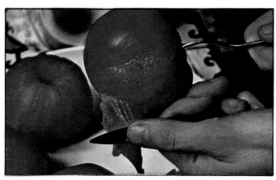

3 Sauté herbs, stirring, over medium heat 5 minutes. If using fresh tomatoes, scald in boiling water; peel skins. Cut tomatoes in quarters; add to Dutch oven. (If using canned tomatoes, add with liquid.) Add tomato paste, sugar, Tabasco and ¾ cup of the wine.

4 Stir to mix well. Place chicken in sauce. Bring to boiling; reduce heat; simmer, covered, 40 minutes. Meanwhile, wash mushrooms; slice through stem, ¼ inch thick. In 2 tablespoons remaining butter in small skillet, sauté mushrooms about 5 minutes, stirring.

5 Add sliced mushrooms to chicken; cook, covered, 10 minutes longer. About 10 minutes before serving, drain chicken livers on paper towels; halve. Sauté livers, chopped onion and chopped mushrooms in 2 tablespoons hot butter, stirring, about 5 minutes.

6 Mash with fork; add 1 tablespoon soft butter; mix well. Cut toast with heart-shape cutter; spread with remaining butter, then with liver mixture. Stir ¼ cup wine into sauce. Arrange chicken, with sauce and toast, on a platter. Sprinkle with parsley. Serves 8.

CHICKEN MARENGO

2 ready-to-cook broiler-fryers
(2-lb size), quartered
3 tablespoons flour
1½ teaspoons salt
⅛ teaspoon pepper
2 tablespoons olive or salad oil
4 tablespoons butter or margarine
1 clove garlic, crushed
½ teaspoon dried thyme leaves

½ teaspoon dried basil leaves
1 tablespoon chopped parsley
4 ripe tomatoes (2 lb) or
1 can (1 lb, 10 oz) Italian plum
tomatoes, undrained
3 tablespoons tomato paste
½ teaspoon sugar
2 drops Tabasco
1 cup dry white wine

½ lb fresh mushrooms

GARNISH
2 chicken livers, washed
¼ cup finely chopped onion
2 mushrooms, finely chopped
¼ cup butter or margarine
8 slices white toast
Chopped parsley

A ONE-DISH MEXICAN MEAL

Our Mexican-inspired tamale pie is a one-dish meal that can be served to family and guests with equal pride. Before baking, the casserole dish is lined with cornmeal mush, filled with chicken that has been cooked in chili sauce, and edged with olives and cornmeal squares. The final touch: a topping of grated Cheddar cheese. Recipe, next page.

1 Wash chicken under cold running water; drain. Dry on paper towels. In hot oil and butter in 6-quart Dutch oven, over medium heat, brown chicken, skin side down, half at a time, turning with tongs—takes about ½ hour in all; remove chicken as it browns.

2 In remaining fat, sauté onion and garlic, stirring, until tender—5 minutes. Add chili powder, cumin and basil; sauté 1 minute, stirring. Add chicken, chicken broth, stewed tomatoes, tomato sauce and 1 teaspoon salt. Bring to boiling, stirring occasionally.

3 Reduce heat; simmer, covered, ½ hour, or until chicken is tender. With tongs, remove chicken pieces; set aside. Boil remaining liquid, uncovered, to reduce to 4½ cups—about 15 minutes. Skim off excess fat. Add corn and chicken; remove from heat.

4 In heavy, 4-quart saucepan, bring 4 cups water and 1½ teaspoons salt to boiling. Slowly stir in cornmeal. Cook over medium heat; stir constantly, until thick—5 minutes. Remove from heat. Add ½ cup cheese. Cool 5 minutes. Preheat oven to 375F.

5 Lightly grease and line bottom and sides of 3-quart shallow baking dish with half of cornmeal mixture. Reserve 1 cup sauce. Turn remaining mixture into dish. On damp surface, between sheets of waxed paper, roll remaining cornmeal mixture.

6 Roll into 9-by-9-inch square, ⅓ inch thick. Remove top paper; cut into 20 rectangles; overlap around edge. Spoon reserved sauce and olives over chicken. Bake, uncovered, 20 minutes. Sprinkle with remaining cheese; bake 10 minutes. Serves 8.

TAMALE PIE

4-lb roasting chicken, cut into 8 pieces
2 tablespoons salad oil
2 tablespoons butter or margarine
2 cups chopped onion
1 clove garlic, crushed

1½ to 2 tablespoons chili powder
1 teaspoon ground cumin
1 teaspoon dried basil leaves
1 can (10¾ oz) condensed chicken broth, undiluted
1 can (1 lb) stewed tomatoes

1 can (8 oz) tomato sauce
Salt
1 can (12 oz) whole-kernel corn
2 cups yellow cornmeal
1 cup grated Cheddar cheese
½ cup pitted ripe olives.

8611-03

CLASSIC ROAST CHICKEN

A plump chicken, roasted to a rich golden brown and served with homemade stuffing and its own giblet gravy, is one of the all-time great dishes—and one well worth learning to prepare correctly. For best results, skewer and tie the stuffed chicken carefully; use a roasting rack and let the bird stand for 15 minutes on a warmed platter before carving. For step-by-step illustrations and directions, turn the page.

1 Wash chicken, inside and out, and giblets under cold water; dry with paper towels. Remove excess fat. Sprinkle inside of cavity with salt and pepper. Chop liver. In medium saucepan, cook rest of giblets, covered, in 1½ cups water 2 hours, until tender.

2 Preheat oven to 350F. Make stuffing: In 2 tablespoons hot butter in medium skillet, sauté onion until golden. Add liver; sauté 1 minute. Remove from heat; stir in bread cubes, parsley, thyme, salt and pepper. Add the milk, tossing mixture with a fork.

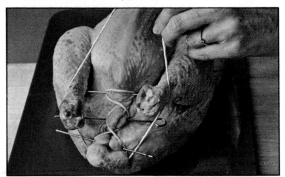

3 Lightly fill cavity with stuffing. Close cavity and fasten neck with poultry pins. Lace cavity with twine, bootlace fashion; tie. Tie legs with twine; tuck wings under. Place on rack in roasting pan. Brush with butter. Roast, uncovered, 2¼ to 2½ hours.

4 During roasting, baste chicken occasionally with pan drippings. Chicken is done when leg joint moves easily. Remove chicken to heated serving platter; remove poultry pins and twine. Let stand 15 minutes before carving. Meanwhile, skim fat from drippings.

5 Strain giblets; set aside. To ½ cup broth from giblets, add canned chicken broth; pour into roasting pan. Cook over medium heat, stirring to dissolve browned bits; simmer, uncovered, to reduce to 1 cup. Chop giblets; add to broth; pour in gravy boat.

6 To carve: Hold end of leg nearest carver; cut thigh joint, pulling leg and thigh away; cut free. Cut nearest wing in same way. Place on extra plate. Slice breast at angle in thin slices, starting near the wing and working upward. Turn platter; repeat. Serves 6.

ROAST CHICKEN WITH STUFFING

1 whole roasting chicken (6 lb)	⅓ cup chopped onion	½ teaspoon salt
Salt, pepper	4 slices white bread, cubed	Dash pepper
	2 tablespoons chopped parsley	¼ cup milk
BREAD STUFFING	½ teaspoon dried thyme leaves	
1 chicken liver		2 tablespoons butter or margarine, melted
2 tablespoons butter or margarine		1 can (13¾ oz) chicken broth

8612-03

No broilers or fryers here—only a plump, old-fashioned roaster, with plenty of tender meat on its bones, will do for this luxury version of a Sunday roast chicken. Stuffed with seasoned bread cubes and chicken liver for richness, it is served with giblet gravy made with extra chicken broth and a touch of celery. But the real secret of this dish is in the roasting method. The herbed butter that is stuffed under the skin of the breast guarantees tenderness and lets the flavors of lemon, parsley, and onion permeate the meat while the bird is cooking.

A CHICKEN TRICK: ROAST IT WITH BUTTER UNDER THE SKIN

1 Preheat oven to 350F. Remove giblets from chicken. Set aside liver for stuffing. Wash chicken inside and out with cold running water, and pat dry with paper towels.

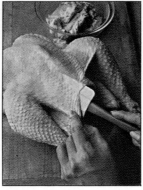

2 Make herb butter (see recipe at right). With a rubber scraper, carefully loosen the skin from either side of the chicken breast, taking care not to break through the skin.

3 Carefully spread half of herb butter over breast meat under skin on each side, using metal spatula or rubber scraper. Cautiously push the herb butter in as far as it will go.

4 Make stuffing (ingredients at right): In ½ cup hot butter, sauté celery, onion, liver until celery is golden. Remove from heat; toss with rest of ingredients in large bowl.

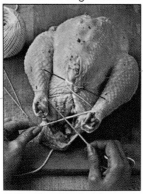

5 Stuff neck, body cavities. Bring neck skin over back. Tuck wings under. Close body cavity with poultry pin. Loop twine around pin; crisscross over opening, under

6 opposite leg, up around legs; bring together. Bring twine under opposite leg, up under wings; tie over back. Roast on rack in roasting pan, uncovered, 1¾ to 2 hours.

7 Baste occasionally with drippings. When done, leg should move up and down easily and flesh feel soft. Remove pins and twine; let stand 15 minutes before carving.

8 Make gravy: In saucepan, mix all ingredients (right) but flour. Add ¾ cup water; simmer, covered, 1½ hours. Strain; add water to make 2 cups. Chop giblets fine.

9 Pour off pan drippings. Return ¼ cup to pan; stir in flour (not on heat) until smooth. Add broth; bring to boil, stirring. Add giblets. Reduce heat; simmer 1 minute. Season.

ROAST CHICKEN WITH HERBS

1 whole, ready-to-cook roasting chicken (about 5 lb)

HERB BUTTER

In a small bowl, using a fork, beat ⅓ cup butter or margarine, softened to room temperature, with 2 teaspoons lemon juice, 2 tablespoons chopped parsley, 1 tablespoon chopped green onion, ½ teaspoon salt, and ⅛ teaspoon pepper.

STUFFING

½ cup butter or margarine
½ cup chopped celery
½ cup chopped green onion
1 chicken liver, chopped
4 cups day-old-white-bread cubes, or 1 pkg (8 oz) seasoned bread cubes
2 tablespoons chopped parsley
½ teaspoon dried thyme leaves
½ teaspoon salt
⅛ teaspoon pepper

GIBLET GRAVY

Giblets and neck
1 onion, peeled and halved
Celery tops from 1 stalk
2 whole black peppercorns
½ teaspoon salt
1 can (10½ oz) condensed chicken broth, undiluted
¼ cup flour

8619-04

MAGICAL MOROCCAN CHICKEN

Here's a way to transform a roasting chicken into an exotic feast: Gild it with spices—ginger, parsley, turmeric and a cinnamon stick—and surround it with a redolent chick-pea-onion-raisin mixture. A one-dish delight. (And what an aroma!) See directions on the next page.

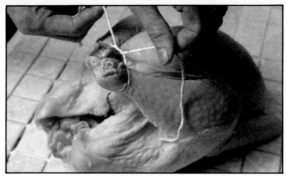

1 Day ahead: Pick over chick-peas; turn into a large bowl; cover with cold water; refrigerate, covered, overnight. Next day, drain chick-peas; turn into a large kettle. Add 2 quarts cold water, 2 teaspoons salt, the quartered onion and bay leaf. Bring to boiling; reduce heat.

2 Simmer, covered, 1½ to 2 hours, or until tender; drain; set aside. Remove and discard onion and bay leaf. Meanwhile, rinse chicken well; dry with paper towels. Sprinkle inside with 1 teaspoon salt. Tuck wings under body; then tie legs together at ends with twine.

3 If necessary, fasten skin at neck with a skewer. In a small bowl, combine garlic, ginger, ½ teaspoon salt, the pepper and 1 tablespoon water; mix well. Brush mixture over entire surface of chicken. Refrigerate chicken in large bowl, covered with plastic wrap or foil, one hour.

4 In 6-quart Dutch oven, combine chopped onion, turmeric, chopped parsley, cinnamon stick, butter and chicken broth. Over medium heat, bring to boiling, stirring constantly. Lower heat; then add chicken, breast side down, and any juices left in bottom of the bowl.

5 Simmer, covered, 1 hour, or until chicken is tender. (Turn chicken frequently in the sauce, using two wooden spoons.) Remove cooked chicken to warm serving platter. Discard cinnamon stick. To liquid left in Dutch oven, add sliced onion, raisins and drained chick-peas.

6 Bring to boiling; cook, stirring frequently with wooden spoon, until onion is soft and flavors have blended—about 15 minutes. Before serving, remove twine. Reheat chicken in chick-pea mixture 5 minutes. Serve chicken and chick-peas together. Makes 8 servings.

MOROCCAN CHICKEN AND CHICK-PEAS

2 cups (1 lb) dried chick-peas	**2 cloves garlic, crushed**	**1 (2-inch) cinnamon stick**
Cold water	**1 teaspoon ground ginger**	**2 tablespoons butter or**
Salt	**¼ teaspoon pepper**	**margarine**
1 onion, peeled and quartered	**½ cup chopped onion**	**1 can (10¾ oz) condensed**
1 bay leaf	**1 teaspoon turmeric**	**chicken broth, undiluted**
4-lb ready-to-cook roasting	**2 tablespoons chopped**	**1 cup sliced onion**
chicken	**parsley**	**½ cup raisins**

8620-04

A PERFECT ONE-POT MEAL

Nothing warms a house like the aroma of a fragrant pot of chicken fricassee. Our creamy version, bursting with carrots and fluffy herbed dumplings, is a meal in itself. And it's not an expensive meal, either. We advise patting the chicken dry with paper towels to make it easier to brown. For really light dumplings, be sure to drop the batter on chicken pieces or vegetables—*not* in the liquid, where they'll get soggy. Step-by-step directions, next page.

1 Wash chicken; dry on paper towels. If legs and thighs are large, cut apart. On waxed paper, combine flour with salt and marjoram; mix well. Dredge chicken in flour mixture, coating evenly. Shake off excess. Reserve leftover flour (about 2 tablespoons).

2 In 2 tablespoons hot butter in 6-quart Dutch oven, sauté chicken, four pieces at a time, skin side down, turning with tongs, until lightly browned all over—about 15 minutes. Lift out with tongs. Continue browning the chicken, adding butter as needed.

3 To drippings, add onion, celery, carrots, bay leaf, cloves and black peppers; sauté, stirring, 5 minutes. Stir in broth and 1 cup water; bring to boiling. Return chicken to Dutch oven. Bring to boiling; reduce heat; simmer, covered, 40 minutes.

4 Dumplings: In medium bowl, combine biscuit mix and 2 tablespoons chives; with fork, blend in egg and milk. Drop batter by 6 rounded tablespoonfuls, 2 to 3 inches apart, onto chicken (not in liquid). Cook, uncovered, over low heat 10 minutes.

5 Cover tightly; cook 10 minutes, or until dumplings are light and fluffy. With slotted spoon, lift dumplings to heated baking dish; keep warm in low oven. In small bowl, combine reserved flour mixture (see Step 1) with the light cream, stirring until smooth.

6 Stir flour mixture gently into fricassee; simmer 5 minutes, or until mixture is thickened. Replace dumplings on top of fricassee to serve. Reheat gently, covered until hot. Before serving, sprinkle with more chives or parsley. Makes 6 servings.

CHICKEN FRICASSEE WITH DUMPLINGS

3 lb chicken parts (legs, thighs, breasts, wings)
⅓ cup flour
1½ teaspoons salt
1 teaspoon dried marjoram leaves
¼ cup butter or margarine
2 medium onions, sliced

1 cup chopped celery
6 large carrots, pared and halved
1 bay leaf
4 whole cloves
9 whole black peppers
1 can (13¾ oz) chicken broth

DUMPLINGS (6 large)
1½ cups packaged biscuit mix
Snipped chives or chopped parsley
1 egg
¼ cup milk
½ cup light cream

8623-03

CHICKEN WITH A RUSSIAN ACCENT

Created in the Russia of the high-living Czars, Chicken Kiev is the most elegant of chicken dishes. Chicken breasts, first boned and skinned, are pounded thin, then wrapped around pats of seasoned frozen butter, coated with egg and crumbs, and deep-fried until golden. By the time chicken is done, butter is just melted and will gush from the chicken breast when you cut into it. Serve with fresh asparagus and fluffy white rice. Chicken Kiev can be cooked ahead and frozen: Cool, wrap in freezer-wrap, and freeze. To serve, unwrap packets, but do not defrost. Bake, uncovered, 35 minutes in 350F oven.

1 In small bowl, with rubber scraper, thoroughly mix butter, parsley, tarragon, garlic, salt, and pepper. On foil, shape into 6-inch square. Freeze until firm—about 40 minutes.

2 Meanwhile, wash chicken; dry well on paper towels. Using a small sharp knife, carefully remove skin. Cut each breast in half. To flatten chicken, place each half, smooth side

3 down, on sheet of waxed paper; cover with second sheet. Using a mallet or side of saucer, pound chicken to about ¼-inch thickness, being careful not to break the meat.

4 Cut frozen butter into 12 pats. Place a pat of herb butter in center of each piece of chicken. Bring long sides of chicken over butter; fold ends over, making sure that

5 no butter is showing; fasten with toothpick. This is important to keep the herb butter inside during frying. Roll each chicken piece in the flour on a sheet of waxed paper.

6 Dip each in beaten egg; roll in crumbs, coating evenly. Then shape each piece, with palms of hands, into triangles (see Picture 7, below). Refrigerate, covered, until chilled—

7 about 1 hour. In a Dutch oven or large, heavy saucepan, slowly heat salad oil (3 inches deep) to 360F on deep-frying thermometer. Add chicken pieces, 3 at a time.

8 Fry, turning with tongs, till browned—5 minutes. Drain. (Do not pierce coating.) Keep warm in 200F oven 15 minutes (no more) in large pan lined with paper towels. Serves 8.

CHICKEN KIEV

HERB BUTTER
1 cup butter or regular margarine, softened
2 tablespoons chopped parsley
1½ teaspoons dried tarragon leaves

1 clove garlic, crushed
¾ teaspoon salt
⅛ teaspoon pepper
_____
6 boned whole chicken breasts (each ¾ lb)

¾ cup unsifted all-purpose flour
3 eggs, well beaten
1½ cups packaged dry bread crumbs
Salad oil or shortening for deep-frying

8624-03

COUSCOUS: AN AFRICAN FAVORITE

Couscous—a fragrant, filling dish that's a staple in Africa—can be a nourishing and enjoyable meal for your own family. Named for the semolina grain that is its key ingredient, couscous can include lamb or beef, but ours is made with chicken—and carrots, cabbage and zucchini. The semolina at its center is strewn with raisins and emboldened by spices—we show you how on the next page.

1 Wash chicken pieces in cold running water; dry well on paper towels. Wash and prepare vegetables: Pare carrots, and halve crosswise; pare turnips, and quarter; cut cabbage in wedges; slice eggplant crosswise ¼ inch thick; slice zucchini ¼ inch thick.

2 In hot oil in 6-quart Dutch oven, brown chicken, turning with tongs on all sides, until browned—30 minutes in all. Brown enough at one time to make single layer in bottom of Dutch oven. As chicken is browned, remove with tongs to shallow pan.

3 Continue browning chicken until all is browned; remove. In remaining fat, in Dutch oven, sauté onion, stirring, until golden—5 minutes. Add 1½ teaspoons turmeric, cumin, allspice, salt, cayenne, garlic and bay leaves; cook, stirring, 5 minutes.

4 Add chicken broth, carrots, turnips and cabbage. Add chicken, along with any juices in pan. Cook, covered, 40 minutes. Add eggplant and zucchini; cook 10 minutes longer. Meanwhile, pour hot water over raisins to cover; let stand ½ hour; drain.

5 Prepare couscous as package label directs. Toss couscous with butter, drained raisins and ½ teaspoon turmeric just to combine. (Keep couscous hot in colander lined with two towels and placed over hot water.) Add chick peas to chicken; cook 5 minutes.

6 To serve, mound couscous in center of large warm platter. With slotted utensil, lift chicken and vegetables to platter, arranging attractively around couscous. Pour sauce in Dutch oven into sauceboat to serve along with couscous. Makes 6 to 8 servings.

COUSCOUS

4-to-5-lb roasting chicken,
cut in 8 pieces
3 carrots
3 white turnips
1 small head cabbage (1 lb)
1 small eggplant (¾ lb)
3 zucchini (1 lb)
¼ cup peanut, olive or salad oil

2 medium onions, peeled and
sliced
Ground turmeric
1 teaspoon ground cumin
¾ teaspoon ground allspice
1½ teaspoons salt
½ to 1 teaspoon cayenne
2 cloves garlic, crushed

3 bay leaves, crumbled
2 cans (10½-oz size) condensed
chicken broth, undiluted
1 cup dark raisins
1 pkg (1 lb) couscous or
semolina
½ cup butter, melted
1 can (1 lb) chick peas, drained

CURRYING FLAVOR

As a company dish, chicken curry has everything going for it. This is no ordinary curry, but a special blend that includes lime juice and grated lime peel, ginger, apple and cardamom to give a lift to prepared curry powder, and (chef's secret) there's a little chutney mixed into the sauce. It's relatively inexpensive to serve—chicken is still the most economical of meats—and can be made ahead and reheated. In fact, reheating improves the flavor. And the chicken breasts look spectacular served on a bed of saffron rice with slices of lime, surrounded by bowls of curry accompaniments for guests to choose from—coconut, pineapple, peanuts, slivered scallions, chutney and chopped green pepper.

1 Wash chicken; dry well on paper towels. Using a small sharp knife, carefully remove skin. Cut each breast in half, making 8. In ¼ cup hot butter in large skillet, over medium heat, brown chicken, 4 pieces at a time, 5 minutes per side. Using tongs,

2 remove chicken as it is browned. Return chicken to skillet. Add 1 can chicken broth; bring to boiling. Reduce heat; simmer, covered, 20 minutes, or just until tender. Remove chicken pieces; keep warm. Measure liquid in skillet; add remaining can of chicken

3 broth and water to make 3 cups; reserve. Make curry sauce: In ¼ cup hot butter in same skillet, sauté garlic, onion, curry powder, and apple until onion is tender—about 5 minutes. Remove from heat. Stir in flour, cardamom, ginger, salt, and pepper; mix

4 well. Gradually stir in reserved 3 cups liquid, lime peel and juice. Bring to boiling, stirring. Reduce heat; simmer, covered, 20 minutes, stirring occasionally. Stir in chutney; add chicken. Cover, and heat gently just to boiling, to reheat chicken—about 5 minutes.

5 Meanwhile, make saffron rice: Mix saffron with 2 tablespoons hot water; set aside. In hot oil and butter in medium saucepan, cook rice and salt, stirring occasionally, 5 minutes. Stir in the saffron mixture and 3 cups water; bring to boiling. Reduce

6 heat; simmer, covered, 15 to 20 minutes, or until liquid is absorbed. Turn rice into center of round platter. Arrange chicken breasts over rice; spoon sauce over chicken. Garnish with slices of lime. Serve with curry accompaniments. Makes 8 servings.

CHICKEN CURRY

4 whole chicken breasts (3¼ lb)
¼ cup butter or margarine
2 cans (10½-oz size) condensed chicken broth, undiluted

CURRY SAUCE
¼ cup butter or margarine
1 clove garlic, crushed
1 cup chopped onion

2 to 3 teaspoons curry powder
1 cup chopped pared tart apple
¼ cup unsifted all-purpose flour
¼ teaspoon ground cardamom
1 teaspoon ginger
½ teaspoon salt
¼ teaspoon pepper
2 teaspoons grated lime peel
2 tablespoons lime juice

¼ cup chopped chutney

SAFFRON RICE
¼ teaspoon saffron, crumbled
2 tablespoons olive or salad oil
2 tablespoons butter or margarine
1½ cups raw long-grain
white rice
1½ teaspoons salt

GLORIOUS GALANTINE

PART I

This culinary classic—boned poultry or meat pressed into a symmetrical shape, glazed in aspic, and served cold—is a magnificent main dish for a summer buffet or first course for an elegant dinner party. It looks very difficult, but if you follow our simple step-by-step directions you will find it to be rather easy. Here, in Part I, you will learn how to skin and bone a whole turkey breast, prepare the ham-and-turkey stuffing, and restuff the skin of the turkey. Be sure to start preparing this galantine one or two days before you plan to serve it. This will give you plenty of time for preparation and chilling.

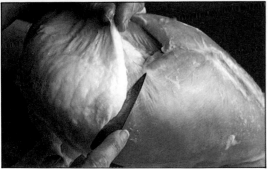

1 Wash turkey under cold water. Dry well on paper towels. Place turkey breast, skin side up, on board. With fingers and sharp knife, carefully remove skin by pulling it away from the flesh so that it comes off in one piece; cut membrane, and remove fat with knife.

2 Do not pierce turkey skin. Cover skin with damp paper towels. With sharp knife, remove breastbone from meat. Slice half of turkey breast into ½-inch slices; then cut into ½-inch lengthwise strips, set aside. Cut up the remaining half of the turkey breast.

3 Put through a food processor or finest blade of food chopper, along with cutup veal, pork and half of sliced fatback. In large bowl, combine meat mixture, ¼ cup brandy, the thyme, salt, nutmeg, pepper, Worcestershire, parsley and beaten eggs; mix well.

4 Cut ham into ½-inch strips. In shallow dish, marinate turkey and ham strips in ¼ cup brandy; refrigerate, covered, 1 hour. Drain; add brandy to meat mixture. Spread large piece of cheesecloth on table. Place turkey skin, outer side down, in center.

5 Spread ⅓ meat mixture in an even layer, 4 inches wide and 14 inches long, in center of skin. Cover with half of turkey and ham strips, in alternating (lengthwise) rows. Spread another third of the meat mixture evenly over strips. Stuff each black olive with a nut.

6 Place olives in row down center. Cover with remaining turkey and ham strips. Spread with remaining meat mixture. Bring up two sides of skin over center to cover filling. The skin will not totally enclose filling; use the rest of the fatback for this.

TURKEY BREAST GALANTINE, PART I

6-lb whole turkey breast	2 teaspoons salt	4 eggs, slightly beaten
½-lb lean boneless veal	½ teaspoon nutmeg	1 lb boiled ham, ½ inch thick
½-lb lean boneless pork	⅛ teaspoon pepper	¼ cup brandy, cognac
½-lb fatback, sliced	2 teaspoons Worcestershire	or Madeira
¼ cup brandy, Cognac or Madeira	sauce	14 pitted black olives
1 teaspoon dried thyme leaves	¼ cup chopped parsley	14 shelled pistachio nuts

GLORIOUS GALANTINE

PART II

If you've followed the steps in Part I correctly, you are now ready to wrap the reshaped turkey breast in cheesecloth (to maintain a uniform shape) and cook it in an herb-seasoned broth. After cooking, the turkey is refrigerated in the cooking broth overnight—this keeps the turkey very moist inside. After draining, remove the cheesecloth and coat the turkey breast in a heavy cream-based aspic and garnish with vegetable flowers. Then add a coat of clear aspic to make the galantine glisten. The result is an unbelievably beautiful turkey-and-ham galatine that is suitable to serve at any elegant special occasion.

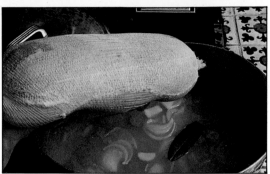

7 Roll filled turkey skin securely in cheesecloth. Tie ends with twine. In 12-quart oval Dutch oven, combine chicken broth, wine, 2 cups water, the onion, celery, carrots, salt, peppers, bay leaf. Bring to boil; add turkey breast seam side down. Return to boil.

8 Reduce heat, simmer gently, covered, until roll is just firm to touch—2 hours. Remove from heat; cool, refrigerate in broth, overnight. Remove roll to tray, skim fat from broth; bring to boil; strain through sieve lined with several thicknesses of cheesecloth.

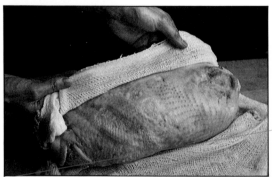

9 To glaze: Carefully remove cheesecloth. Place galantine, seam side down, on rack on tray. Refrigerate. Make glaze: In small saucepan, sprinkle gelatine over ½ cup broth; let stand 5 minutes to soften; add 3 cups broth. Heat, stirring, to dissolve gelatine.

10 In medium bowl, combine 1½ cups gelatine mixture and the cream. Set bowl in large bowl of ice water; let stand 15 minutes, until chilled and consistency of unbeaten egg white; stir occasionally. Remove from ice water. Spoon glaze over galantine.

11 Refrigerate on tray until glaze sets—about ½ hour. Scrape glaze from tray; reheat; chill again in ice water; spoon over galantine. Refrigerate. Cut cucumber skin to make leaves and olives into petals. Use chives for stems, capers for centers.

12 Cut carrot into rounds. Press flowers into surface. Refrigerate. Chill rest of clear glaze in ice water, stirring until thickened. Reglaze galantine, covering completely. Refrigerate on serving platter. To serve: Cut into slices ¼ inch thick. Makes 20 servings.

TURKEY BREAST GALANTINE, PART II

2 cans (10½-oz size) chicken broth	2 teaspoons salt	1 cup heavy cream
1½ cups dry white wine	6 whole black peppers	
1 large onion, quartered	1 bay leaf	**DECORATION**
2 celery stalks, cut up		Cucumber, pitted
3 medium carrots, pared, cut up	**GLAZE**	black olives, chives,
	2 env unflavored gelatine	capers, carrot, watercress

HUNTER-STYLE CHICKEN

Chicken Cacciatore literally means chicken hunter-style—an Italian way of cooking chicken with tomatoes, herbs and red wine. Even the heartiest of appetites will be satisfied when this flavorful mixture is served over a bed of polenta—cooked yellow cornmeal. Serve it with zucchini sautéed in olive oil and minced garlic, a tossed green salad and a hearty red wine.

1 Wash chicken; pat dry with paper towels. Heat oil and butter in 5- or 6-quart Dutch oven. Add chicken to hot fat, a few pieces at a time; brown well, turning on all sides. With tongs, remove pieces as they are browned and set aside—takes about 10 minutes in all.

2 Add onion, garlic, carrot, celery, parsley, salt, pepper, bay leaf and basil to Dutch oven. Sauté, stirring, until golden-brown—about 5 minutes. Add tomatoes and tomato sauce; mix well, mashing tomatoes with a fork. Bring to boiling, stirring.

3 Reduce heat; simmer, uncovered, 20 minutes. Add browned chicken with drippings and wine; gently simmer, covered, 45 to 50 minutes, until tender. Make polenta: In heavy, 6-quart kettle, bring 4 cups water and the salt to a full, rolling boil.

4 Slowly add cornmeal to the boiling water (it should not stop boiling), stirring constantly with wire whisk—mixture will become very thick. Turn heat very low; cook, uncovered and without stirring, until a very thick crust forms and leaves side of the pan.

5 This takes about 20 minutes. Spoon into a lightly greased, 9-inch, 1½-quart casserole, spreading evenly. (Keep warm in low oven if not serving at once.) To serve: With spatula, loosen around edge and underneath. Invert on large, heated platter.

6 Shake gently to release polenta in a large mound. Spoon chicken and some of sauce around polenta. Pass rest of sauce in gravy boat. If desired, sprinkle with chopped parsley. For each person, serve a chicken quarter with polenta and sauce. Serves 8.

CHICKEN CACCIATORE WITH POLENTA

2 (2-lb size) ready-to-cook broiler-fryers, quartered	½ cup pared, chopped carrot	1 can (1 lb, 1 oz) Italian tomatoes, undrained
3 tablespoons olive or salad oil	½ cup chopped celery	1 can (8 oz) tomato sauce
2 tablespoons butter or margarine	2 tablespoons chopped parsley	½ cup red wine
1½ cups sliced onion	1½ teaspoons salt	**POLENTA**
1 clove garlic, crushed	¼ teaspoon pepper	1 tablespoon salt
	1 bay leaf	2 cups yellow cornmeal
	½ teaspoon dried basil	

CHICKEN BREASTS TONNATO

This festive and light entrée, which can be made a day ahead, if you like, and served cold, is perfect for a luncheon or late evening buffet. Chicken breasts are poached and chilled in wine-flavored broth, then served on a bed of lettuce and topped with a traditional tuna-and-anchovy sauce. Garnishes of tomatoes and anchovies complete this picture-perfect, tasty dish.

1 Cut out core of iceberg lettuce with pointed knife; discard core. Hold cut part of lettuce under cold running water to separate leaves. Drain well on paper towels, in colander or salad spinner. Refrigerate, stored in plastic bag in crisper or plastic container with tight-fitting lid.

2 Wipe chicken breasts with damp paper towel. With sharp knife, split in half. In large 10-inch skillet, combine onion, celery stalk, carrot, parsley, 1 teaspoon salt, the thyme, bay leaf, undiluted chicken broth and water. Over medium heat, bring to boiling; add the chicken.

3 Bring to boiling; reduce heat; simmer, covered, 30 minutes, or until chicken is fork-tender. Remove skillet from heat; cool chicken breasts in broth 1 hour. Meanwhile, make tonnato sauce: Drain anchovy fillets; with sharp knife, chop 2 fillets; reserve the rest for garnish.

4 Drain tuna; discard liquid. In blender or food processor, combine chopped anchovies with tuna, mayonnaise, chopped celery, salt, pepper and lemon juice. Blend until smooth. Turn into 2-cup container with tight-fitting lid; refrigerate, covered. Makes about 2 cups.

5 Remove cooled chicken breasts from broth; strain broth, and refrigerate, covered, to use another time. Remove and discard skin and bone from chicken breasts. With sharp knife, shred lettuce. To serve: Cover large round serving platter with shredded lettuce.

6 Arrange breasts on lettuce in a circle. Spoon tonnato sauce over each breast. Garnish each breast with 2 whole anchovy fillets. Place tomato wedges between breasts and a whole tomato, cut into wedges, in the center. Garnish with watercress. Makes 8 servings.

CHICKEN BREASTS TONNATO

1 head iceberg lettuce	1 small bay leaf	1 cup mayonnaise
4 (1-lb size) whole chicken breasts	1 can (10¾ oz) condensed	½ cup finely chopped celery
1 large onion, sliced	chicken broth, undiluted	½ teaspoon salt
1 celery stalk, sliced	1 cup water	Dash black pepper
1 carrot, pared and sliced		1 tablespoon lemon juice
2 parsley sprigs	**TONNATO SAUCE**	
1 teaspoon salt	1 can (2 oz) anchovy fillets	2 tomatoes, each cut in 8 wedges
½ teaspoon dried thyme leaves	1 can (7 oz) tuna	Watercress sprigs

8634-03

French country cooks are famous for their chicken recipes—especially ones that use a long, slow cooking process with lots of wine and herbs added for flavor. This recipe for French Country-Style Chicken will be a valuable addition to your recipe collection, and you'll serve it often. Whole chickens are browned in a large Dutch oven and then are cooked with tomatoes, sherry wine, onion, celery, bay leaves, thyme, marjoram and cloves. The result is a delicious mélange of seasonings that combine to make a flavorful sauce for the tender chicken.

CHICKEN COOKED IN SHERRY WINE

1 Remove giblets from chickens; wash chickens and giblets under cold running water. Pat dry with paper towels and set aside while vegetables are being sautéed. Peel and thinly slice onion.

2 Put oil and butter in a large, heavy Dutch oven; heat over high heat until butter melts. Add onion, celery leaves, bay leaves, thyme, marjoram and clove. Sauté for about 5 minutes, stirring constantly, until onions are lightly browned.

3 Add one chicken to Dutch oven and cook for about 15 minutes, turning frequently until chicken is thoroughly browned on all sides. Remove from Dutch oven and set aside. Repeat with remaining chickens, one at a time, to brown thoroughly.

4 Return all chickens to Dutch oven; add drained tomatoes, pepper, 1 teaspoon salt and giblets (except livers). Cover and simmer over low heat for 1 hour. Add the chicken livers and 1 cup sherry wine; cover and cook 15 minutes longer or until chicken is tender.

5 Transfer chickens to serving platter; place in a warm oven to keep hot. Strain broth remaining in Dutch oven; remove chicken livers and discard remaining vegetable-giblet mixture. Return broth to Dutch oven; chop livers and reserve.

6 Stir remaining ¼ cup sherry into flour; stir flour mixture into broth in Dutch oven. Bring to a boil over high heat, stirring until thickened. Stir in chicken livers and season with salt. Serve sauce with chickens. Makes 6 servings.

FRENCH COUNTRY-STYLE CHICKEN

3 (2-lb size) whole chickens
1 medium onion
2 tablespoons salad oil
2 tablespoons butter or margarine

¼ cup chopped celery leaves
3 small bay leaves
¼ teaspoon dried thyme leaves
¼ teaspoon dried marjoram leaves
1 whole clove

1 can (1 lb) tomatoes, drained
¼ teaspoon pepper
Salt
1¼ cups dry sherry wine
3 tablespoons all-purpose flour

Cicero/Fimage Inc.

8636-04

A TASTY WAY TO TREAT A TURKEY

Turkey Tetrazzini was originally created for the Italian soprano Luisa Tetrazzini, back in the days when divas didn't count calories. Actually, the first version was made with chicken, but turkey gives it an even richer flavor. And what better way to use the remnants of a holiday bird? Pieces of cooked turkey are bathed in a rich wine-and-cream sauce, placed in a baking dish in a ring of spaghetti, topped with grated cheese and baked till hot. Or make it ahead of time, freeze and bake at the last minute.

1 Make sauce: Melt butter in large saucepan. Remove from heat. Stir in flour, 3 teaspoons salt and the nutmeg until smooth. Gradually add milk and turkey stock; bring to boiling, stirring constantly; boil 2 minutes, or until slightly thickened.

2 In small bowl, with wire whisk or wooden spoon, beat egg yolks with cream. Beat in a little of the hot mixture. Pour back into saucepan; cook over low heat, stirring constantly, until sauce is hot—do not boil. Remove from heat. Stir in the sherry.

3 Meanwhile, in 8-quart kettle, bring 6 quarts water to boiling; add 2 tablespoons salt and the spaghetti; cook as label directs; drain in colander. Return spaghetti to kettle. Add 2 cups sauce; toss lightly until spaghetti and sauce are well combined.

4 Divide spaghetti in half and place in two 12-by-8-by-2-inch baking dishes, arranging around edges. Add 2 cups sauce to turkey and mushrooms; mix well. Spoon half of turkey mixture into center of each dish. Reserve rest of sauce for later use.

5 Sprinkle cheese over spaghetti in each dish. Cover with foil; refrigerate 1 hour or overnight. About 1 hour before serving, preheat oven to 350F. Bake, covered, 45 minutes. Reheat sauce; spoon over spaghetti in each dish. Serves 12.

6 To freeze: Line baking dish with foil; assemble as directed. Fold foil over to seal; freeze right in dish. When frozen, lift out foil; remove dish from freezer. To serve: Unwrap; let stand 1 hour to thaw. Bake, covered, for 1 hour at 350F, or until bubbly.

TURKEY TETRAZZINI

SAUCE
¾ cup butter or margarine
¾ cup all-purpose flour
Salt
⅛ teaspoon nutmeg
1 quart milk
2 cups turkey stock* or

canned condensed chicken
broth, undiluted
4 egg yolks
1 cup heavy cream
½ cup dry sherry

1 pkg (1 lb) thin spaghetti

6 cups cooked leftover
turkey or chicken, cut
into 1½-inch pieces
2 cans (6-oz size) whole
mushrooms, drained
1 pkg (8 oz) sharp Cheddar
cheese, grated (2 cups)

*Turkey stock: Break up carcass. Place in 6-quart kettle with 3 cups water; 3 parsley sprigs; 2 carrots, pared and halved; 3 celery tops; 2 onions, halved; 2 teaspoons salt; 10 black peppercorns; 1 bay leaf. Bring to boiling; reduce heat; simmer, covered, 2 hours. Strain. Boil gently, uncovered, to reduce stock to 2 cups.

PERFECT POACHED CHICKEN

Here's a traditional French technique for preparing a whole chicken: Poach it slowly, on a nest of fresh carrots and leeks, in a Dutch oven on top of the range. The bird's delicate flavor is enhanced by the vegetables—and, later, by gravy with a subtle hint of white wine. The key to the recipe: careful prebrowning of the chicken. See the next page for step-by-step instructions.

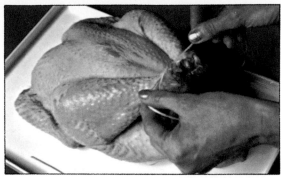

1 Remove giblets from chicken; rinse; set aside on paper towels. Rinse chicken well; dry with paper towels. Sprinkle inside with 1½ teaspoons salt and the pepper. Tuck wings under body; tie legs together. If necessary, fasten skin at the neck with a skewer.

2 In ¼ cup hot butter in 6-quart Dutch oven, brown chicken well all over—takes ½ hour. Turn chicken carefully with two wooden spoons; do not break skin. Coarsely chop giblets. Wash leeks; cut off and discard roots. Remove some leaves; add to giblets.

3 Halve leeks lengthwise; set aside. Place giblet-leek mixture under chicken. Cover; simmer over low heat ½ hour. Arrange carrots (if large, halve lengthwise) around chicken. Simmer, covered, 1 hour, till chicken and carrots are done. Remove from heat.

4 Meanwhile, scrub potatoes. Pare a strip of skin, about ½ inch wide, around center of each potato. Cook potatoes in 1 inch boiling salted water in medium saucepan, covered, 20 to 25 minutes, or until tender. Drain; drizzle with 2 tablespoons butter.

5 Cook leeks in 1 inch boiling water in medium pan, covered, 10 minutes, until tender. Drain; pour on 2 tablespoons butter. Lift chicken and carrots to heated platter; keep warm. Strain drippings; return liquid to Dutch oven. Stir in flour until smooth.

6 Gradually stir in wine and chicken broth; bring to boiling. Reduce heat; simmer, stirring, 3 minutes. Taste; add salt, if needed. Arrange potatoes, leeks and parsley sprigs around chicken. Sprinkle potatoes with chopped parsley. Pass gravy. Serves 6 to 8.

POACHED CHICKEN WITH VEGETABLES

5-to-5½-lb ready-to-cook roasting chicken, with giblets
Salt
⅛ teaspoon pepper
¼ cup butter or margarine

4 leeks (1 lb)
1½ to 2 lb small carrots, pared
1½ lb small new potatoes
¼ cup butter or margarine, melted
¼ cup flour

½ cup dry white wine
½ cup canned chicken broth

Parsley sprigs
Chopped parsley

8639-03

Arroz con pollo, that classic Spanish casserole of chicken, vegetables and saffron rice, has become a favorite dish throughout the world. We love it for its zesty flavor and the way it lends itself to easy, informal entertaining. It's colorful, economical and can be cooked and served in the same pot. And once it's in the oven, it requires very little attention —leaving you plenty of time to enjoy the party. Step-by-step instructions on the next page.

CHICKEN WITH A SPANISH ACCENT

1 Wash chicken pieces under cold running water; drain well. Wipe dry with paper towels so fat won't spatter when chicken is browning. Combine oregano, pepper and 2 teaspoons salt. Sprinkle chicken all over with mixture; rub in well. Let stand 10 minutes.

2 In heavy, 6-quart round or oval Dutch oven, heat olive oil over medium heat. Brown chicken, a third at a time, until golden-brown all over, using tongs to turn chicken—this takes about 30 minutes in all. Remove chicken as it browns. Preheat oven to 350F.

3 Wash green pepper; cut into quarters; remove ribs and seeds; cut into lengthwise strips, ¼ inch wide. To drippings in Dutch oven, add onion, garlic, green pepper, bay leaf and red pepper; sauté, stirring, over medium heat until onion is tender—5 minutes.

4 Using back of spoon, crush saffron threads on small piece of foil, or use a mortar and pestle. Add with 2 teaspoons salt and the rice to Dutch oven; cook, stirring, until rice is lightly browned—about 10 minutes. Add undrained tomatoes and chicken broth.

5 Arrange browned chicken pieces over rice mixture. Bring just to boiling, uncovered. Bake in oven, tightly covered, 1 hour. Remove from oven; add ½ cup water. Do not stir. Sprinkle peas and olives over top. Drain pimientos; cut into ¼-inch strips.

6 Arrange pimiento strips attractively over top. Bake, covered, 20 minutes longer, or until chicken is tender, peas are cooked and rice has absorbed all liquid. Remove from oven. Let stand, covered, 10 minutes. Serve right from Dutch oven. Serves 6.

ARROZ CON POLLO

2 (2½-lb size) roasting chickens, each cut into 6 pieces
2 teaspoons dried oregano leaves
½ teaspoon pepper
Salt
½ cup olive or salad oil
1 medium green pepper

2 cups chopped onion
1 clove garlic, crushed
1 bay leaf
⅛ to ¼ teaspoon crushed red pepper
1 teaspoon saffron threads
2 cups converted raw white rice

1 can (1 lb, 12 oz) tomatoes, undrained
1 can (13¾ oz) chicken broth
½ pkg (10-oz size) frozen green peas
½ cup pimiento-stuffed green olives, sliced
1 can (4 oz) pimientos

8640-04

A HUNGARIAN SUPPER

Chicken Paprikash with Galuska is traditional Hungarian fare: hearty and filling and so good you just can't stop eating! Galuska— tiny dumplings cut bit-by-bit and dropped into rapidly boiling water—are tossed with lots of butter and served with chicken in a paprika sauce laced with lots of sour cream. It's very rich and very good!

1 Wash chicken; dry on paper towels. Cut each breast in half. Brown chicken, half at a time, in 2 tablespoons hot butter in large skillet with tight-fitting cover, turning to brown well—takes about 20 minutes in all. With tongs, lift out chicken as it browns.

2 In 2 tablespoons butter in same skillet, sauté whole and chopped onions with 1 tablespoon paprika until lightly browned. Cut carrots diagonally into 1½-inch pieces. Add to onions; sauté 2 minutes. Stir in undiluted chicken broth and 2 teaspoons salt.

3 Arrange chicken on top of vegetables; bring to boiling. Reduce heat; simmer, covered, 45 minutes. Meanwhile, make Galuska: In large bowl, combine 2¾ cups flour, eggs, 1 teaspoon salt and 1 cup water. Beat with spoon until smooth.

4 When chicken is tender, remove with vegetables to platter, reserving liquid; cover. Keep warm in 300F oven while cooking Galuska and making gravy. In kettle, bring 2 quarts water and 2 teaspoons salt to boil. Spread dough on pancake turner, covering surface.

5 Cook Galuska: With moistened spatula, cut off small pieces of dough, letting them drop into boiling water. Cook one fourth dough at a time. Boil gently, uncovered, until firm and rise to top. Remove with slotted spoon to dish. Add butter. Keep warm.

6 In small bowl, mix flour with wine until smooth. Stir into liquid (there should be 3½ cups) in skillet. Bring to boil, stirring. Reduce heat; simmer 2 minutes. Slowly add sour cream; heat gently 1 minute. Pour some gravy over chicken. Add parsley. Serves 8.

CHICKEN PAPRIKASH WITH GALUSKA

6 whole chicken breasts (about ¾ lb each)
4 tablespoons butter or margarine
16 small white onions (1½ lb)
1 cup chopped onion
1 tablespoon paprika
8 small carrots (1 lb)
2 cans (10¾-oz size) condensed

chicken broth, undiluted
2 teaspoons salt

GALUSKA
2¾ cups sifted all-purpose flour (sift before measuring)
3 eggs
Salt

Water
2 tablespoons butter or margarine

GRAVY
⅓ cup flour
½ cup dry white wine
2 cups sour cream
Parsley or watercress

A NEW TWIST ON POTPIE

This old-fashioned one-pot meal is called Chicken-and-Noodle Potpie. It is not the traditional crusted pie you usually think of as a potpie, but instead is a chunky chicken stew made hearty with the addition of potatoes and wide homemade egg noodles. The broth is thin like a soup but rich in flavor. Serve it in deep bowls with chunks of black bread or potato bread and butter. Have a large salad to complete the meal—we suggest the Caesar Salad (Recipage—Salads 4).

1 Rinse chicken under cold running water; pat dry with paper towels. Put chicken pieces in a 6-quart Dutch oven and add water, celery, salt, peppercorns and saffron. Bring to a boil over high heat; reduce heat and simmer, covered, for 1 hour or until tender.

2 Remove chicken pieces from broth; reserve broth. Remove and discard skin and bones from chicken; leave chicken meat in large pieces. Set aside. Add potatoes and onion to broth; bring to a boil; reduce heat and simmer 15 minutes or until tender.

3 While potatoes cook, make noodles: In a medium-sized bowl, combine flour, butter and salt; mix with a fork to combine. Make a well in center of flour mixture. Add egg and 2 tablespoons water; beat with a fork until ingredients are blended. Press into a ball.

4 On a lightly floured pastry cloth or on a wooden surface, roll dough out to ⅛ inch thickness. Using a sharp knife or pastry wheel, cut noodles in strips 4 inches long and 1 inch wide. Remove potatoes, onions and celery from broth; set aside and keep warm.

5 Bring broth in Dutch oven to a rolling boil over high heat; add noodle strips, all at once, and return broth to a boil. Cook, uncovered, for about 10 to 15 minutes, stirring occasionally, until noodles are tender but not overcooked.

6 To serve: Add reserved chicken pieces, potatoes, onions and celery to broth and noodles in Dutch oven. Bring to a simmer and cook for about 5 minutes or until hot. Sprinkle top of Chicken-and-Noodle Potpie with chopped parsley. Makes 6 servings.

CHICKEN-AND-NOODLE POTPIE

5-lb roasting chicken, cut up
6 cups water
1 celery stalk, cut up
1½ teaspoon salt
6 whole black peppercorns
¼ teaspoon saffron threads,

crumbled
4 medium potatoes (2 lb), pared
and sliced ¼ inch thick
1 cup sliced onion

NOODLES
1 cup unsifted all-purpose flour

1 tablespoon butter or margarine
1 teaspoon salt
1 egg
2 tablespoons water

Chopped parsley

This is a great party dish: skillet-browned chicken topped with melted Parmesan cheese on top of a bed of seasoned spinach and al dente-cooked pasta. It's festive and delicious!

ITALIAN-STYLE CHICKEN PARMIGIANA

1 Rinse chicken thighs under cold running water and then pat them dry with paper towels; set aside. Peel onion. Using a large sharp knife, cut onion into thin slices; set aside. Peel garlic. Using a garlic press, crush garlic and set aside.

2 In a large skillet, melt butter over moderately high heat. Cook chicken a few pieces at a time, skin side down, for 5 minutes or until golden brown. Return all chicken to skillet, add onion and garlic; cover skillet and cook 5 minutes.

3 Uncover skillet and push chicken to one side. Add frozen block of spinach to skillet; sprinkle with ½ teaspoon salt and the basil. Cover skillet and simmer 15 minutes longer, separating the spinach with a fork as it cooks.

4 Meanwhile, cook spaghetti: Bring water and 1½ teaspoons of the salt to a boil in a large saucepot. Add spaghetti, all at once; stir to separate strands and return to a boil. Cook for 7 minutes or until tender but firm to the bite. Drain thoroughly.

5 Uncover skillet and stir spinach together with onion and butter to mix thoroughly. Turn chicken skin side up and sprinkle with ¼ cup Parmesan cheese. Cover skillet and simmer 10 minutes longer or until chicken is tender and thoroughly cooked.

6 Remove skillet from heat. Arrange drained spaghetti on a large platter and top with cooked spinach mixture. Arrange cheese-topped chicken thighs on top and serve immediately. Makes 4 to 6 servings.

CHICKEN THIGHS PARMIGIANA

8 chicken thighs (about 2 lb)	**1 pkg (10 oz) frozen chopped**	**1 teaspoon dried basil leaves**
1 medium onion	**spinach**	**4 quarts water**
2 cloves garlic	**Salt**	**1 pkg (8 oz) spaghetti**
¼ cup butter or margarine		**¼ cup grated Parmesan cheese**

CRUMB-COATED CHICKEN WITH SOUR-CREAM SAUCE

These baked chicken breasts are easy to prepare: Simply dip pieces into mushroom soup, coat with packaged herb-seasoned stuffing mix and bake. Then use more mushroom soup and sour cream to make a rich velvety sauce. Delicious and perfect for an impromptu dinner!

1 Rinse chicken breasts thoroughly under cold running water; pat dry with paper towels. Split chicken breasts; pull skin from chicken breasts and discard. Preheat oven to 375F.

2 Put one can of condensed cream of mushroom soup in a medium-sized bowl. Add milk and stir with a wire whisk or a wooden spoon until thoroughly combined. Put stuffing mix in a shallow plate or pie dish. Peel and finely chop onion; add to mix with parsley.

3 Dip skinned side of chicken into soup mixture, coating well. Press into stuffing mix, making sure that it sticks to the chicken. Place in a shallow baking pan, crumb side up. Place in oven on center rack and bake for 1 hour.

4 While chicken bakes, prepare sour-cream sauce: Put mushroom soup-milk mixture, left over from dipping chicken, in a medium-sized saucepan. Add the remaining can of mushroom soup and stir in an equal amount of sour cream. (You will use about 1½ cups.)

5 Heat soup-and-sour-cream mixture over moderate heat, stirring frequently, until mixture is hot but not boiling. If desired, stir in a can of tomato soup and season to taste with the seasoned salt. Heat again until mixture is hot.

6 Transfer baked chicken to a decorative serving platter. Spoon some of the sour-cream sauce over the baked chicken. Serve the rest of the sauce separately. Garnish with fresh sprigs of watercress. Makes 8-10 servings.

SOUR-CREAM CHICKEN BREASTS*

5 whole chicken-breasts	**¼ cup milk**	**Sour cream (about 1½ cups)**
2 cans (10¾ oz each) condensed	**1 pkg (8 oz) herb-seasoned**	**1 can (10¾ oz) condensed**
cream of mushroom soup or	**stuffing mix, finely crushed**	**tomato soup, undiluted (optional)**
golden mushroom soup	**1 small onion**	**Seasoned salt (optional)**
(undiluted)	**1 tablespoon dried parsley flakes**	**Fresh watercress sprigs**

*Recipe contributed to McCall's by Beth Tartan, *Winston-Salem Journal*, Winston-Salem, NC.

David Viens

8646-03

STIR-FRIED TURKEY AND VEGETABLES WITH CHINESE FRIED NOODLES

Traditionally this Chinese dish is called *chow mein*—literally interpreted as "fried noodles." In Chinese kitchens, cooks boil plain noodles (similar to our spaghetti), dry and chill them, and then, just before serving, drop them into hot fat to fry until crispy and browned. These crisp noodles make the base for stir-fried meat-and-vegetable mixtures. Follow our step-by-step directions for Turkey Chow Mein: a stir-fried turkey-and-vegetable mixture spooned over store-bought Chinese fried noodles. It's delicious!

1 Wash and trim green onions. Using a small, very sharp knife, make several lengthwise cuts through the dark green ends. Place onions in a bowl of ice water; cover and refrigerate about 20 minutes. (During chilling, the green tops will crisp and curl.)

2 To make turkey easier to slice, store in freezing compartment until partially frozen. Using a sharp chef's knife, slice turkey into ⅛-inch slivers. (You should have about 3 cups.) Pour oil into a large skillet or wok and heat over moderately high heat.

3 When oil is very hot, add sliced onion and celery and cook, stirring constantly, until onion is golden brown and celery is tender. Push the onion and celery to one side, then add turkey slivers; cook, stirring constantly, 5 minutes.

4 Add gravy, cream-of-mushroom soup, ½ cup water and soy sauce to turkey, onion and celery in skillet. Continue to heat over moderately high heat, stirring constantly, until mixture comes to a boil. Add sprouts; reduce heat to moderately low, cover skillet, and simmer 5 minutes.

5 Meanwhile, in a small bowl, mix cornstarch with ½ cup cold water until no lumps remain. Add about ½ cup of the hot gravy mixture from the skillet to the cornstarch mixture, stirring thoroughly. Return to turkey mixture in skillet and mix well.

6 Bring turkey mixture to a boil over moderately high heat, stirring constantly, until gravy thickens and turns translucent. To serve: Gently spoon hot turkey mixture over Chinese noodles and garnish with the scallion brushes. Good served with rice. Serves 6.

TURKEY CHOW MEIN

4 green onions or scallions	**½ cup canned chicken gravy**	**1 can (14 oz) bean sprouts**
1 lb turkey cutlets	**1 can (10¾ oz) condensed cream-**	**(drained)**
2 tablespoons vegetable oil	**of-mushroom soup (undiluted)**	**1 tablespoon cornstarch**
1 cup thinly sliced onion	**Water**	**1 can (3 oz) crisp Chinese**
2 cups diagonally sliced celery	**¼ cup soy sauce**	**noodles**

David Viens

8648-03

COUNTRY CAPTAIN CHICKEN

Legend has it that "Country Captain" was the nickname given to British officers of Indian troops who served in England long ago.

This exotic recipe probably came from the blending of these two extremely different cuisines: The curry of India was combined with the foods available at the time in

England, such as chicken, onions and tomatoes. The result is this unusual and delicious Country Captain Chicken.

1 Using a large butcher knife or poultry shears, cut chickens in half along breast bone and back bone. Cut each half into two pieces, cutting between breast and leg. (You should have 8 pieces of chicken.) If you prefer, you can purchase 2 chickens, quartered.

2 Wash chicken pieces under cold running water and pat dry with paper towels. (Be sure to dry thoroughly.) Put flour, salt and pepper in a large plastic bag. Twist top of bag to close and shake to thoroughly combine flour and seasonings.

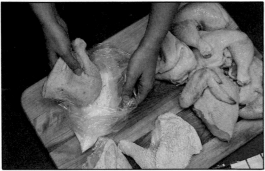

3 Add one or two pieces of chicken to the plastic bag; twist top closed and shake until chicken is thoroughly coated with seasoned-flour mixture. Remove chicken pieces from bag, shaking off excess flour. Repeat until all chicken pieces are coated.

4 Put butter and oil in a 6-quart Dutch oven and heat over moderately high heat. When oil is hot, add chicken, a few pieces at a time, and cook for several minutes, turning to brown well on all sides. Remove browned chicken to platter; repeat for all pieces.

5 Add onion, green and red pepper, garlic and curry powder to drippings remaining in Dutch oven. Sauté vegetables, stirring constantly until onion is soft (about 5 minutes). Stir in tomatoes, crushing with a fork, and the raisins. Bring to a boil.

6 Return chicken to sauce; simmer, covered, for 50 to 60 minutes or until chicken is just tender. To serve: Arrange chicken on serving platter; spoon some sauce over chicken. Spoon rice around edge of platter and serve with remaining sauce. Makes 8 servings.

COUNTRY CAPTAIN CHICKEN

2 (2½-lb size) broiler-fryer chickens
¼ cup all-purpose flour
1½ teaspoons salt
½ teaspoon pepper

2 tablespoons butter
2 tablespoons vegetable oil
1 cup chopped onion
½ cup cubed green pepper
½ cup cubed red (sweet) pepper
1 clove garlic (crushed)

1 tablespoon curry powder
1 can (1 lb) whole peeled tomatoes (undrained)
½ cup dark seedless raisins
4 cups hot cooked rice

David Viens

8649-05

A TRADITIONAL ROAST TURKEY PART I

When you're in the mood for an old-fashioned roast turkey or when it's holiday time and you're elected to cook the traditional feast, you can relax, knowing that all you have to do is follow our easy step-by-step directions. Here, in Part I of this series, you will learn how to stuff and truss the turkey and how to roast it. Turn to Part II (Recipage—Chicken, Poultry 30) to learn how to make the delicious Cranberry-Orange Stuffing and the Giblet Gravy; see Part III (Recipage—Chicken, Poultry 31) for the Fresh-Cranberry Sauce in Orange Shells and the Candied Orange-Ring Chain garnish. You'll be amazed at how easy it all is!

1 Remove giblets and neck from turkey; wash and set aside (see Note). Wash turkey, inside and out, under running water; dry with paper towels. Remove excess fat; discard. Cover and chill until ready to stuff. Prepare stuffing as directed (Recipage—Chicken, Poultry 30).

2 Spoon some stuffing into neck cavity of the turkey. Bring skin of neck over back; fasten with a poultry pin. Spoon the remaining dressing loosely into body cavity; do not pack. Insert 4 or 5 poultry pins at regular intervals; lace cavity closed with kitchen twine.

3 Bend wing tips under body of turkey; tie ends of legs together with more kitchen twine. Insert a meat thermometer in inside of thigh at the thickest part, being sure that it does not touch bone. Place the turkey on a rack in an open shallow roasting pan.

4 Brush turkey with some of the melted butter and sprinkle with salt and pepper. Roast turkey, uncovered, for about 4½ hours, brushing frequently with more butter and pan drippings. (When turkey begins to turn golden brown, cover loosely with aluminum foil.)

5 The turkey is done when the meat thermometer registers 185F in the thigh or 165F in the center of the stuffing. The thickest part of the drumstick should feel very tender and the thigh joint should move freely. Meat juices should be clear and not pink.

6 Place turkey on heated platter. Remove twine and pins. Let stand 20 minutes while you make Giblet Gravy (Recipage—Chicken, Poultry 30). Before serving, garnish with Fresh-Cranberry Sauce in Orange Shells, Candied-Orange-Ring Chain and parsley. Makes 14 servings.

OLD-FASHIONED ROAST TURKEY

14- to 16-lb ready-to-cook turkey (thawed, if frozen)
Cranberry-Orange Stuffing (Recipage—Chicken, Poultry 30)
1 cup butter or margarine (melted)

Salt
Pepper
Giblet Gravy (Recipage— Chicken, Poultry 30)

Fresh-Cranberry Sauce in Orange Shells (Recipage— Chicken, Poultry 31)
Candied-Orange-Ring Chain (Recipage—Chicken, Poultry 31)
Fresh parsley sprigs

Note: Save giblets and neck, roasting pan and pan drippings for preparing Giblet Gravy (Recipage—Chicken, Poultry 30).

David Viens

9800-03

A TRADITIONAL ROAST TURKEY PART II
CRANBERRY-ORANGE STUFFING
AND GIBLET GRAVY

**This delicious stuffing and vegetable-giblet gravy are perfect
accompaniments for the succulent roast turkey described in Part I of this
series (see Recipage—Chicken, Poultry 29). Our step-by-step directions
will make your next Thanksgiving feast as easy as one, two, three!**

1 Preheat oven to 350F. In hot butter in medium skillet, sauté onion, celery and Brazil nuts, stirring frequently with a wooden spoon, for about 5 minutes or until onion is tender. Add cranberries, sugar, orange juice and orange peel.

2 Cook cranberry mixture over medium heat until cranberries start to pop. Remove from heat; set aside to cool 20 minutes. Meanwhile, cut bread into ½-inch cubes (10 cups). Spread on baking sheet and put in oven to toast for 5 minutes.

3 In a large bowl, toss cranberry mixture with salt, poultry seasoning, savory and pepper. Add toasted bread cubes and toss until thoroughly combined. Makes about 12 cups stuffing. Use to stuff Old-Fashioned Roast Turkey (see Recipage—Chicken, Poultry 29).

4 Make Giblet Gravy: Place giblets (reserve liver and chill until ready to use), neck, water, celery, onion, carrot, salt, peppercorns and bay leaf in 2-quart saucepan. Bring to boil, reduce heat and simmer, covered, for 2½ hours.

5 Add turkey liver to giblet mixture in saucepan and simmer 15 minutes longer. Discard neck. Remove giblets and chop coarsely; set aside. Strain broth; press vegetables through a sieve. Add enough chicken broth to vegetables to make 2½ cups total.

6 Put ⅓ cup fat in roasting pan; stir in flour until smooth. Stir over low heat to brown flour slightly. Remove from heat; stir in vegetable-broth mixture. Bring to a boil, stirring constantly. Add giblets and simmer 5 minutes. Makes 3 cups gravy.

CRANBERRY-ORANGE STUFFING AND GIBLET GRAVY

STUFFING
½ cup butter or margarine
½ cup chopped onion
½ cup chopped celery
1 pkg (6 oz) chopped Brazil nuts (1 cup)
2 cups fresh cranberries (washed)
½ cup sugar
½ cup orange juice
1 tablespoon grated orange peel
2 loaves (1-lb size) raisin bread (sliced)

1½ teaspoons salt
½ teaspoon poultry seasoning
½ teaspoon dried savory
⅛ teaspoon pepper

GRAVY
Giblets and neck reserved from Old-Fashioned Roast Turkey (See Recipage—Chicken, Poultry 29)
3 cups water
1 stalk celery (cut up)

1 onion (quartered)
1 pared carrot (cut up)
1 teaspoon salt
4 whole black peppercorns
1 bay leaf
Undiluted canned chicken broth
⅓ cup fat reserved from Old-Fashioned Roast Turkey (See Recipage—Chicken, Poultry 29)
⅓ cup all-purpose flour

David Viens

9801-03

A TRADITIONAL ROAST TURKEY PART III
CRANBERRY-FILLED ORANGE SHELLS AND AN ORANGE-RING GARLAND

Complete your holiday feast by garnishing
your turkey with a Candied-Orange-Ring Chain
studded with cranberries and fluted orange
cups filled with homemade cranberry sauce.

1 Prepare Fresh-Cranberry-Sauce in Orange Shells up to two days before serving. Wash cranberries; remove and discard stems and soft berries. (If berries are frozen, do not thaw.) Put sugar and water in a large saucepan. Bring to a boil and stir until sugar dissolves.

2 Cook sugar syrup 10 minutes on medium-low heat, stirring occasionally. Add cranberries; return mixture to a boil over high heat. Reduce heat to low and simmer 8 to 10 minutes, stirring occasionally. Remove from heat; transfer to a bowl. Makes 4 cups sauce. Cover and chill.

3 Cut oranges in half crosswise, making a zigzag pattern. Scoop out pulp (use for orange juice). If desired, cover and chill shells until you are ready to garnish the turkey. Just before serving, fill shells with cranberry sauce and arrange around turkey.

4 Prepare Candied-Orange-Ring Chain up to 2 days before serving. Wash oranges. With a 2½-inch round cookie cutter, cut four rounds of orange peel from each orange, pressing and turning cutter into orange. With 1¾-inch cutter, cut out centers of large rounds to make rings.

5 Put sugar, corn syrup and water in 4-quart saucepan. Bring to boil; stir constantly, until sugar dissolves. Boil, uncovered, 10 minutes. Add rings; reduce heat; simmer 50 to 60 minutes or until rings are glazed. Remove from heat. Turn into shallow dish, covering rings with syrup.

6 Cover dish; let stand at room temperature several hours. Drain rings by threading on handle of wooden spoon, balanced over pan. Make chain: Make a cut in half of the rings and weave together on turkey breast, alternating cut and uncut rings to form chain. Garnish with cranberries.

FRESH-CRANBERRY-SAUCE IN ORANGE SHELLS AND CANDIED-ORANGE-RING CHAIN

SAUCE
4 cups fresh or frozen cranberries
1½ cups sugar

1½ cups water
4 small oranges

CHAIN
6 large navel oranges

2¼ cups sugar
¾ cup light corn syrup
3 cups water

THE MOST ELEGANT CUSTARD

Rich, heavy cream whipped with egg yolks and crowned with caramelized brown sugar, crème brûlée is the crème de la crème of custard desserts. Make it a day ahead (it must be refrigerated overnight), and serve with fresh fruit (we love frosted grapes and strawberries). Directions on the next page.

1 Day before serving, over low heat, heat heavy cream in a heavy, 2½-quart saucepan just until bubbles form around the edge of the pan. Remove from heat. In double-boiler top, with electric mixer at medium speed, beat yolks until very thick and light.

2 Gradually beat in ⅓ cup granulated sugar, a tablespoon at a time, beating until very thick—about 4 minutes. Gradually stir in cream, using wooden spoon. Cook, over hot, not boiling, water, stirring constantly, until thickened—about 15 minutes.

3 Mixture should be thick enough to form a coating on a metal spoon. Add vanilla. Strain custard into attractive 9-inch shallow baking dish, 1 inch deep, or 9-inch pie plate. Or turn into 6 (½ cup) individual soufflé dishes. Refrigerate 8 hours or overnight.

4 An hour or two before serving, set in large baking pan; surround completely with ice. Sift brown sugar through strainer evenly over surface. Run under broiler, 4 inches from heat, just until sugar melts slightly and caramelizes—it forms a hard crust.

5 Refrigerate until serving. Meanwhile, prepare frosted grapes: Wash and dry bunches of grapes on paper towels. With soft brush, coat grapes with slightly beaten egg white. Quickly roll in granulated sugar to coat well. Place on rack on tray to dry.

6 If necessary, roll grapes in sugar to coat once again. Place in freezer a few minutes. To serve: Place crème brûlée on silver platter; surround with galax leaves and small bunches of frosted grapes, alternating with large strawberries. Makes 8 servings.

CRÈME BRÛLÉE

3 cups heavy cream	**⅓ cup light-brown sugar, packed**	**2 egg whites**
6 egg yolks		**Granulated sugar**
⅓ cup granulated sugar	**1 lb seedless green grapes,**	**8 large whole strawberries**
1 teaspoon vanilla extract	**cut into small bunches**	**with stems on**

8602-4

Some occasions call for a spectacular dessert, like this *vacherin glace au chocolat:* crisp meringue layers filled with ice cream and topped with chocolate sauce. The secret of a perfect meringue is to add the sugar to beaten egg whites *very* gradually; then beat until it looks—and feels—absolutely smooth. Complete recipe, next page.

SWEET NOTHING: CHOCOLATE-FILLED MERINGUE

1 Day ahead, make meringue: In large mixer bowl, let whites warm to room temperature—1 hour. Line two cookie sheets with brown paper. On each, draw a 9-inch round, using cake pan as guide. At high speed, beat egg whites with cream of tartar and salt.

2 Continue to beat just until soft peaks form when beater is slowly raised. Gradually beat in 2 cups sugar, 2 tablespoons at a time, beating well after each addition. Beat in vinegar and vanilla; continue beating until stiff peaks form—10 minutes longer.

3 Preheat oven to 200F. Spread half of meringue on paper on each cookie sheet, to make 9-inch rounds. Bake 2 hours; turn off heat, and leave in oven overnight, to dry out the meringue layers. Turn ice cream into bowl; let stand in refrigerator to soften slightly.

4 Line a 9-inch layer pan with plastic wrap; fill with ice cream; freeze until firm—overnight. Next day, to serve, make chocolate sauce: In top of double boiler, combine sugar and 2 tablespoons heavy cream; cook over boiling water, stirring to dissolve the sugar.

5 Remove double boiler from heat; leave top over bottom. Cut up ½ square unsweetened and the sweet chocolate; stir into cream mixture to melt. Beat in remaining cream. Invert ice cream over one meringue on serving plate. Top with meringue.

6 Frost sides with half of whipped cream. With remainder in pastry bag with number-5 star tip, make rosettes around top. Spoon chocolate sauce inside ring to form a "lake." Grate remaining chocolate. Sprinkle over whipped cream. Makes 12 servings.

VACHERIN GLACE AU CHOCOLAT

MERINGUE LAYERS
1 cup egg whites (about
7 large)
1 teaspoon cream of tartar
¼ teaspoon salt
2 cups sugar
2 teaspoons white vinegar

1 teaspoon vanilla extract

2 pints chocolate, strawberry
or coffee ice cream

CHOCOLATE SAUCE
2 tablespoons sugar

¼ cup heavy cream
1 square (1 oz) unsweetened
chocolate
½ pkg (4-oz size) sweet
cooking chocolate

1¾ cups heavy cream, whipped

A RICH DESSERT
THAT COSTS LITTLE

An ordinary low-cost dessert can become special when you use a little extra imagination in preparing and serving it. To make simple rice custard more impressive: Bake the mixture of rice, eggs, sugar, milk and vanilla in an attractive soufflé dish set in a pan of simmering water. Cook it a day ahead and chill. At the last-minute, on goes a caramelized-sugar design. Recipe, next page.

1 Day before: In top of double boiler, combine rice and 4 cups milk. Cook over boiling water, stirring occasionally, 45 minutes, until rice is tender (add water to lower part if necessary). Remove from hot water. Let cool slightly—10 minutes. Preheat oven to 350F.

2 Lightly butter a 2-quart soufflé dish or casserole; place in shallow baking pan. In large bowl, with wire whisk, beat eggs with remaining 1 cup milk. Add ¾ cup sugar, the salt and vanilla extract; mix well. Gradually stir in the hot rice mixture, and mix well.

3 Pour into prepared soufflé dish. Pour hot water to 1-inch depth around soufflé dish. Bake, uncovered, 50 to 60 minutes, or until knife inserted in custard 1 inch from edge comes out clean. Use pot holders to remove soufflé dish from hot water to wire rack.

4 Cool at room temperature 1 hour. Then refrigerate, covered with plastic wrap, until very well chilled—overnight. Next day, about 1 hour before serving, make caramel syrup: Sprinkle ⅓ cup sugar evenly over the bottom of a small, heavy skillet.

5 Cook slowly over very low heat, stirring occasionally with wooden spoon, just until sugar melts and turns golden. (If sugar is cooked too long or at too high a temperature, it will be too dark and have a burned flavor.) Remove from heat, and cool slightly.

6 Using a teaspoon, drizzle syrup over top of custard crisscross, to form pattern as pictured. Refrigerate the custard until serving. (Caramel will melt and become runny if it is refrigerated too long.) Nice served with whipped cream. Makes 8 servings.

CARAMEL RICE CUSTARD

⅓ cup raw (short grain)* regular white rice 5 cups milk	3 eggs ¾ cup sugar 1 teaspoon salt	2 teaspoons vanilla extract CARAMEL SYRUP ⅓ cup sugar

*Short-grain rice is softer than long-grain rice. It is preferred for use in desserts.

SNOWY, SHOWY
MERINGUE WITH FRUIT

From the land of ice and snow comes a dessert as refreshing as Scandinavia itself. This delectable mountain made of meringue, whipped cream and fruit is popular there: Puffs of foamy meringue are baked till firm, then mounded over a creamy base filled with bits of pineapple, orange and green grapes—and chocolate is shaved over the finished confection. To see how it's done, turn the page.

1 In large bowl, let whites warm to room temperature—1 hour. Section oranges: Hold fruit over bowl; with sharp knife, remove peel and white membrane by cutting around in a spiral. Cut on each side of dividing membranes; lift out sections. Refrigerate.

2 With mixer at high speed, beat whites with cream of tartar and salt until soft peaks form when beater is slowly raised. Beat in granulated sugar, 2 tablespoons at a time, until stiff peaks form when beater is slowly raised (they should be moist and shiny).

3 Preheat oven to 275F. Lightly butter and flour two large cookie sheets. Drop meringue by tablespoonfuls; with rubber scraper, push meringue from spoon to form mounds 1 inch apart. There will be about 40. Bake 1 hour, or just until crisp and light golden.

4 Cool on wire rack. Drain fruit; save juices for another time. Beat cream with confectioners' sugar until stiff. Gently fold in three fourths of drained fruit. To assemble dessert: Arrange 12 meringues on round serving platter to form a 9-inch round layer.

5 Spoon half of whipped-cream mixture on center of meringues, mounding. Arrange more meringues around and on top of whipped cream. Continue to form pyramid with meringues and whipped cream. Fill spaces between meringues with whipped cream.

6 Place one meringue on top. Decorate with orange sections, grapes and bananas, as pictured. Sprinkle all over with shaved chocolate. Refrigerate to chill well—4 hours. To serve: Spoon several meringues with cream and fruit on each plate. Serves 12.

ROYAL MERINGUE DESSERT

6 egg whites (1 cup)	¾ cup well-drained pineapple chunks, chilled	2 cups heavy cream
2 navel oranges	¾ cup seedless green grapes	½ cup confectioners' sugar
½ teaspoon cream of tartar	1 banana, sliced and dipped in orange juice, chilled	1 square German sweet chocolate, shaved with a sharp knife
½ teaspoon salt		
1½ cups granulated sugar		

8605-04

A GOLDEN FLOATING ISLAND

Floating island, a favorite American dessert adapted from the French, is a soft, creamy custard with a deliciously light and fluffy meringue floating on top. Ours is an especially elegant version of this classic. We baked the meringue in a fancy mold to make it more glamorous. Then we poured a golden caramel syrup over it and decorated the custard with whole fresh strawberries. Remember to chill the custard well, and take care with the caramel syrup—it burns easily; cook it slowly just until it turns golden. For the complete, illustrated step-by-step instructions, please turn the page.

1 Heat milk in top of a metal double boiler, over direct heat, until tiny bubbles form around edge. In small bowl, using rotary beater, beat egg yolks, ⅓ cup sugar and dash salt. Slowly beat hot milk into egg mixture. Pour back into top of double boiler.

2 Place over gently simmering water. (Water in lower part of double boiler should not touch upper part.) Cook, stirring constantly, until a thin coating forms on metal spoon—8 to 10 minutes. Pour immediately into a medium bowl. Set bowl in cold water.

3 When cool, add vanilla. Place sheet of waxed paper directly on surface. Refrigerate several hours. Meanwhile, in large electric mixer bowl, let whites warm to room temperature—about 1 hour. Lightly butter inside of a 5-cup mold. Preheat oven to 350F.

4 Meringue: At high speed, beat whites with cream of tartar and salt until foamy. Beat in ½ cup sugar, 2 tablespoons at a time; beat after each addition. Beat until stiff peaks form when beater is slowly raised. Spoon into mold. Press to remove air pockets.

5 Place in deep pan. Add boiling water, 1¾ inches deep. Bake, uncovered, 25 minutes, or until knife inserted in center comes out clean. Cool on rack 5 minutes. Spoon custard into serving dish. With spatula, loosen edge of mold. Unmold on custard.

6 Sprinkle ¼ cup sugar over bottom of small, heavy skillet. With spoon, stir occasionally over low heat until sugar turns to a golden syrup. Slowly stir in hot water; stir to melt sugar. Spoon over meringue. Refrigerate 1 hour. Decorate with berries. Serves 8.

A GOLDEN FLOATING ISLAND

CUSTARD SAUCE
2 cups milk
4 egg yolks
⅓ cup sugar
Dash salt
¾ teaspoon vanilla extract

MERINGUE
4 egg whites (½ cup)
⅛ teaspoon cream of tartar
Dash salt
½ cup sugar
Boiling water

CARAMEL SYRUP
¼ cup sugar
¼ cup hot water

8 large strawberries, washed, with hulls left on

This golden pastry ring crowned with sliced almonds and confectioners' sugar takes its name— Paris-Brest—from the French train route on which it is believed to have first been served. The secret of its airy consistency is basic cream-puff dough, called *pâte à choux*, which is baked first, then split open and filled with whipped cream. To learn how it's done, turn the page.

A CREAMY FRENCH DESSERT

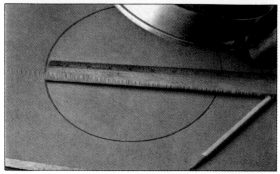

1 Preheat oven to 400F. In medium saucepan, combine 1 cup water, the butter and salt. Over medium heat, bring to boiling. Remove from heat. With wooden spoon, beat in flour all at once. Over low heat, beat until mixture forms ball and leaves pan.

2 Remove from heat. Add whole eggs, one at a time. With portable electric mixer or wooden spoon, beat hard after each addition. Beat until mixture is shiny and breaks into strands. On baking sheet lined with brown paper, draw an 8-inch circle, to use as guide.

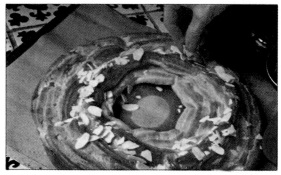

3 Spoon dough into pastry bag with number-8 star tip. Pipe an 8-inch circle of dough (1 inch in diameter) on guide, pressing down hard on bag. Pipe a circle inside and touching 8-inch circle. Pipe third circle on top. Press out rest on top of third circle.

4 Bake 50 minutes. In small bowl, with fork, beat egg yolk with 1 tablespoon water. Remove cream-puff ring from oven. Brush egg mixture lightly over top (not side) of ring. Sprinkle top with almonds. Bake 5 minutes longer, or until ring is deep golden-brown.

5 Cool on wire rack. Make whipped-cream filling: In medium bowl, combine cream, 1 cup confectioners' sugar and vanilla and almond extracts; mix well. Refrigerate, covered, 1 hour. Place in bowl of ice water. With mixer at high speed, beat until stiff.

6 To assemble: With sharp knife, split ring in half crosswise. Scoop out filaments of soft dough. Place bottom on serving platter. To fill, pipe filling through pastry bag with number-8 tip. Set top in place, and sprinkle with confectioners' sugar. Serves 12.

PARIS-BREST

CREAM-PUFF DOUGH
½ cup butter or regular margarine
¼ teaspoon salt
1 cup unsifted all-purpose flour
4 whole eggs

1 egg yolk
¼ cup sliced blanched almonds

WHIPPED-CREAM FILLING
2 cups heavy cream, chilled

1 cup confectioners' sugar
2 teaspoons vanilla extract
¼ teaspoon almond extract

Confectioners' sugar

THE ULTIMATE CHEESECAKE

One of New York's most famous restaurants was Lindy's; it was jammed night after night with Broadway's brightest stars, but the main attraction was its famous cheesecake. Though Lindy's is gone now, you can still enjoy what many think is the greatest cheesecake ever made. Serve it glazed with pineapple, un-glazed, or with sour cream spread thick and smooth on top. With only a few minor changes, our recipe is just like the one used at Lindy's. You'll find the same crisp cookie crust and the daringly rich cream-cheese filling, touched with just a hint of lemon. For instructions, turn page.

1 Preheat oven to 400F. Grease inside of 9-inch springform pan (3 inches high). Remove side. Make crust: In medium bowl, combine flour, sugar, lemon peel, vanilla. Make well in center; with fork, blend in yolk and butter. Mix with fingertips until smooth.

2 On bottom of pan, form half of dough into ball. Place waxed paper on top; roll pastry to edge of pan. Remove paper. Bake 6 to 8 minutes, or until golden. Cool. Meanwhile, divide rest of dough into three parts. Cut six strips of waxed paper, 3 inches wide.

3 On dampened surface, between paper strips, roll each part 2¼ inches wide and 9 inches long. Assemble springform pan with crust on bottom. Line inside of pan with pastry strips, overlapping ends. Remove waxed-paper strips. Preheat oven to 450.

4 Filling: In large mixer bowl, blend cheese, sugar, flour, peels and vanilla at high speed. Beat in eggs and yolks, one at a time; beat until smooth, occasionally scraping bowl with spatula. Beat in cream. Pour into pan. Bake 10 minutes. Lower oven to 250F.

5 Bake 1 hour longer. Remove to rack to cool—2 hours. Make glaze: In small saucepan, combine sugar and cornstarch. Stir in remaining ingredients. Over medium heat, bring to boiling, stirring; boil 1 minute, or until thickened and translucent. Cool.

6 Spread surface of cheesecake with glaze; refrigerate until well chilled—3 hours or overnight. To serve: Loosen pastry from side of pan with spatula. Remove side of springform pan. Garnish with sliced strawberries, if desired. Cut into wedges. Serves 16.

CHEESECAKE

CRUST:
1 cup sifted all-purpose flour (sift before measuring)
¼ cup sugar
1 teaspoon grated lemon peel
½ teaspoon vanilla extract
1 egg yolk
¼ cup butter or regular margarine, softened

FILLING:
5 pkg (8-oz size) cream cheese, softened
1¾ cups sugar
3 tablespoons flour
2 teaspoons grated lemon peel
1½ teaspoons grated orange peel
¼ teaspoon vanilla extract
5 eggs, plus 2 egg yolks

¼ cup heavy cream

PINEAPPLE GLAZE:
2 tablespoons sugar
4 teaspoons cornstarch
2 cans (8¼-oz size) crushed pineapple in heavy syrup, undrained
2 tablespoons lemon juice
2 drops yellow food color

8608-04

Everybody's favorite Italian dessert is that sweet and creamy confection known as tortoni. It's basically a super-rich form of frozen mousse, made with sugar syrup, stiffly beaten egg white and whipped cream, flavored with almond extract and sprinkled with toasted almonds. Make it as the Italians do, in fluted paper cups (use the kind you bake cupcakes in); top with a maraschino cherry. Instructions, next page.

ITALIAN DELIGHT

1 Separate eggs: Crack shell; turn yolk from one half into the other, letting white run into small bowl, yolk into another. Turn each white into the small bowl of electric mixer as it is separated. (Take care that none of the yolk gets into the white.) Refrigerate yolks.

2 Let whites warm to room temperature—1 hour. Mix ¼ cup water with the sugar in 1-quart saucepan; stir over low heat to dissolve. Boil, uncovered, without stirring, to 236F on candy thermometer (syrup spins 2-inch thread when dropped from spoon).

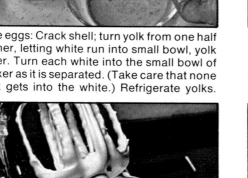

3 Meanwhile, at high speed, beat whites with salt just until stiff peaks form when beater is slowly raised. Pour hot syrup in thin stream over whites; beat constantly until very stiff peaks form when beater is raised. Refrigerate, covered, 30 minutes.

4 Meanwhile, preheat oven to 350F. Place blanched almonds in shallow baking pan; bake just until lightly toasted—8 to 10 minutes. Chop almonds finely or grind finely in electric blender. Turn into small bowl. Stir in 1½ teaspoons almond extract. Set aside.

5 In medium bowl, beat cream, using portable electric mixer, with ¼ teaspoon almond extract and the vanilla until quite stiff. With wire whisk or rubber scraper, using an under-and-over motion, gently fold into egg-white mixture until well combined.

6 Spoon into 12 paper-lined, 2½-inch-size muffin-pan cups. Sprinkle with almond mixture; top with cherry. Cover with foil; freeze until firm—several hours or overnight. Makes 12. (For longer storage, remove from pan; wrap each well. Keeps 1 month.)

BISCUIT TORTONI

3 eggs	¼ cup whole blanched	1½ cups heavy cream
¾ cup sugar	almonds	¾ teaspoon vanilla extract
Dash salt	Almond extract	12 candied cherries

To make a fancy mold instead of individual desserts: In Step 6, turn the mixture into a 1-quart mold or bowl; cover with foil. Freeze until firm enough to unmold, or overnight. To unmold: Run a small spatula around the edge of mold; dip quickly into hot water; invert onto serving dish. Sprinkle with ground-almond mixture. Return to freezer until serving. Decorate with whipped cream and candied cherries. Makes 8 to 10 servings.

A MAGNIFICENT FRENCH DESSERT

Baba au rhum, that glorious yeast cake baked with raisins and citron, soaked in rum syrup and gleaming with apricot glaze, is one of the great desserts of French *haute cuisine.* To add it to your repertoire, see the directions on the following page. Serve with whipped cream.

1. Grease a 10-by-4-inch tube pan. Check temperature of water with thermometer. Sprinkle yeast over water in electric-mixer bowl; stir to dissolve. Add ¼ cup sugar, the salt, eggs and 2¼ cups flour. At medium speed, beat 4 minutes, or until smooth.

2 While beating, scrape side of bowl and guide mixture into beater with rubber scraper. Add butter; beat 2 minutes, or until well blended. At low speed, beat in rest of flour until smooth—2 minutes. Stir in the citron and currants; mix well. Batter will be thick.

3 Turn into tube pan; spread evenly. Cover with towel. Let rise in warm place (85F), free from drafts, about 1 hour and 10 minutes, or until dough has risen to ½ inch from top. Preheat oven to 400F. Place pan on oven rack; do not jar or baba may fall.

4 Bake 45 minutes, until brown and tester inserted comes out clean. Make syrup: In pan, combine sugar and 2 cups water; bring to boil; stir to dissolve. Boil, uncovered, 10 minutes; reduce heat. Add fruit; simmer 10 minutes. Remove from heat; add rum.

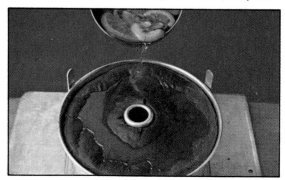

5 With spatula, loosen side of baba from pan. Turn out of pan onto rack; cool 15 minutes. Return baba to pan; place on cookie sheet. Gradually pour hot syrup, with fruit slices, over baba. Continue until all syrup is absorbed. Let stand 2 hours or longer.

6 Meanwhile, make glaze: Over low heat, melt preserves. Stir in the lemon juice; strain. Refrigerate ½ hour. To serve: Turn baba out on platter. Arrange fruit slices on top, as pictured. Brush with glaze. If desired, serve with whipped cream. Serves 12.

BABA AU RHUM

¾ cup warm water (105 to 115F)
2 pkg active dry yeast
¼ cup sugar
1 teaspoon salt
6 eggs
3¾ cups sifted*
all-purpose flour
*Sift before measuring.

¾ cup butter, softened
½ cup finely chopped citron
or grated orange peel
¼ cup currants or seedless
raisins

RUM SYRUP
2½ cups sugar

1 unpeeled, medium-size orange,
sliced crosswise
½ unpeeled lemon, sliced
1 to 1½ cups light rum

APRICOT GLAZE
1 cup apricot preserves
2 teaspoons lemon juice

A COOL GOLDEN DESSERT

Sunny as a summer day, refreshing as a breeze, this cool and sumptuous lemon mousse can be whipped up without sending yourself into a froth. Egg whites beaten into snowy peaks are combined with a lemony base; and it's all folded with clouds of whipped cream. How to do it? See next page.

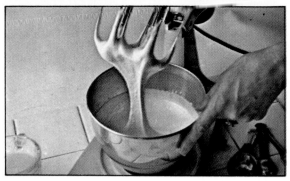

1 Fold waxed paper, 26 inches long, in thirds. With string, tie collar around 1-quart soufflé dish, to form rim 2 inches high. Let egg whites warm to room temperature—1 hour. In double-boiler top, combine gelatine with ½ cup granulated sugar and the salt.

2 In small bowl, with mixer at high speed, beat egg yolks until thick—3 minutes. Gradually beat in ½ cup granulated sugar, 2 tablespoons at a time; beat until very thick. Slowly add lemon juice and ¼ cup water; mix to combine. Stir into gelatine mixture; mix well.

3 Cook, stirring constantly, over boiling water (water in bottom should not touch top of double boiler) until gelatine dissolves and mixture is thickened—15 to 20 minutes. Remove from hot water. Stir in lemon peel and Grand Marnier. Turn into bowl to cool slightly.

4 Set in bowl of ice cubes, stirring occasionally, 15 minutes. Then stir constantly until mixture thickens and mounds when dropped from a spoon. In large bowl, at high speed, beat whites (clean beaters) until soft peaks form when beater is slowly raised.

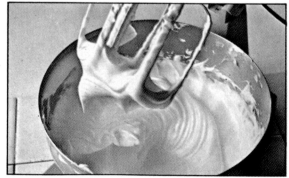

5 Beat in remaining ½ cup granulated sugar, 2 tablespoons at a time; beat well after each addition. Beat until stiff peaks form when beater is raised. With whisk, using an under-and-over motion, gently fold gelatine mixture into egg whites just to combine.

6 Beat 1½ cups cream with confectioners' sugar until stiff. Gently fold into gelatine. Turn into soufflé dish. Refrigerate 3 hours. To serve: Remove collar. Whip remaining cream; put through pastry bag with number-6 tip. Garnish with lemon. Serves 8.

LEMON MOUSSE

4 egg whites (½ cup)	4 egg yolks	¼ cup Grand Marnier
2 env unflavored gelatine	¾ cup lemon juice	2 cups heavy cream
1½ cups granulated sugar	⅓ cup finely grated lemon	¼ cup confectioners' sugar
Dash salt	peel	Lemon slices, halved

Our delicate soufflé is a light and refreshing way to conclude a good meal. The sweet yet tart savor of dried apricots gives it a very special flavor. What's more, the ingredients can be combined ahead of time, re-

A VERY SPECIAL SOUFFLÉ

frigerated and popped into the oven just as everyone is sitting down to dinner. Fifty minutes later, it's ready to serve—in a soufflé dish or, as shown, unmolded and topped with apricot preserves.

1 Let egg whites warm to room temperature in large bowl of electric mixer at least one hour to give more volume. Meanwhile, in medium saucepan, combine dried apricots with 1¼ cups water; bring to boiling. Remove from heat; let stand, covered, 20 minutes.

2 Puree apricots and liquid in blender or press through food mill. Puree will measure 1½ cups. Add almond extract; turn into large bowl. Preheat oven to 350F. Lightly butter inside of 3-quart mold or pyrex bowl. Sprinkle evenly with 2 to 3 tablespoons sugar.

3 Add cream of tartar and salt to egg whites; beat at high speed just until soft peaks form when beater is slowly raised. Then gradually beat in 1 cup granulated sugar, 2 tablespoons at a time, beating well after each addition. Continue to beat at high speed.

4 Beat until very stiff peaks form when beater is slowly raised. With wire whisk, using an under-and-over motion, gently fold one third of egg whites into puree to combine well. Fold in rest of egg whites just to combine. Do not overmix. Turn into mold.

5 Set in pan containing 1 inch hot water. On low shelf in oven, bake 50 minutes, or until puffed and golden-brown. Meanwhile, beat cream with 2 tablespoons confectioners' sugar just until stiff. Turn into serving bowl; refrigerate to chill very well.

6 Melt preserves in small skillet; strain, if desired. To unmold soufflé, loosen around edge of mold with small spatula; invert on warm serving platter. Shake gently to release. Lift off mold. Brush melted preserves over top. Serve with whipped cream. Serves 8.

MOLDED APRICOT SOUFFLE

8 egg whites (1⅓ cups)	2 tablespoons butter	½ teaspoon salt
1 cup dried apricots, packed,	or margarine	1 cup heavy cream
about 36 (6 oz)	Granulated sugar	Confectioners' sugar
½ teaspoon almond extract	½ teaspoon cream of tartar	½ cup apricot preserves

8619-05

STRAWBERRIES SABAYON IN SHELLS

Who could resist a dessert as delectable as this one? Grand Marnier spikes creamy sabayon custard sauce cascading over a luscious mound of fresh strawberries—all tucked into a delicate, fluted, wafer-thin cookie shell and topped with chopped pecans. (The pastry cups can be prepared in advance and stored in a tight container.) For complete step-by-step directions, turn the page.

1 Make cookie shells: Preheat oven to 300F. Grease and flour two large cookie sheets. In medium bowl, with electric beater, beat egg until light and fluffy. Add confectioners' sugar and brown sugar; beat until mixture is smooth and the sugars dissolve—about 3 minutes.

2 Add vanilla. Using wooden spoon, stir in flour and salt; mix well. Blend in melted butter. Spoon about 2 tablespoons batter onto prepared cookie sheet for each cookie. Spread evenly into a 5-inch round. Bake, one sheet at a time, 8 to 10 minutes, till lightly browned.

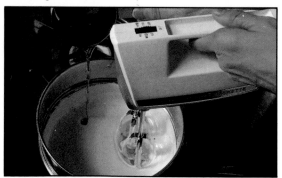

3 With spatula, loosen edge of cookie. Immediately place each cookie over outside of 6-ounce custard cup; press with hand to form shell. If cookies are too brittle, reheat briefly in oven. Cool about 30 minutes before removing from custard cups. Makes 6 cookie shells.

4 Wash strawberries under cold running water in colander. Drain; hull. Refrigerate. Make sauce: In top of double boiler, with electric beater at high speed, beat egg yolks until thick. Gradually add granulated sugar, beating until peaks form when beater is slowly raised.

5 Place double-boiler top over simmering water (water in bottom should not touch base of top). Slowly beat in Grand Marnier; continue beating until mixture is fluffy and mounds—about 5 minutes. Turn into medium bowl. Place the bowl in a larger bowl of ice water.

6 Beat custard mixture until cool. Gently fold in whipped cream. Refrigerate sauce, covered. To serve: Spoon the strawberries into cookie shells. Stir sauce; spoon over berries. Sprinkle with the chopped nuts. *Note:* Sift confectioners' sugar before measuring.

STRAWBERRIES SABAYON IN COOKIE SHELLS

COOKIE SHELLS
1 egg
⅓ cup confectioners' sugar
(see Note, step 6)
2 tablespoons light-brown sugar
½ teaspoon vanilla extract
¼ cup unsifted all-purpose flour
Dash salt

2 tablespoons butter or margarine, melted

1½ pints fresh strawberries

SAUCE
4 egg yolks

2 tablespoons granulated sugar
¼ cup Grand Marnier or Cointreau
½ cup heavy cream, whipped stiff

½ cup chopped pecans or walnuts

8620-05

CARAMEL CUSTARD: HANDLE WITH CARE

Old-fashioned caramel custard is one of the most delightful and healthful desserts you can serve your family. It's also one of the trickiest. As with any egg mixture, it demands careful handling. Our custard is made in a ring mold instead of individual cups, since this makes it easier both to prepare and to serve. Custard that is overcooked becomes watery and is not smooth. Our method is to place the mold in a pan of hot water while the custard is baking. There's a trick to caramelizing the sugar, too. It should be cooked over low heat just long enough to make a light-golden syrup. If cooked over high heat or too long, it develops a burned flavor. For an extra bit of drama, we've topped our custard with fresh fruit.

1 Preheat oven to 325F. Sprinkle ½ cup sugar evenly over bottom of a small, heavy skillet (see picture 1). Cook slowly over very low heat, stirring occasionally with a wooden spoon, just until sugar melts to a golden syrup (picture 2). If the sugar is cooked too long

2 and at too high a temperature, it will be too dark and taste burned. Immediately pour syrup (picture 3) into bottom of 5-cup ring mold (8½ inches across and 2 inches deep). Tilt mold (picture 4), while syrup is still liquid, to coat bottom and side. (Caramel syrup will

3 harden.) Let cool. In large bowl, with wire whisk, beat eggs with sugar, salt and vanilla to mix well. Gradually add milk, beating until smooth, not frothy. Place prepared ring mold in shallow baking pan. Remove 1 cup egg mixture; reserve. Pour rest of mixture into mold.

4 Place baking pan on middle rack in oven; pour reserved mixture into mold (this eliminates spilling). Pour hot water into pan (picture 5) 1 inch deep around mold. Bake 55 to 60 minutes, or until a silver knife inserted 1 inch from edge comes out clean (picture 6).

5 Do not overbake; custard continues to bake after removal from oven. Remove mold from hot water to rack to cool completely; then refrigerate to chill —at least 1 hour. (Custard can be made day ahead.) The custard will settle slightly on cooling. To unmold:

6 Loosen edge with spatula. Place serving plate upside down on mold and reverse the two; shake gently to release; caramel will run down side. Toss fruit together lightly; use to fill center of custard. Spoon some of caramel sauce over each serving. Makes 6 to 8 servings.

CARAMEL CUSTARD

SYRUP
½ cup granulated sugar

CUSTARD
5 eggs

½ cup granulated sugar
¼ teaspoon salt
1 teaspoon vanilla extract
3½ cups milk

FRUIT FOR CENTER
½ pint fresh strawberries, washed and hulled (1 cup)
1 cup drained pineapple cubes
½ lb seedless green grapes

8623-04

BLINTZES—THE DIETER'S DOWNFALL

Golden pancakes filled with creamy cheese and topped with jam and sour cream, blintzes belong to that select group of dishes capable of melting the willpower of even the strictest dieter. And they're wonderfully versatile. Serve them for brunch or supper—the cheese provides plenty of protein—or have them for dessert. Cheese is the classic filling, but you can also make blueberry blintzes, strawberry blintzes, even apple blintzes. Best of all, you can make and fill them several hours in advance. Simply refrigerate, then sauté just before serving.

1 Make batter: In medium bowl, with portable electric mixer or rotary beater, beat eggs, salad oil and milk to blend well. Add flour and salt; continue to beat until batter is smooth and flour is dissolved. Refrigerate, covered, 30 minutes, or until ready to use.

2 Make cheese filling: In medium bowl, combine egg yolk and granulated sugar; beat with portable electric mixer until thick and yellow. Add cheeses and vanilla; stir until well combined. Makes 3 cups. Refrigerate until ready to use. Slowly heat an 8-inch skillet.

3 To test temperature, drop a little cold water onto hot skillet; water should roll off in drops. For each blintz, brush inside of pan lightly with melted butter. Measure 3 tablespoons batter into ¼ cup. Pour in all at once, rotating skillet quickly to spread evenly.

4 Batter should be like heavy cream. If it seems too thick, dilute with a little milk. Cook until golden on underside—1 minute; remove, loosening edge with spatula. Dry on paper towels. Stack, browned side up, with waxed paper between blintzes. Makes 16.

5 To fill: Spread 3 level tablespoons filling on browned side of each blintz, making rectangle 4 inches long. Fold two opposite sides over filling; then overlap ends, covering filling completely. Melt 1 tablespoon butter in large skillet over medium heat.

6 Add half of blintzes, not touching, seam side down; sauté until golden-brown on underside; turn; sauté other side. Keep warm in a low oven while cooking rest. Serve hot, sprinkled with confectioners' sugar, with sour cream and preserves. Serves 8.

BLINTZES

3 eggs
3 tablespoons salad oil
1½ cups milk
1 cup unsifted all-purpose flour
½ teaspoon salt
⅓ cup butter or margarine, melted

CHEESE FILLING
1 egg yolk
2 tablespoons granulated sugar
1 pkg (8 oz) cream cheese, softened
2 cups (1 lb) creamed cottage cheese

¼ teaspoon vanilla extract
2 tablespoons butter or margarine
Confectioners' sugar
1 cup sour cream
1 cup strawberry or cherry preserves

THE PERFECT DESSERT SOUFFLÉ

Even the inexperienced cook will have success with this light-as-a-feather chocolate dessert soufflé. If this is your first attempt at making a soufflé, forget serving a big dinner and have your friends in for just dessert and coffee. Then you won't have to worry about timing the soufflé to come out of the oven just as dinner is over. Before your guests arrive, have all your ingredients ready, prepare your soufflé dish (put the collar on, butter, and sprinkle with sugar), and preheat your oven. If you're familiar with the recipe directions, it will take only about 10 minutes of preparation time to get the soufflé ready to go into the oven after your guests arrive. During baking, don't keep opening the oven door for progress checks—a soufflé needs an even oven temperature and doesn't want to be disturbed during baking! Serve the soufflé immediately after it is removed from the oven—it will be a most impressive dessert.

1 Separate eggs: Crack shell, keeping yolk in one half, white in other. Turn yolk from one half into the other, letting white run into a small bowl, yolk into another. Pour each white into large bowl; let stand to warm 1 hour.

2 With 1 tablespoon butter, grease 2-quart soufflé dish. Fold 26-inch piece waxed paper lengthwise in thirds. Grease with 1 tablespoon butter. Form 2-inch collar around dish; tie. Sprinkle dish, paper with 2 tablespoons sugar.

3 In medium-size, heavy saucepan, with wire whisk, mix flour, cocoa, ¾ cup granulated sugar, the salt. Gradually blend in milk. Cook, stirring, over medium heat, until mixture comes to boil (large bubbles break on surface).

4 Beat yolks with a wire whisk. Beat in some of cocoa mixture. Gradually stir yolk mixture into rest of mixture in saucepan. Add 2 tablespoons butter and the vanilla, stirring until they are combined. Set aside to cool slightly

5 Add cream of tartar to egg whites. With electric mixer at high speed, beat just until soft peaks form when beater is slowly raised; scrape side of bowl several times with rubber scraper so that egg whites are beaten throughout.

6 Add ¼ cup granulated sugar, 2 tablespoons at a time, beating well after each addition. Beat just until stiff peaks form when beater is raised. Whites will be shiny and satiny. Turn a third of cocoa mixture over top of

7 egg whites. Using a wire whisk or rubber scraper, gently fold mixture into whites, using under-and-over motion, just until combined. Fold in rest of cocoa mixture a half at a time. Caution: Overfolding reduces the volume.

8 Using a rubber scraper, gently turn soufflé mixture, without stirring, into prepared dish set in a large baking pan; clean out bowl with scraper. Smooth top with a metal spatula. Place pan and dish in oven on bottom rack.

9 Pour hot water into pan to measure 1 inch. Bake 1¼ hours. With rotary beater, beat cream with confectioners' sugar until stiff. Chill. To serve, remove collar. Break the top of the soufflé with fork. Serve with whipped cream.

CHOCOLATE SOUFFLÉ

8 egg whites	½ cup all-purpose flour	2 cups milk
6 egg yolks	¾ cup Dutch-process	1 teaspoon vanilla extract
4 tablespoons butter or regular	unsweetened cocoa	¼ teaspoon cream of tartar
margarine, softened	1 cup granulated sugar	1 cup heavy cream, chilled
2 tablespoons granulated sugar	¼ teaspoon salt	¼ cup confectioners' sugar

Preheat oven to 350F. Place oven rack on lowest rung in oven. Start with step 1, above.

8626-06

FILLED WITH SWEETNESS—AND LIGHT

Éclairs are a true luxury dessert—enticingly rich custard on the inside, soft, buttery pastry on the outside. They take various toppings: We chose creamy chocolate and powdered sugar. The dough, called pâte à choux, is basic to many cream-puff desserts. Be sure mixture is cool when you add the eggs; then beat vigorously for extra lightness and puff. Instructions are on next page.

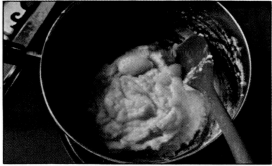

1 Preheat oven to 400F. In medium saucepan, bring water, ⅓ cup butter and the salt to boiling. Remove from heat. Quickly add flour all at once. With wooden spoon, beat constantly over low heat until mixture forms ball and leaves side of pan. Remove from heat.

2 Using portable electric mixer or wooden spoon, beat in eggs, one at a time, beating very well after each addition. Continue beating vigorously until dough is shiny and satiny and breaks away in strands. Dough will be stiff and hold its shape.

3 Drop dough by rounded tablespoons, 3 inches apart, on ungreased cookie sheet. With spatula, shape into 4-by-1½-inch strips, rounding ends and slightly indenting sides. Bake 35 to 40 minutes, or until puffed and golden. Cool on rack.

4 Filling: In small, heavy saucepan, heat 1½ cups milk until bubbling around edge. Mix sugar and cornstarch; stir, all at once, into hot milk. Over medium heat, cook, stirring, until bubbling. Reduce heat; simmer 1 minute. Beat a little of hot mixture into yolks.

5 Return to saucepan; cook, stirring, over medium heat until thickened. Add vanilla. Turn into bowl; refrigerate—with waxed paper on surface—1½ hours. Fold in cream. To fill: With sharp knife, cut off tops of éclairs crosswise. Remove some of soft dough inside.

6 Fill each with ¼ cup custard. Replace tops. Make glaze: In top of double boiler, over hot water, melt chocolate with butter. Blend in corn syrup and milk. Cool 5 minutes. Spoon over éclairs, placed on rack on tray. Serve at once or refrigerate. Makes 8.

ÉCLAIRS

¾ cup water	**CUSTARD FILLING**	**CHOCOLATE GLAZE**
⅓ cup butter or regular margarine	1½ cups milk	1 cup (6 oz) semisweet chocolate pieces
⅛ teaspoon salt	¼ cup sugar	2 tablespoons butter or regular margarine
¾ cup all-purpose flour (sift before measuring)	1½ tablespoons cornstarch	2 tablespoons corn syrup
3 large eggs	2 egg yolks, slightly beaten	3 tablespoons milk
	1 teaspoon vanilla extract	
	½ cup heavy cream, whipped	

Note: Or fill éclairs with sweetened whipped cream: Beat 1 cup chilled heavy cream with 3 tablespoons confectioners' sugar until stiff. Add 1 tablespoon vanilla extract. Fill éclairs; sprinkle tops with confectioners' sugar.

What's Kuchen? Peach Kuchen!

One of the delights of summer in Germany is fruit kuchen, an open-face fresh-fruit pie served warm from the oven. It's made with pastry crust or raised yeast-dough crust; a custard mixture is poured over the fruit before baking. We've used fresh ripe peaches for our version, plus a crispy, rich biscuit crust, somewhat like shortcake. Kuchen can also be made with canned or frozen fruit.

Fragrant peach kuchen is especially delicious with whipped cream or à la mode. Time the kuchen to bake during dinner so that it will be at just the right temperature to serve for dessert. The batter may be mixed ahead of time, turned into a baking pan and refrigerated for as long as 3 hours. At brunch, serve kuchen instead of coffeecake.

1 Pour enough boiling water over peaches in large bowl to cover. Let stand 1 minute to loosen skins; then drain, and plunge into cold water for a few seconds to prevent softening of fruit. With paring knife, pare peaches; place in large bowl.

2 Preheat oven to 400F. Sprinkle peaches with lemon juice to prevent darkening. Slice into the bowl; toss to coat with lemon juice; set aside. Onto sheet of waxed paper, sift flour with the sugar, baking powder, and salt. In large mixing

3 bowl, using fork, beat eggs with milk and lemon peel. Add flour mixture and melted butter, mixing with fork until smooth—1 minute. Do not overmix. Butter a 9-inch springform pan, pictured, or a 9-inch round layer-cake pan. (If

4 cake pan is used, kuchen must be served from pan.) Turn batter into pan; spread evenly over bottom. (At this point, kuchen may be refrigerated several hours, or until about ½ hour before baking.) Combine sugar and cinnamon; mix well.

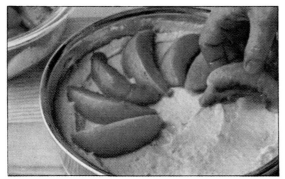

5 Drain peach slices; arrange on batter, around edge of pan, as pictured; fill in center with 5 peach slices. Sprinkle evenly with sugar-cinnamon mixture. Bake 25 minutes. Remove kuchen from oven. With a fork, beat egg yolk with cream.

6 Pour over peaches. Bake 10 minutes longer. Cool 10 minutes on wire rack. To serve, remove side of springform pan. Serve kuchen warm, cut into wedges, with sweetened whipped cream or soft vanilla ice cream. Makes 8 to 10 servings.

FRESH PEACH KUCHEN

Boiling water
2 lb ripe peaches, peeled and sliced (about 6); or
2½ pkg (10-oz size) frozen sliced peaches, drained
2 tablespoons lemon juice
KUCHEN BATTER
1½ cups sifted
all-purpose flour

½ cup sugar
2 teaspoons baking powder
½ teaspoon salt
2 eggs
2 tablespoons milk
1½ tablespoons grated lemon peel
¼ cup butter or regular margarine, melted

TOPPING
¼ cup sugar
½ teaspoon ground cinnamon
1 egg yolk
3 tablespoons heavy cream

Sweetened whipped cream or soft vanilla ice cream

8629-04

A PERFECT PEAR TART

This elegant dessert is neither as difficult to make nor as calorific as it looks. A more delicate version of the classic *tarte Tatin*, which uses apples, our recipe calls for caramelized pears. They're placed on top of a pastry round, then garnished with whipped-cream rosettes. For simple step-by-step instructions, please see the next page.

1 In colander, drain pears; reserve liquid for later. Cut pears in half lengthwise; drain on paper towels. Preheat oven to 450F. Caramelize sugar: Sprinkle granulated sugar evenly over bottom of medium-size, heavy skillet. Cook slowly over very low heat.

2 Stir occasionally with a wooden spoon until sugar melts and becomes a light-brown syrup. (If sugar is cooked too long or at too high a temperature, it will be too dark and have a burned flavor.) Pour syrup into the bottom of an 8½-inch round baking dish.

3 Arrange pears, rounded side down, spoke fashion, on caramelized sugar. Top with second layer, rounded side up, fitting over bottom layer to fill open spaces. Dot with butter. Bake, uncovered, 25 minutes, or just until the caramel is melted and bubbly.

4 Let stand in baking dish on wire rack until cooled to room temperature—1 to 1½ hours. Meanwhile, prepare pastry as package directs. On lightly floured pastry cloth, roll out to a 9-inch circle. Place on ungreased cookie sheet; prick pastry well with fork.

5 Refrigerate ½ hour. Bake pastry, at 450F, 10 minutes, or until golden-brown. Cool on wire rack. Beat cream and confectioners' sugar in medium bowl until stiff; refrigerate. To serve: Place pastry over pears. Place serving plate over top of pastry circle.

6 Invert; remove baking dish. Press whipped cream through pastry bag with number-4 star tip in a 1-inch circle, twisting to form a rosette. Form 8 rosettes around edge and a large one in center. Garnish, if desired, with candied violets. Makes 8 to 10 servings.

PEAR TARTE TATIN

2 cans (1-lb, 14-oz size) pear halves
1 cup granulated sugar

1 tablespoon butter or margarine
½ pkg piecrust mix (pastry for 1-crust pie)

½ cup heavy cream, chilled
2 tablespoons confectioners' sugar
Candied violets (optional)

8629-05

A LUSCIOUS DESSERT

Cannoli are a traditional Sicilian dessert: crisp pastry shells filled with creamy ricotta cheese, whipped cream and bits of candied fruit. The extra-rich version pictured here is a specialty of TV's popular Italian cooking team, Margaret and Franco Roma- gnoli. The pastry is wrapped around cannoli forms (available in stores that carry European cooking ware) and deep-fried. Make them ahead; fill before serving.

1 Pastry: Place flour in a mound on pastry board. Make well in center; put in salt, sugar and dabs of soft butter. Add wine, and with fork stir in center. Keep stirring until most of flour is absorbed. You can work paste with your hands. Knead until smooth.

2 Almost all the remaining flour will have been picked up. Roll out no thicker than a noodle; cut into 3½-inch squares, if using 5-inch-long, 1-inch-diameter forms. Place forms diagonally on squares. Wrap pastry around form, one corner over the other.

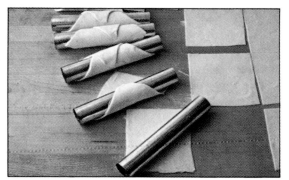

3 Press corners together. If corners don't stick, moisten finger with water; apply to contact point and press again. Cover the bottom of the frying pan with about ¾ inch vegetable oil; heat to 375F. If you don't have a thermometer, drop in a bit of the dough.

4 If it immediately blisters and turns toast color, the temperature is right. Cannoli cook very fast and swell in size; three is a good number to cook at a time. Put them in the hot oil, turning carefully when one side is done. Remove from pan as soon as they are crisp.

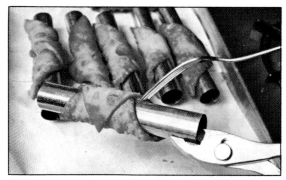

5 They should be a uniform toast color and rather blistered all around. Forms get hot; pointed pliers are best for lifting them out. Hold form with pliers; give a gentle push with fork to slip the fried cannoli off. Drain on paper towels. Put forms aside to cool.

6 When cooled, rewrap; continue frying Using spatula or broad knife, fill cannoli first from one end and then the other. Press filling in gently to make sure centers are full. Scrape ends to smooth cream; dip ends in remaining candied fruit. Makes 16 to 18.

CANNOLI

FILLING
2 cups ricotta cheese
1 cup whipped heavy cream
3 tablespoons sugar
2 tablespoons candied fruit

1½ teaspoons vanilla extract

PASTRY
1 cup flour
¼ teaspoon salt

1 scant tablespoon sugar
1 tablespoon soft unsalted butter
¼ cup white wine
Vegetable oil for frying

For filling: Put ricotta in a bowl; fold in whipped cream, adding sugar as you fold. Chop candied fruit into tiny slivers; fold in all but a teaspoonful. Add vanilla. Refrigerate until shells are cooked and ready to be filled.

8630-05

FRENCH ORANGE CRÊPES

Crêpes Suzette may be the most elegant and exciting dessert you can serve—especially if you plan to assemble and flambé the crêpes at the table in front of your guests. Make the crêpes ahead of time, fill with the orange butter and fold as directed. At the table prepare the orange sauce in a chafing dish over a high flame; add the crêpes and flambé. If you've never made a flambéed dessert before, you might want to practice one time with your family before performing in public!

1 Crêpe batter: In medium bowl, combine flour, oil, eggs, egg yolks and ½ cup milk; beat with rotary beater until smooth. Add rest of milk, beating until blended and smooth. Refrigerate, covered, for 2 hours or longer (overnight is better).

2 Orange sauce: In medium skillet, melt ¼ cup butter. Stir in ⅓ cup sugar, shredded orange peel and juice; cook over low heat, stirring occasionally, until peel is translucent—10 minutes. Add oranges and ¼ cup Grand Marnier or Cointreau.

3 Crêpes: Slowly heat a 7-inch skillet until a drop of water sizzles and rolls off. For each crêpe, brush skillet lightly with butter. Pour in 2 tablespoons batter, rotating pan to cover bottom of skillet evenly. Cook until lightly browned. Turn; brown slightly.

4 Cool on rack; stack with waxed paper between. Orange butter: In small bowl, with electric beater, cream sweet butter with sugar until fluffy. Blend in Grand Marnier and orange peel. Use to spread on crêpes—about 1 tablespoon for each one.

5 Fold each in half, then in half again. Arrange in pattern in orange sauce in chafing dish or skillet; cook over low heat just until sauce is hot and crêpes are heated through. (Crêpes and sauce may be made ahead and refrigerated separately.)

6 To serve flaming: Bring crêpes to table right in chafing dish or skillet. Gently heat brandy in small saucepan just until vapor rises, no longer. Ignite with match and pour flaming brandy over heated crêpes. Serve with sauce. Makes 6 to 8 servings.

CRÊPES SUZETTE

CRÊPES
1 cup unsifted all-purpose flour
¼ cup salad oil
2 eggs, 2 egg yolks
1½ cups milk

ORANGE SAUCE
¼ cup sweet butter

⅓ cup sugar
1 tablespoon coarsely shredded orange peel
⅓ cup orange juice
1 cup orange sections
¼ cup Grand Marnier or Cointreau

Butter or margarine

ORANGE BUTTER
¾ cup sweet butter
½ cup sugar
⅓ cup Grand Marnier or Cointreau
¼ cup grated orange peel

¼ cup brandy

FANCY FINALE

This quick-and-easy Black Forest Trifle is a variation of the traditional English trifle. It is made of luscious layers of chocolate pudding and cherries, laced with cookie crumbs—either vanilla, shortbread or chocolate chip. With that combination it is sure to be a hit with kids both little and big!

1 Put 4 cups of the milk into a large, heavy saucepan. Add unsweetened chocolate and heat over moderate heat, watching carefully, until bubbles form on milk around edges of pan—milk is then scalded. Remove from heat and set aside.

2 Put cornstarch, sugar, salt and remaining ½ cup milk into a small bowl. Use a small whisk to stir cornstarch mixture until all dry ingredients are moistened and no lumps remain. Be sure mixture is well stirred just before adding to hot milk.

3 Using a large wire whisk, stir hot-milk mixture in saucepan while gradually adding cornstarch-milk mixture. Return saucepan to heat and cook over moderately high heat, stirring constantly, until milk mixture begins to boil. Boil 1 minute longer, stirring constantly.

4 Remove from heat and stir in vanilla extract. (If you must stop for a short while, place a piece of plastic wrap on surface of pudding to prevent a skin from forming.) Spoon ⅓ of the chocolate pudding into a 2-quart soufflé dish or glass bowl. Top with ⅓ of the cookie crumbs.

5 Set aside ½ cup cherry-pie filling. Gently spoon half of remaining filling onto crumbs in bowl. Repeat layering with another third of chocolate pudding, crumbs, the remaining cherry-pie filling and the remaining chocolate pudding.

6 Spoon remaining cookie crumbs around chocolate pudding to form a border. Top chocolate pudding layer with remaining ½ cup cherry-pie filling, placing it in the center. Refrigerate trifle, covered, until pudding is well chilled—5 to 6 hours. Makes 8 servings.

BLACK FOREST TRIFLE

4½ cups milk
3 squares (1 oz each) unsweetened chocolate
⅓ cup cornstarch

½ cup sugar
¼ teaspoon salt
2 teaspoons vanilla extract
2 cups cookie crumbs (made

from vanilla wafers, shortbread
or chocolate-chip cookies)
1 can (20 oz) cherry-pie filling, re-
duced-calorie if available.

A FROZEN-FRUITED PARFAIT

This is a lovely creamy dessert—it's loaded with lots of whipped heavy cream and tiny pieces of marshmallow and it's laced with crushed pineapple and sherry wine. Make it well ahead of time and freeze so that the flavors have time to mellow. It's the perfect ending to a light meal!

1 Using a sharp knife or oiled kitchen shears, cut each marshmallow into 8 pieces; place in large bowl. Add either wine or pineapple juice. Sherry will give the parfaits a rich flavor. Use juice for children. Add undrained pineapple.

2 Stir mixture until marshmallows and pineapple are well blended. Cover bowl tightly with plastic wrap or aluminum foil and set aside at room temperature, away from heat, for mixture to marinate at least 8 hours.

3 Meanwhile, put beaters and small bowl of electric mixer in the refrigerator to chill thoroughly. After marshmallow mixture has marinated at least 8 hours, you are ready to beat the heavy cream. Remove bowl and beaters from refrigerator and pour in heavy cream.

4 Beat heavy cream with electric mixer set at high speed until cream stands in stiff peaks when beater is lifted from bowl. Be sure you don't overbeat the cream: It will turn into butter! Put whipped cream into bowl with marshmallows and fold together gently.

5 Turn marshmallow mixture into a 13-by-9-by-2-inch pan, spreading evenly with a rubber spatula or the back of a wooden spoon. Cover with plastic wrap and place in freezer for 3 hours or longer until the mixture is completely frozen.

6 To serve: Spoon marshmallow mixture into a large glass compote, as pictured on the front of this Recipage or into individual parfait glasses. If desired, garnish with rosettes of whipped cream, pineapple chunks and candied cherries. Makes 8 to 10 servings.

FROZEN PINEAPPLE-MARSHMALLOW PARFAIT

1 lb large marshmallows
1 cup canned pineapple juice or dry sherry wine

1 can (20 oz) crushed pineapple in pineapple juice, undrained
2 cups heavy cream

Whipped cream, pineapple chunks and candied cherries (optional for garnish)

Cicero/Fimage Inc.

8636-05

COLD POWER COOKING

This delicate summer cheesecake can be made a day ahead, refrigerated overnight, and glazed just before serving. Points to remember: (1) Let cream cheese stand at room temperature 1 hour to soften —it's easier to combine, makes a smoother mixture; (2) For a deep cheesecake, use a springform pan so that sides can be removed while cake itself stands on the bottom of the pan; (3) For serving, cut with a sharp knife, lift up with a pie server.

1 Make Graham-Cracker Crust: In small bowl, combine crumbs, 2 tablespoons sugar and the butter; mix well with fork. Reserve ¼ cup. With back of spoon, press rest of mixture on bottom of a 9-inch springform pan. Refrigerate. Make Filling: In small, heavy saucepan, combine gelatine, ¾ cup sugar and the salt. In small bowl, with wire whisk, beat egg yolks with milk until smooth; gradually stir into gelatine mixture; mix well.

2 Cook over medium heat, stirring until gelatine is dissolved and custard is thickened slightly (should form coating on metal spoon)—about 5 minutes. Remove from heat; cool 10 minutes. In large bowl, with electric mixer at medium speed, beat cream cheese, lemon peel, lemon juice and vanilla until smooth—3 minutes. Slowly add cooled custard, beating at low speed just to blend.

3 Set in a bowl of ice water to chill, stirring occasionally, until mixture mounds (partially set) when lifted with spoon. Meanwhile, at medium speed and using clean beaters, beat egg whites until soft peaks form when beater is slowly raised. Gradually add ¼ cup sugar, beating until stiff peaks form. Add beaten egg whites and sour cream to cheese mixture; beat at low speed just until smooth. Turn into the prepared pan, spreading evenly.

4 Refrigerate until firm and well chilled—at least 4 hours or overnight. Glaze 1 hour before serving: In small saucepan, combine sugar and cornstarch. With fork, crush 2 cups berries. Stir into sugar mixture with ¼ cup water. Bring to boiling, stirring, until thickened and translucent. Strain; cool. To serve, loosen side of pan with spatula; remove. Arrange some of berries over cake. Top with some of glaze. Sprinkle reserved crumbs around edge. Serve rest of berries in glaze. Serves 10 to 12.

NO-BAKE STRAWBERRY CHEESECAKE

GRAHAM-CRACKER CRUST
1 cup graham-cracker crumbs
2 tablespoons sugar
⅓ cup butter or regular margarine, melted

CHEESE FILLING
2 env unflavored gelatine
¾ cup sugar
¼ teaspoon salt
3 egg yolks
1 cup milk
3 pkg (8-oz size) cream cheese
(at room temperature)

2 tablespoons grated lemon peel
2 tablespoons lemon juice
1 teaspoon vanilla extract
3 egg whites (at room
temperature)
¼ cup sugar
1 cup (8-oz) sour cream

GLAZE
½ cup sugar
1 tablespoon cornstarch
2 pints fresh strawberries,
washed and hulled

8637-04

A SPECIAL SUMMER DESSERT

Fresh-fruit kuchen is Europe's answer to our shortcake. A layer of biscuit dough is covered with slices of cinnamon-sprinkled fruit. We chose plums; you could also use peaches, green apples or alternating layers of all three. Serve warm from the oven with whipped cream, custard or cinnamon ice-cream sauce— or, for breakfast, all by itself. Step-by-step directions on the next page.

1 Grease a 13-by-9-by-2-inch baking pan or dish. Wash plums; drain. For easier slicing, cut each plum in half; then cut each half into 4 slices to measure 4½ cups. (If using apples, pare, quarter, core and slice thinly; measure 3 cups.) Preheat oven to 400F.

2 Into medium bowl, sift flour with ¼ cup sugar, the baking powder and salt. With fork or pastry blender, cut in ¼ cup butter until mixture resembles coarse crumbs. In small bowl, beat egg slightly with fork; then add milk and vanilla, blending well with fork.

3 Add to flour mixture, beating vigorously with fork until smooth—about 1 minute; batter will be quite stiff. Using spatula or rubber scraper, spread batter evenly over bottom of prepared pan. Arrange plum slices over batter, to cover completely, as shown.

4 Place thin sides down, slightly overlapping, in five parallel rows. Place any extra slices between rows. Topping: Mix ¼ cup sugar, 1 teaspoon cinnamon and the melted butter. Spoon over fruit. Bake 35 minutes, or until fruit is tender and pastry is golden.

5 Remove to wire rack to cool slightly. (Meanwhile, remove ice cream from freezer to soften.) In small skillet, over medium heat, mix preserves with 1 tablespoon water, stirring until melted. Brush over plums. Cut between rows of fruit into 10 rectangles.

6 Serve warm with whipped cream or Cinnamon Ice-Cream Sauce. Sauce: In medium bowl, combine softened ice cream, sugar and cinnamon; mix well with wooden spoon until smooth. Turn into chilled serving dish. Freeze if not using at once. Serves 10.

FRESH PLUM KUCHEN

2 lb plums or 1½ lb tart apples
1¼ cups all-purpose flour
(sifted before measuring)
¼ cup sugar
1½ teaspoons baking powder
½ teaspoon salt
¼ cup butter or regular margarine

1 egg, ¼ cup milk
1 teaspoon vanilla extract
TOPPING
¼ cup sugar
1 teaspoon ground cinnamon
¼ cup butter or margarine, melted

⅓ cup strawberry preserves
Whipped cream or
CINNAMON ICE-CREAM SAUCE
1 quart vanilla
ice cream
1 tablespoon sugar
2 teaspoons ground cinnamon

COLD CARAMEL SOUFFLÉ — OLÉ!

In Venezuela, when a hostess wants an especially elegant dessert, she serves this cold caramel soufflé called *esponjosa*. A delightfully rich mixture of cara- melized sugar and sweetly flavored meringue, it is baked until firm, chilled and topped with English Cus- tard Sauce.

1 In large mixer bowl, let whites warm to room temperature—1 hour. Meanwhile, place 1½ cups sugar in a heavy, medium-size skillet. To caramelize, stir with wooden spoon, over high heat until melted and begins to boil—syrup will be a medium brown.

2 Holding a 3-quart oven-glassware casserole with pot holders, pour in hot syrup, all at once. Tilt and rotate casserole until bottom and side are thoroughly coated. Set on wire rack to cool. Beat egg whites, at high speed, until very stiff—8 minutes. (See Note 1.)

3 Continue beating, slowly pouring in 1 package (1 lb) sugar, in continuous stream, scraping bowl with rubber scraper—takes 3 minutes. Beat 15 minutes. About 5 minutes before beating time is up, place ¾ cup sugar in heavy skillet; caramelize, Step 1.

4 Remove from heat; immediately place skillet in cold water for a few seconds, or until syrup is thick; stir constantly. At medium speed, gradually pour syrup into beaten egg whites. Scrape bowl with scraper. At high speed, beat 12 minutes. Preheat oven to 250F.

5 Turn egg-white mixture into prepared dish; spread evenly. Set in large baking pan; pour boiling water to 1-inch depth around dish. Bake 1 hour, until firm when gently shaken and rises about 1 inch above dish. Remove casserole from water; cool on rack.

6. Refrigerate to chill at least 6 hours. To unmold: Run a small spatula around edge to loosen. Hold casserole in pan of very hot water at least 1 minute. Invert on serving dish. Spoon caramel over meringue. Serve with Custard Sauce. (See Note 2.) Serves 16.

ESPONJOSA (COLD CARAMEL SOUFFLÉ)

12 egg whites (1⅔ cups)	**ENGLISH CUSTARD SAUCE**	2 tablespoons butter or margarine
2 pkg (1-lb size) superfine granulated sugar	⅓ cup sugar 1 tablespoon cornstarch 2 cups milk	6 egg yolks 1½ teaspoons vanilla extract ½ cup heavy cream

Note 1: This dessert requires long beating in an electric mixer. We do not advise using a portable electric mixer.

Note 2: To make English Custard Sauce: 1 In medium saucepan, combine sugar and cornstarch. Gradually add milk; stir until smooth; add butter. 2 Cook over medium heat, stirring constantly, until mixture is thickened and comes to boil. Boil 1 minute; remove from heat. 3 In medium bowl, slightly beat egg yolks. Gradually add a little hot mixture, beating well. 4 Stir into rest of hot mixture; cook over medium heat, stirring constantly, just until comes to boil. Remove from heat; stir in vanilla. 5 Strain custard immediately into bowl. Refrigerate, covered, until cool. Stir in heavy cream. Refrigerate until well chilled. Makes about 2½ cups.

"If you want to know how good a restaurant is," says a gentleman of our acquaintance, "order the chocolate mousse." This classic French dessert is meltingly rich and totally delectable. We think our version would win four stars for any restaurant, and it's surprisingly easy to make. For extra lightness, let the egg whites warm to room temperature before beating. Mousse can be stored for a day or two in the refrigerator, a week or two in the freezer without damaging its delicate texture. Instructions on next page,

MOUSSE AU CHOCOLAT

1 Make mousse a day or two ahead. Separate eggs, putting whites into a large bowl, yolks in a small one. Let whites warm to room temperature—1 hour. In top of double boiler, over hot, not boiling, water, melt semisweet chocolate with butter, stirring constantly.

2 Remove top of double boiler from water. With wooden spoon, beat in yolks, one at a time, beating well after each addition. Let cool 10 minutes; stir in Cognac. With portable mixer, beat whites until stiff, moist peaks form when beater is slowly raised.

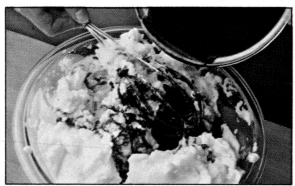

3 With wire whisk or rubber scraper, using an under-and-over motion, gently fold chocolate mixture into egg whites just enough to combine thoroughly; there should be no white streaks. Turn into an attractive, 1-quart serving dish. Refrigerate.

4 Several hours before serving, decorate mousse. To make chocolate curls, warm chocolate bar, still wrapped. Place in a warm spot just until soft, not melting. Then, with vegetable peeler pressing lightly, pare along bar in a long, thin stroke, to form a curl.

5 Make 8 curls. Lift with toothpick to plate; refrigerate. In small bowl, whip cream stiff. Turn into pastry bag with a number-6 star tip, pushing cream to end of bag. With tube held upright, squeeze whipped cream out in a 1-inch circle, twisting to form rosette.

6 Form about 8 whipped-cream rosettes around mousse, 1 inch from edge of bowl, with one large rosette in center. Using a toothpick, carefully place chocolate curls between rosettes, as pictured. Refrigerate until serving time. Makes 8 to 10 servings.

CHOCOLATE MOUSSE

8 eggs	10 tablespoons sweet or	1 bar (4 oz) milk chocolate
2 pkg (6-oz size) semisweet	very lightly salted butter	¾ cup heavy cream
chocolate pieces	¼ cup Cognac or brandy	

Note: The chocolate mousse may be made through Step 3, wrapped in foil and frozen for a week or two. To serve: Let thaw in refrigerator 4 to 5 hours; then decorate mousse, starting with Step 4.

CHARLOTTE AUX POMMES

This is an extremely tasty dessert: Fresh apple slices laced with cinnamon-sugar and raisins are layered with bread cubes in a bread-lined charlotte mold and baked until the bread turns a crisp golden brown and the apples are tender. Removed from the mold, the warm Apple Charlotte is glazed with apricot preserves and served with a custard sauce.

1 Make custard: Heat milk in top of double boiler over direct heat until tiny bubbles appear around edge of pan. Beat egg yolks, ¼ cup sugar and the salt, to mix well. Slowly pour hot milk into egg mixture, beating constantly. Return to double boiler.

2 Place over hot, not boiling, water (water in bottom of double boiler should not touch top part). Cook, stirring, until coating forms on metal spoon—10 minutes. Immediately pour into bowl; stir in lemon peel; place sheet of waxed paper directly on surface.

3 Refrigerate until very cold—several hours. Butter well the inside of a 2-quart charlotte mold or a straight-sided Pyrex bowl. Trim crust from 7 slices bread; reserve crusts. Cut bread slices in half, and use to line inside of mold, overlapping, as shown.

4 Using 2-inch heart-shape cutter, cut out 6 bread hearts; fit in bottom of mold; reserve trimmings. With sharp knife, cut trimmings into ¼-inch cubes (4 cups). In large bowl, mix sugar, cinnamon and nutmeg. Thinly slice apples to make 5½ cups.

5 Toss lightly with cinnamon-sugar mixture and raisins. Preheat oven to 350F. In bottom of mold, layer 1⅓ cups apple-raisin mixture; dot with 1 tablespoon butter; top with 1 cup bread cubes. Make three more layers of apple mixture, butter and bread cubes.

6 Bake 1 hour and 15 minutes. Cool on rack 20 minutes. In small saucepan, bring preserves and rum to boiling, stirring. To serve: Carefully loosen around edge of mold with spatula; turn out. Brush with apricot glaze. Serve warm with custard to 8.

APPLE CHARLOTTE WITH CUSTARD SAUCE

CUSTARD SAUCE
1½ cups milk
3 egg yolks
¼ cup sugar
Dash salt
1 teaspoon grated lemon peel

CHARLOTTE
Butter or margarine, softened
13 slices white bread
1 cup sugar
4 teaspoons ground cinnamon
⅛ teaspoon nutmeg
2 lb greening or McIntosh apples,
pared and cored
½ cup seedless raisins

GLAZE
½ cup apricot preserves
1 tablespoon rum

8643-04   George Ratkai

LUSCIOUS ALMOND CUSTARD

You'll please both the dieters and nondieters at your table with this Almond Custard. It tastes remarkably good even though it has only 109 calories per serving! We've cut the calories by leaving out the egg yolks and using much less sugar than your taste buds will suspect.

1 Preheat oven to 325F. Put milk in a small saucepan; place over medium heat until bubbles begin to form around the edge of pan. (Watch carefully so that milk doesn't come to a boil.) Remove from heat when milk is scalded.

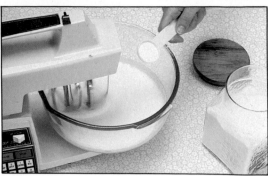

2 Meanwhile, in a medium-sized bowl, combine egg whites, vanilla and almond extracts, and the salt. Beat with a wire whisk or electric mixer until mixture is frothy. Gradually beat in sugar, 1 tablespoon at a time, beating well after each addition.

3 After beating, the egg-whites-and-sugar mixture should be stiff, like a meringue. With a wire whisk and using an under-and-over motion, gently fold warm milk into egg-white mixture. Pour into an 8-inch pie plate or a 1-quart shallow baking dish.

4 Place pie plate or baking dish in a larger shallow baking pan; pour hot water into pan around dish to measure ½-inch in depth. Arrange sliced almonds decoratively around outer edge of custard mixture.

5 Place custard, in its hot-water bath, on the center rack in oven; bake for 40 minutes or until a silver knife inserted ½-inch into the center of custard comes out clean. Remove from oven; remove custard from the hot-water bath.

6 Place custard on a wire rack to cool. When at room temperature, place custard in the refrigerator to chill for several hours. This can be done the day before you plan to serve it. To serve, spoon into individual bowls and serve with fruit. Makes 6 servings.

ALMOND CUSTARD

2 cups milk
3 egg whites (⅓ cup), at room temperature

½ teaspoon vanilla extract
¼ teaspoon almond extract

¼ teaspoon salt
2 tablespoons sugar
1 tablespoon sliced almonds

Cicero/Fimage Inc.

8643-05

A GRAND FINALE

You'll really impress your guests if you serve them this Pineapple Savoy Trifle. All you have to do is line a bowl with sliced, store-bought jelly rolls and fill it with a rich, homemade Bavarian cream. Chill until the Bavarian cream sets, unmold and serve. Everyone will think you spent hours preparing it. Only you will know how simple it really was!

1 Sprinkle gelatine over 1 cup milk; let stand 5 minutes to soften. Heat remaining milk in top of double boiler, over direct heat, until tiny bubbles appear around edge of milk. In medium bowl, beat egg yolks with salt and ½ cup sugar until well blended.

2 Add softened gelatine to egg-yolk mixture; gradually add hot milk while stirring egg-yolk mixture rapidly. Return mixture to top of double boiler; place over simmering water. Cook, stirring constantly, until mixture coats a metal spoon (about 15 minutes).

3 Remove from heat; cool slightly and stir in rum and pineapple. Hasten chilling by placing pan over ice water. Stir occasionally until mixture is thicker than unbeaten egg whites or until it mounds slightly when lifted with a spoon (about 30 minutes).

4 Meanwhile, line a 3-quart bowl with plastic wrap. Using a serrated knife, cut each jelly roll into 7 slices. Arrange 4 to 5 slices in single layer to cover bottom of bowl; refrigerate. Set remaining slices aside, covered with plastic wrap for use later.

5 Beat egg whites with electric mixer until soft peaks form when beater is lifted; gradually beat in ¾ cup sugar until stiff peaks form. Add whipped cream and chilled-gelatine mixture; beat at low speed just until combined. Cover bottom of prepared bowl with cream mixture.

6 Place two rows of reserved jelly-roll slices around sides of bowl. Fill with gelatine mixture; chill several hours or until firm. To serve: Invert bowl on chilled serving dish; remove bowl and plastic wrap. Serve with additional whipped cream if desired. Makes 12 servings.

PINEAPPLE SAVOY TRIFLE

3 env unflavored gelatine
3¾ cups milk
6 eggs, separated
¼ teaspoon salt

1¼ cups sugar
¼ cup dark rum
1 can (8½ oz) crushed
pineapple, drained

4 (3-oz size) bakers' miniature
jelly rolls
1 cup heavy cream, whipped

BLACK-BOTTOM CHEESECAKE

This Chocolate Marble Cheesecake is rich — very rich! The creamy cheesecake filling is marbled with semisweet chocolate and is underlaid with a chocolate cookie-crumb crust. The entire cake is covered with chocolate sour-cream frosting and decorated with chocolate nonpareils!

1 Prepare Cheesecake: In a small bowl, combine crumbs and butter. Lightly grease the bottom of a 9-inch springform pan; press crumb mixture evenly over the bottom. Preheat oven to 300F. Put cream cheese, sugar and vanilla in the large bowl of electric mixer.

2 With mixer set at medium speed, beat cheese mixture, scraping bowl and beaters as necessary, until mixture is smooth and no lumps of cheese remain. Add eggs, one at a time, beating well after each addition. Set 1 cup of cheese mixture aside; pour rest into prepared pan.

3 Fold melted chocolate into the cup of reserved cheese mixture; spoon into pan and cut through batter in a spiral motion for a marbled effect. Bake 50 to 55 minutes, or until the mixture is just set. Remove to wire rack; cool completely. Chill 2 hours.

4 Prepare Chocolate Sour-Cream Frosting: Melt chocolate pieces in top of double boiler over hot water, stirring constantly. Add sour cream and salt. Remove top of double boiler from bottom and beat frosting with a wooden spoon until it is creamy and of spreading consistency.

5 Frost Cheesecake: With small spatula, loosen cheesecake from side of springform pan. Place cake on serving platter. Frost top and sides with Chocolate Sour-Cream Frosting.

6 Decorate top of cake with miniature chocolate nonpareils as shown. Chill the decorated cake for at least 4 hours. Cover any leftover cheesecake with plastic wrap and store in the refrigerator. Makes 1 large cake, 12 servings.

CHOCOLATE MARBLE CHEESECAKE

CHEESECAKE
½ cup chocolate-wafer crumbs
1 tablespoon butter or
margarine, softened
3 pkg (8-oz size) cream cheese,
softened

1 cup sugar
1½ teaspoons vanilla extract
5 eggs
2 squares semisweet chocolate,
melted

CHOCOLATE SOUR-CREAM FROSTING
1 pkg (6 oz) semisweet-chocolate pieces
½ cup sour cream
Dash salt

Miniature chocolate nonpareils

8646-04   David Viens

This fabulous ice-cream dessert is perfect for the holidays—vanilla ice cream rippled with mincemeat and toasted almonds. If you're really ambitious, make home-made vanilla ice cream and flavor it with a little brandy or dark rum. Serve it with demitasse cups of espresso.

A MOLDED ICE-CREAM-AND-MINCEMEAT DESSERT

1 Preheat oven to 350F. Place sliced almonds in a shallow baking pan and put on center rack in oven. Bake for 10 minutes, stirring once or twice with a wooden spoon, until almonds are toasted to a light golden brown. Remove from oven and cool completely.

2 Put mincemeat and cooled, toasted almonds in a medium-sized bowl. Mix well. Spoon about ¼ cup of the mincemeat mixture into the bottom of an 8-cup decorative mold. (A tall fluted mold will give a more dramatic effect in the end!)

3 With a spatula or the back of a large spoon, press about one-fourth of the vanilla ice cream into the bottom of the mold on top of the mincemeat mixture. Then press 1 cup of the mincemeat mixture irregularly around inside of the mold.

4 Pack mold with remaining ice cream, filling in any crevices with the remaining mincemeat mixture. Cover mold with plastic wrap and place in the freezer. Freeze overnight or longer until ice cream is very firm. (This can be made several days before serving.)

5 To unmold and serve: Run the tip of a sharp knife around the ice cream at the edge of the mold. Invert mold onto a round of aluminum foil or onto a serving platter. Place a hot, damp cloth around mold to melt ice cream slightly; then shake ice cream out of mold.

6 Return Mincemeat Glacé to the freezer until you are ready to serve it. (If it is to be stored longer than several hours, cover with plastic wrap.) Remove from freezer a few minutes before serving. Cut into pieces to serve. Makes 16 servings.

MINCEMEAT GLACÉ

½ cup sliced almonds
2 cups prepared mincemeat

2 quarts vanilla ice cream
(softened slightly)

David Viens

8648-04

LIGHT-AS-A-CLOUD

This delicate, fluffy, light-and-airy Kahlua Mocha Mousse is flavored with real brewed coffee and crème de cacao liqueur. It is made "light-as-a-cloud" by the addition of beaten egg whites and whipped heavy cream. In all, it's a truly magnificent and elegant dessert that is extremely easy to prepare if you follow our directions. Make it ahead of time and chill in the refrigerator—you'll have no last-minute preparations before serving.

1 In top of double boiler, combine Kahlua, crème de cacao, brewed coffee, ¾ teaspoon coffee granules, 1 cup sugar, extract, gelatine and egg yolks; mix well. Cook over boiling water (do not let water touch bottom of pan), stirring until mixture thickens (10 to 15 minutes).

2 Meanwhile, fold a 26-inch-long strip of waxed paper lengthwise into thirds. With string, tie this paper around a 1-quart soufflé dish to form a collar 2 inches high. When coffee mixture is thick, remove from heat and set top of double boiler in a bowl of ice cubes.

3 Let coffee mixture stand, stirring occasionally, until mixture thickens and mounds when dropped from a spoon. Meanwhile, in a large bowl, beat egg whites with electric mixer at high speed until stiff peaks form when beaters are lifted; set aside.

4 In medium bowl, beat 1½ cups heavy cream until stiff. Using a wire whisk, fold coffee mixture and whipped cream into beaten egg whites, using an under-and-over motion. Turn mixture into the prepared soufflé dish. Place in the refrigerator and chill for several hours or overnight.

5 Before serving: In a chilled bowl, combine ½ cup heavy cream and 2 tablespoons confectioners' sugar. Beat with a portable electric mixer set at high speed until stiff peaks hold when beaters are lifted. Spoon into pastry bag fitted with a number-6 star tip.

6 Take soufflé dish from refrigerator; remove and discard paper collar. Pipe whipped cream decoratively into swirls around top edge of mousse. Sprinkle cream with more coffee granules and press finely chopped pecans around edge. Makes 8 to 10 servings.

KAHLUA MOCHA MOUSSE

½ cup Kahlua (coffee-flavored liqueur)
½ cup dark crème de cacao
¾ cup strong brewed coffee
Instant decaffeinated coffee granules

1 cup confectioners' sugar
¼ teaspoon almond extract
1 env unflavored gelatine
7 egg yolks (beaten)
7 egg whites

2 cups heavy cream
2 tablespoons confectioners' sugar
Finely chopped pecans

David Viens

8649-06

What makes our Orange Snow Pudding so satisfyingly sweet yet light? Foamy egg whites and the natural sweetness of fresh orange juice, a touch of lemon juice and a sprinkling of sugar. All these are combined into a molded pudding that has only 50 calories a serving. It's the perfect ending to a heavy meal!

A LIGHT ORANGE DESSERT

1 In a small saucepan sprinkle gelatine over orange juice and let stand for 5 minutes to soften. Place over low heat and cook, stirring constantly, until gelatine dissolves completely. Remove from heat and stir in 2 tablespoons of the sugar; stir until sugar is completely dissolved.

2 Pour gelatine mixture into a medium-sized bowl. Add lemon juice and set bowl into a large bowl filled with ice cubes or crushed ice. Stir gelatine mixture frequently until it is the consistency of unbeaten egg whites (about 10 minutes).

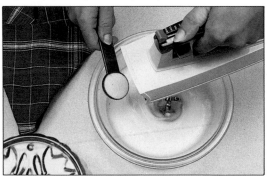

3 Put egg whites and salt in the small bowl of an electric mixer. Beat at high speed with a portable electric mixer until foamy. Gradually add remaining 2 tablespoons sugar, beating well after each addition. Continue beating until soft peaks form when the beaters are slowly raised.

4 Using the same beaters (no need to wash), beat the gelatine mixture until foamy. Using a wire whisk or a rubber spatula and an under-and-over motion, gently fold beaten egg whites into gelatine mixture until thoroughly combined.

5 Using a rubber spatula, scrape the gelatine mixture into a 4-cup mold and place in the refrigerator for 2 to 4 hours (longer if desired) or until very firm. (Select a mold that is high and fluted. It will give a dramatic effect when pudding is unmolded.)

6 To unmold: Run a small metal spatula around edge of mold to loosen orange-gelatine mixture. Invert over serving platter. Place a hot, damp dishcloth over mold; shake to release. If desired, garnish with orange slices and fresh mint sprigs. Makes 8 servings.

ORANGE SNOW PUDDING

1 env unflavored gelatine	2 tablespoons lemon juice	Dash salt
1 cup orange juice	4 egg whites (½ cup)	Orange slices and fresh mint
¼ cup sugar	(at room temperature)	sprigs (optional for garnish)

9800-04   David Viens

AN ICE-CREAM SURPRISE

This is a fabulous dessert: a frozen vanilla ice-cream mold filled with brandy-soaked seedless green grapes and topped with an apricot sauce. It can all be made ahead of time and un-molded just before serving.

1 Select a metal 2-quart mold, preferably a tall, gently fluted one. Soften the ice cream and quickly spoon it into the mold, packing firmly so that no air bubbles are trapped inside. Freeze until ice cream is very hard (several hours).

2 Meanwhile, using a small, sharp paring knife, peel the green grapes and cut each in half. Put grape halves in a small bowl and add ½ cup mirabelle. Toss well; cover and let marinate for several hours while the ice cream is freezing.

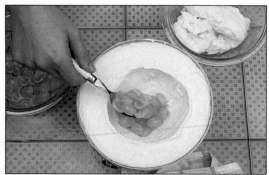

3 When the ice cream is firm, use a small spoon to scoop out the center, leaving a 1½- to 2-inch-thick shell. Fill the resulting cavity with drained marinated grapes. Soften the scooped-out ice cream and pack it over the grapes to seal. Freeze 1 to 1½ hours, no longer.

4 Just before serving, put the apricot preserves in a small saucepan. Heat over low heat, stirring constantly, until preserves are hot and thin out. Add ¼ to ½ cup of the mirabelle or kirschwasser, according to your taste. Remove from heat and keep warm.

5 Remove mold from freezer and loosen ice cream around edges with tip of a small knife. Turn ice cream mold upside down on a well-chilled serving platter. Place a hot-water-soaked towel or cloth on top of mold; shake firmly to release ice cream; remove mold.

6 Return ice cream on platter to freezer for a few minutes until ready to garnish and serve. At the moment of serving, spoon warm apricot sauce on the ice cream, garnish with clusters of green grapes, galax or lemon leaves, and canned drained apricot halves. Makes 6 servings.

VANILLA ICE-CREAM BOMBE SURPRISE

2 quarts vanilla ice cream
1 lb seedless green grapes
¾ to 1 cup mirabelle (yellow-plum brandy) or kirschwasser (cherry brandy)

2 jars (12 oz) apricot preserves
Small clusters of green grapes, galax or lemon leaves and canned apricot halves (optional for garnish)

9801-05   David Viens

This glamorous puffy omelet, light and delicate as a soufflé, is substantial enough to serve as a main dish for lunch or supper. It's economical, too. Made with six eggs, it serves four to six people. There's a trick to making it puff: Let egg whites warm to room temperature before beating them to give maximum volume. Serve with a rich cheese sauce, a seafood sauce or a Spanish-style tomato sauce. A green vegetable and light dessert completes the meal. Step-by-step instructions are on the following page.

THE PERFECT PUFFY OMELET

1 Separate whites into large bowl, yolks into small bowl. Let whites warm to room temperature 1 hour. Preheat oven to 350F. With portable mixer at high speed, beat whites with cream of tartar just until stiff peaks form when beater is slowly raised.

2 Using same beater, beat yolks until thick and lemon-colored. Add salt, mustard and pepper. Gradually add milk; beat until blended. With wire whisk or rubber scraper, using an under-and-over motion, gently fold yolk mixture into whites just to combine.

3 Slowly heat a 10- or 11-inch heavy skillet with a heat-resistant handle. Test temperature: Sprinkle with a little cold water; it will roll off in drops. Heat oil and butter to sizzling—don't brown; tilt pan to coat side. Spread egg mixture evenly in pan.

4 Cook over low heat, without stirring, until lightly browned on underside—about 2 minutes. Transfer skillet to oven; bake, uncovered, 15 minutes, or until golden-brown and top seems firm when gently pressed with finger. Meanwhile, make Cheese Sauce.

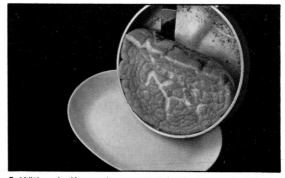

5 In small saucepan, melt butter; remove from heat. Stir in flour, mustard, salt, pepper, cayenne and milk until smooth. Bring to boiling, stirring until thickened. Reduce heat; add the grated cheese; cook, stirring, until cheese is melted and mixture is smooth.

6 With a knife, make a cut, 1 inch deep, slightly to right of center of omelet. Fold smaller part over larger part. Turn out onto heated platter, loosening with spatula. Spoon sauce over omelet. Sprinkle with paprika. Garnish with parsley. Makes 4 servings.

OMELET

6 egg whites (¾ cup)
6 egg yolks
¼ teaspoon cream of tartar
¾ teaspoon salt
½ teaspoon dry mustard
Dash pepper
⅓ cup milk
2 teaspoons salad oil

2 tablespoons butter or margarine

CHEESE SAUCE
2 tablespoons butter or margarine
2 tablespoons flour
½ teaspoon dry mustard

¾ teaspoon salt
Dash pepper
Dash cayenne
1 cup milk
1 cup grated sharp Cheddar cheese (¼ lb)
Paprika
Parsley sprigs

Here's how to add a special shimmering touch to any meal. Eggs en gelée make an elegant first or main course for lunch or supper, especially if the weather is warm. The eggs are soft-cooked and then encased in a crystal-clear aspic, flavored with wine and tarragon—and here we've adorned them with ribbons of chives and rosettes of pâté. Everything is refrigerated, then unmolded and served with a creamy sauce verte. Easy directions begin on the next page.

ELEGANT EGGS IN ASPIC

1 With a pin, prick a hole in large end of each egg. Place in medium saucepan; cover with water to an inch above them. Bring rapidly to a boil. Remove from heat; cover; let stand 5 minutes. Cool eggs under cold running water; carefully remove shells.

2 Sprinkle gelatine over 1 cup broth in small saucepan; let stand 5 minutes to soften. Stir over low heat to dissolve gelatine. Stir in rest of broth, the white wine, vinegar and salt. Set aside. Pour boiling water over chive strips; drain; plunge into ice water.

3 Mix pâté and heavy cream until smooth. Place in pastry bag with small star tip. Place 6 (6-ounce) oval molds or custard cups in pan of ice and water. Spoon 2 tablespoons gelatine mixture into bottom of each mold or cup. Let stand 10 minutes, or until just set.

4 Arrange 3 or 4 chives on gelatine in each mold. Pipe liver pâté in little stars or in a ring around chives. Cover with another tablespoon gelatine mixture, keeping decoration intact. Let stand until gelatine is firm. Place an egg in center of each mold.

5 Pour in enough gelatine mixture to cover eggs and fill molds. Refrigerate until firm enough to unmold— several hours. Make sauce verte: In small bowl, combine mayonnaise, lemon juice, parsley, chives and watercress. Refrigerate, covered, several hours.

6 To unmold: Dip bottom of mold quickly in hot water; invert onto individual serving plates; shake gently to release. Garnish with watercress. Serve with sauce verte. Makes 6 servings. *Note:* The yolks should be soft in center; be careful not to overcook.

EGGS EN GELÉE

6 eggs (see Note, Step 6)
3 env unflavored gelatine
2 cans (10¾-oz size) condensed chicken broth, undiluted
1 cup dry white wine
1 tablespoon tarragon vinegar

¼ teaspoon salt
Boiling water
12 fresh chives, cut into 3-inch strips
4 tablespoons liver pâté
1 teaspoon heavy cream

SAUCE VERTE
1 cup mayonnaise or cooked salad dressing
2 tablespoons lemon juice
2 tablespoons chopped parsley
1 tablespoon chopped chives
1 tablespoon chopped watercress

A NEW ROLE FOR SOUFFLÉ

When you're looking for something light, tasty and just a little special, try a soufflé roll. It's a delicate cheese soufflé baked in a jelly-roll pan, then rolled around a spinach filling. Top with sliced Cheddar, and brown. Serve with salad, white wine and a fresh-fruit dessert. Directions, next page.

1 Place whites and yolks in separate bowls. Let whites warm to room temperature—1 hour. Grease bottom of 15-by-10½-by-1-inch jelly-roll pan; line bottom with waxed paper; then grease with butter. Heat oven to 350F. Melt ⅓ cup butter in saucepan.

2 Remove from heat. With wire whisk, stir in flour, cayenne, ½ teaspoon salt until smooth. Gradually stir in milk. Bring to boil, stirring. Reduce heat; simmer, stirring, until thick and leaves bottom of pan. Beat in ½ cup Parmesan and ½ cup Cheddar.

3 With whisk, beat yolks; beat in cheese mixture. With mixer at high speed, beat whites with ¼ teaspoon salt and cream of tartar until stiff peaks form when beater is slowly raised. With under-and-over motion, fold one third whites into the cheese mixture.

4 Carefully fold in remaining whites to combine. Turn into pan. Bake 15 minutes, or until surface is puffed and firm when pressed with fingertip. Meanwhile, make filling: Cook spinach as package label directs. Turn into sieve; press to remove the water.

5 In hot butter in medium skillet, sauté onion until golden. Add spinach, salt, ¼ cup Cheddar and the sour cream; mix well. With metal spatula, loosen edges of soufflé. Invert on waxed paper sprinkled lightly with Parmesan. Peel off waxed paper.

6 Spread surface evenly with filling. From long side, roll up; place, seam side down, on greased cookie sheet. Arrange cheese slices over top. Broil, about 4 inches from heat, just until cheese melts. Use large spatula to remove to serving dish or board. Serves 8.

CHEESE SOUFFLÉ ROLL

CHEESE SOUFFLÉ
7 eggs, separated
Butter or regular margarine
6 tablespoons unsifted
all-purpose flour
Dash cayenne
¾ teaspoon salt
1¼ cups milk

Grated Parmesan cheese
½ cup coarsely grated
sharp Cheddar cheese
¼ teaspoon cream of tartar

SPINACH FILLING
2 pkg (10-oz size) frozen
chopped spinach

2 tablespoons butter or
margarine
¼ cup finely chopped onion
¼ teaspoon salt
¼ cup grated sharp Cheddar
cheese
½ cup sour cream
¼ lb Cheddar cheese, sliced

8612-05

The Rise of the Soufflé

Soufflés are among the trickiest dishes in a cook's repertoire. However, if you follow each of the steps in this recipe, your soufflé will turn out puffy and perfect every time.

1 Separate eggs—whites into one large bowl and yolks into another. Let whites warm to room temperature—1 hour. Butter a 1½-quart, straight-sided soufflé dish (7½ inches in diameter). Dust lightly with grated Parmesan cheese—about 1 tablespoon.

2 Fold a sheet of waxed paper, 26 inches long lengthwise into thirds. Lightly butter one side. Wrap waxed paper around soufflé dish, with buttered side against dish and a 2-inch rim extending above top edge to make a collar. Tie with string.

3 Preheat oven to 350F. Melt 5 tablespoons butter in medium saucepan; remove from heat. Using a wire whisk or wooden spoon, stir in flour, 1 teaspoon salt and the cayenne until smooth. Gradually stir in milk. Bring to boiling, stirring constantly.

4 Reduce heat; simmer, stirring, until mixture is thick and leaves bottom and side of pan. Beat egg yolks with wire whisk or wooden spoon. Gradually beat cooked mixture into yolks. Beat in ½ cup Parmesan cheese and the grated Swiss cheese.

5 At high speed, beat whites with ½ teaspoon salt and the cream of tartar until stiff peaks form when beater is slowly raised. With wire whisk, using an under-and-over motion, gently fold one third of whites into warm cheese mixture to combine well.

6 Carefully fold in remaining egg whites just until combined. Turn into prepared soufflé dish. Bake 40 minutes, or until soufflé is puffed and golden-brown. Carefully remove collar just before serving. Serve soufflé at once. Makes 4 servings.

FABULOUS CHEESE SOUFFLÉ

6 eggs	6 tablespoons unsifted	1¼ cups milk
Butter or regular	all-purpose flour	½ cup coarsely grated
margarine	1½ teaspoons salt	natural Swiss cheese
Grated Parmesan cheese	Dash cayenne	¼ teaspoon cream of tartar

A soufflé must come to the table straight from the oven the very moment it is ready—it cannot wait for guests. To remove any risks, we suggest preparing the soufflé up to the point of baking. Refrigerate it until guests have arrived (it will keep up to 2 hours). Then, while cocktails are being served, remove to oven and bake as directed, increasing baking time by 10 to 15 minutes, since soufflé will be cold.

8619-06

CHEESE LOVERS' MACARONI AND CHEESE!

If you love Cheddar cheese, this macaroni-and-cheese loaf will be an all-time favorite! It's the ultimate—macaroni, laced with a creamy Cheddar-cheese-and-pimiento sauce, surrounding a heart of more Cheddar cheese. It's all baked into a loaf, unmolded, and topped with Cheddar cheese slices and a mustard-cheese sauce. What more could a cheese lover ask for?

1 Preheat oven to 350F. Line a 9-by-5-by-3-inch loaf pan with aluminum foil; grease well. Cook macaroni according to package directions; drain well. In a medium skillet sauté onion in 2 tablespoons butter for about 3 minutes or until tender.

2 In a large bowl gently toss cooked macaroni with sautéed onion, hot milk, bread crumbs, 2 cups cheese, the chopped pimiento, 2 tablespoons chopped parsley, and the eggs; mix well. Turn half of the mixture into the prepared pan; set aside.

3 To make two triangular pieces of cheese, cut the 10-ounce bar diagonally in half lengthwise. Place ends together to make one strip. Trim strip to measure 8½ inches in length. Shred remaining cheese and set aside for use in making cheese sauce.

4 Arrange the 8½-inch-long strip of cheese in loaf pan: Place it lengthwise on top of macaroni with ends touching and point down. Gently spoon remaining macaroni mixture on top. Smooth out surface and press down gently. Bake 1 hour or until firm.

5 Cheese Sauce: Melt butter in pan; stir in flour, mustard, salt, and pepper. Cook 1 minute, stir constantly; remove from heat and stir in milk. Bring to a boil; cook, stir constantly until thick. Add ½ cup cheese and reserved cheese; stir until melted. Keep warm.

6 Unmold onto heated serving platter. Peel off foil. Top with sauce, pimiento strips, and chopped parsley, if desired. The cheese lovers in your family will love the creamy cheese center and the rich cheese sauce. Makes 8 servings.

BAKED MACARONI-AND-CHEESE LOAF WITH CHEESE SAUCE

2 cups (8 oz) elbow macaroni
1 cup finely chopped onion
2 tablespoons butter or margarine
2 cups hot milk
2 cups fresh bread crumbs
2 cups grated sharp Cheddar cheese (½ lb)
2 tablespoons chopped pimiento

2 tablespoons chopped parsley
6 eggs, well beaten
1 package (10 oz) sharp Cheddar cheese (rectangular)

CHEESE SAUCE
2 tablespoons butter or margarine
2 tablespoons flour

½ teaspoon dry mustard
¾ teaspoon salt
Dash pepper
1 cup milk
½ cup grated sharp Cheddar cheese (⅛ lb)
3 strips pimiento (optional)
Chopped parsley (optional)

8623-05   Gordon E. Smith

A SAVORY VEGETABLE BREAD PUDDING

This is a truly magnificent vegetable side dish — broccoli, cheddar cheese, and bread cubes baked in a basil-flavored egg custard and topped with rings of fresh bread. Prepare it up to 1 day in advance and then pop it into the oven to bake just before serving. The abundance of eggs and cheese makes this dish high in protein, and for a light lunch or dinner you need only add a big tossed salad.

1 Put frozen broccoli into a small saucepan; add water as package directs. Cover and cook until tender, separating broccoli as directed. Drain and set aside. Use butter or margarine to thoroughly grease the inside of a 9-by-9-by-2-inch ovenproof baking pan.

2 Using a large knife, trim off and set aside crusts from bread slices. Using a 2¾-inch-diameter doughnut cutter, cut doughnut-shaped rounds from 8 slices of the bread. Cut bread trimmings and remaining 2 slices of bread into ¼-inch cubes.

3 Using a four-sided food shredder or a food processor fitted with a coarse shredding blade, coarsely shred Cheddar cheese. Put cheese, bread cubes, and drained chopped broccoli into a large mixing bowl. Toss well and spoon into the prepared baking pan.

4 Arrange doughnut-shaped bread rings on top of broccoli mixture, overlapping them if necessary. Put eggs into the mixing bowl; beat with a wire whisk or a rotary or portable electic mixer. Add milk, dried basil leaves, salt, and pepper. Beat until smooth.

5 Pour seasoned egg-milk mixture over broccoli and bread in pan. Let stand 30 minutes. (This much can be done up to 1 day in advance. Cover broccoli mixture with aluminum foil and refrigerate until about 1¼ hours before you plan to serve dinner.)

6 Heat oven to 350°F. Put uncovered pan on center rack in oven. Bake 60 to 65 minutes or until mixture is puffed and lightly browned. It is done when a knife inserted in center of puff comes out clean. Serve immediately. Makes 8 servings.

BROCCOLI-CHEESE PUFF

1 pkg (10 oz) frozen chopped broccoli	12 oz sharp Cheddar cheese	½ teaspoon dried basil leaves
2 tablespoons butter or margarine, softened	6 eggs	1 teaspoon salt
10 slices day-old white bread	3½ cups milk	⅛ teaspoon pepper

Gordon E. Smith

8627-05

The winter is a good time to make this hearty, low-cost casserole, when good rutabagas and firm, fresh potatoes are in season. You can do all the preparation and assemble in advance and then, about 50 minutes before you're ready to have dinner, just pop the casserole into the oven for final baking and browning. It's sure to be a winner — especially with those with hearty appetites. Serve it with tomato soup and a big tossed salad.

A HEARTY CASSEROLE MEAL

1 Preheat oven to 375F. Lightly grease a 2½-quart casserole. Using a sharp knife, peel rutabaga; cut lengthwise in half and then crosswise into ¼-inch-thick slices. Peel potatoes and slice thinly. You should have about 5 cups sliced potatoes.

2 Bring 2 cups water to a boil in a large skillet over high heat. Add rutabaga and 2 teaspoons salt. Cover and cook 10 minutes. Add potatoes and onions; cover and cook 5 minutes or until vegetables are partly tender. Drain well; set aside.

3 Make Cheese Sauce: Melt butter in a small saucepan over moderately high heat. Stir in flour and cook 1 minute, stirring constantly while butter and flour bubble. Remove from heat and gradually stir in milk; stir in 1 teaspoon salt, pepper, and cayenne.

4 Return sauce to heat and cook, stirring constantly, for 4 to 5 minutes until sauce thickens and just comes to a boil. Reduce heat to low and add ½ cup of the cheese. Cook, stirring constantly, until cheese is melted. Sauce should be smooth and creamy.

5 Arrange half of the rutabaga, potato, and onion in casserole; pour on half of the cheese sauce. Then top with remaining vegetables and sliced luncheon meat; Add remaining cheese sauce. Sprinkle with ½ cup of the Cheddar cheese. (This much may be done ahead.)

6 Cover casserole with lid or aluminum foil and bake for 30 minutes or until potatoes and rutabaga are tender when pierced with a fork. If desired, remove cover for the last 10 minutes of baking time to brown top. Makes 8 servings.

CHEESE-SCALLOPED POTATO CASSEROLE

1 rutabaga (yellow turnip)
(about 1 lb)
2 lb all-purpose potatoes
Water
2 teaspoons salt
1½ cups sliced, peeled onion

CHEESE SAUCE
3 tablespoons butter or margarine
2 tablespoons all-purpose flour
1½ cups milk
1 teaspoon salt
⅛ teaspoon pepper

Dash cayenne
½ cup grated sharp Cheddar cheese
1 can (12 oz) luncheon meat, or 12 oz
canned or boiled ham, cut into 8 slices,
cut each slice in half crosswise
½ cup grated sharp Cheddar cheese

Gordon E. Smith

8630-06

The traditional quiche is time-consuming to make: First comes the preparation of the pastry, then rolling it out, fitting it into the quiche dish, and fluting the crust. Only then can you begin to make the filling, and it must be baked immediately. Instead of going to all that work, try our

Quiche-Without-A-Crust. Simply place a layer of toasted bread cubes on the bottom of the dish, top with the traditional quiche filling, and chill until you are ready to bake it, or bake immediately and serve. It's easy and delicious—you'll never return to the old standard again!

THE
CRUSTLESS
QUICHE

1 Preheat oven to 350F. Butter a 10-inch ceramic quiche dish or a 10-inch pie plate, using ½ teaspoon of the butter. Spread bread cubes on a baking sheet in a single layer and bake about 5 minutes, stirring occasionally, until cubes are lightly browned.

2 Spread toasted bread cubes in the bottom of the prepared dish. Melt remaining ½ teaspoon butter in a large skillet. Add onion and sauté about 3 to 5 minutes, stirring occasionally, until onion has turned a light golden brown.

3 Using a 2-inch heart-shaped cookie cutter, cut 6 hearts from ham slices. Coarsely chop trimmings from ham and sprinkle them over the bread cubes in the dish. Spoon onion over ham and top with grated Swiss cheese.

4 Put eggs in a medium-sized bowl. Using an electric mixer or rotary beater, beat eggs thoroughly. Add flour, half-and-half, salt and cayenne pepper. Beat on low speed until thoroughly combined but not frothy. (This much can be done ahead—cover and chill until ready to bake.)

5 Open oven and pull out center rack. Place baking dish on rack and pour in egg mixture, making sure all ingredients are moistened. Top with ham hearts, arranging them so that the points are all directed in toward the center of the dish.

6 Gently push rack back into oven, being careful not to spill milk mixture. Bake 50 to 60 minutes or until top is golden and a knife inserted into center of quiche comes out clean. Let cool 10 minutes before cutting. Makes 8 servings.

QUICHE-WITHOUT-A-CRUST

1 teaspoon butter or margarine
1½ cups bread cubes, made from
2 or 3 slices fresh bread
1 cup chopped onion

½ lb ham, sliced ⅛ to ¼ inch thick
1½ cups (6 oz) grated natural
Swiss cheese
4 eggs
1 tablespoon all-purpose flour

1½ cups dairy half-and-half
cream
Dash salt
Dash ground cayenne pepper

Gordon E. Smith

8634-05

THE BRUNCH SPECIAL

This recipe for Eggs Mornay with Fresh Tomato Sauce is perfect for a special weekend brunch. Soft-cooked eggs wrapped in Swiss cheese are placed in individual ramekins on top of fresh tomato sauce and broiled until the cheese melts. You may think this recipe is complex, but it's not—if you are organized. Make the tomato sauce and the soft-cooked eggs ahead of time. About 1 hour before serving you can wrap eggs in cheese and assemble the ramekins. Just before serving place under the broiler to reheat. Don't forget to toast the bread!

1 Make Fresh Tomato Sauce: Using a large French chef's knife, cut tomatoes into thin wedges. Cut off and discard cores. Put oil in a large skillet and heat over moderately high heat until oil is hot. Add garlic and basil; cook for 1 minute, stirring constantly.

2 Add fresh tomato wedges and salt to garlic-and-basil mixture in skillet. Cook several minutes, tossing frequently with a wooden spoon, until tomatoes are just heated through. Remove skillet from heat; cover and set aside to keep warm.

3 Prepare soft-cooked eggs: Put eggs in a medium-sized saucepan and add cold water to measure 1-inch above eggs. Put pan over high heat and bring water to a boil. Remove pan from heat; cover and let stand 4 minutes. Cool eggs under running water to stop cooking.

4 When eggs are cool enough to handle, gently crack shells. Using fingers, gently remove and discard shells, being careful not to break the whites of the eggs. Wrap each egg in one-half slice of Swiss cheese. Set aside.

5 Divide tomato sauce evenly in four shallow au-gratin dishes (each about 6 inches in diameter). Top sauce with a cheese-wrapped egg. Place under hot broiler, about 4 inches from heat source, and broil 3 to 5 minutes or until cheese is melted and turns golden brown.

6 Meanwhile, toast bread slices and spread with butter. Cut each slice into quarters, cutting on the diagonal. Arrange 5 pieces of bread around inner rim of au-gratin dishes, in a spokelike fashion. Serve immediately. Makes 4 servings.

EGGS MORNAY WITH FRESH TOMATO SAUCE

FRESH TOMATO SAUCE
3 medium-sized ripe tomatoes
2 tablespoons olive or salad oil
1 clove garlic, crushed

½ teaspoon dried basil leaves
½ teaspoon salt

4 large eggs

2 slices natural Swiss cheese, halved lengthwise
5 slices toast, white or whole wheat

Cicero/Fimage Inc.

8637-05

AN UNUSUAL GERMAN SALAD

Substantial and savory—this is the food that is the delicious, hearty heritage of the Germans who first settled in Pennsylvania nearly 300 years ago and who developed ingenious ways of using the simple supplies in their larders. Vegetables from the fields and meal from local mills went into crusty breads, buttery and bubbly pies, stews chunky and fragrant enough to satisfy any farmer's family, and unique salads. Here is a traditional salad recipe—Red-Beet Eggs—a remarkable way to pickle and preserve eggs and beets for use in salads or to serve with sandwiches. You'll be amazed at how delicious this is.

1 Put eggs in a medium-sized saucepan and add water to measure 1 inch above tops of eggs. Place over high heat and bring water to a boil. Remove from heat; cover pan and let stand 20 minutes. Plunge eggs into cold water to stop cooking. Place in refrigerator.

2 Gently turn beets into a strainer; drain thoroughly and reserve the beet juice. Place the drained beets in a 1½-quart jar or glass bowl. Measure beet juice and add water, if necessary, to measure a total of 1 cup liquid.

3 Put liquid from beets, cider vinegar, sugar and salt in a small saucepan. Bring to a boil over high heat, stirring constantly, and pour over beets in jar or bowl. Cover tightly with plastic wrap and place in the refrigerator for 24 hours.

4 The next day: Remove eggs from the refrigerator and tap sharply on a hard surface to crack shells. Gently peel eggs; discard shells. (Holding egg under cold running water while peeling will help to release shell smoothly from egg.)

5 Remove beets from liquid in jar or bowl. Place in another glass bowl; cover tightly with plastic wrap and return to refrigerator. Add peeled, hard-cooked eggs to liquid remaining in jar or bowl; cover tightly with plastic wrap and refrigerate for about 24 hours.

6 To serve: Drain eggs and use a sharp knife to cut each in half lengthwise. Arrange salad greens on a serving platter and top with beets and red-beet eggs. If desired, slice beets before serving. Makes 6 servings.

RED-BEET EGGS

6 large eggs	2 cans (1-lb size) small whole	½ cup sugar
Water	beets, undrained	1 teaspoon salt
	1 cup cider vinegar	Salad greens

Cicero/Fimage Inc.

8642-05

A FRENCH OPEN-FACE CHEESE TART

This classic French Quiche Lorraine is rich with cream, eggs, bacon and Swiss cheese. It is delicious served hot from the oven or cold as a snack. Serve it with broiled tomatoes, French bread and a dry white wine. For dessert serve assorted fresh fruits and a raspberry sorbet. Altogether a perfect lunch or supper menu!

1 Make piecrust as label directs, sprinkling some water over all of pastry mix; toss lightly with fork after each addition, pushing dampened portion to side. Shape three fourths of the pastry into a ball; flatten to make a 6-inch round. Freeze the remaining dough.

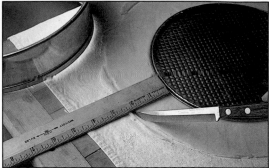

2 On lightly floured pastry cloth or surface, with light strokes, roll pastry from center to edge, alternating directions, to form a 13-inch circle. Trim edge to make 12-inch circle. Fold pastry in half; place, with fold in center, in bottom of 9-inch springform pan.

3 Unfold pastry; fit carefully into pan. Pastry will measure 2 inches high on side of pan. Pat pastry to fit snugly and evenly in pan. Brush bottom and side of pastry lightly with egg white. Refrigerate to chill slightly, until ready to use. Preheat oven to 375F.

4 Make Filling: Fry bacon until crisp; drain; crumble. Sprinkle over bottom of pie shell. Sprinkle cheese over bacon. In large bowl, with wire whisk or rotary beater, beat eggs and egg yolk, salt, nutmeg, pepper and cayenne slightly. Gradually beat in cream.

5 Beat mixture just until well combined, not frothy. Slowly pour over bacon and cheese in pie shell. Bake 50 to 55 minutes, or until top is golden-brown and puffy and the center seems firm when it is gently pressed with fingertip. Remove to wire rack.

6 Let cool 15 minutes on wire rack. With sharp knife, loosen edge of pastry from side of pan; gently remove side of springform pan. Place, still on bottom of springform pan, on plate. Serve warm. Makes 6 to 8 main-course or 12 hors-d'oeuvre servings.

QUICHE LORRAINE

PIE SHELL
1 pkg (10 oz) piecrust mix
1 egg white, slightly beaten

FILLING
½ lb sliced bacon
¾ lb natural Swiss cheese, grated (3 cups)
6 whole eggs
1 egg yolk

1¼ teaspoons salt
⅛ teaspoon nutmeg
⅛ teaspoon black pepper
Dash cayenne
3 cups light cream

8646-05   George Ratkai

MEXICAN RANCH-STYLE EGGS

These Mexican-style eggs are perfect to serve for brunch or supper: Soft-fried corn tortillas are topped with a spicy tomato sauce, fried eggs, shredded Cheddar cheese and sliced green pepper. You may want to spread the tortillas with hot re-fried beans before adding the other toppings. Either way, it's delicious.

1 Make Ranchero Sauce: In a medium-sized saucepan, heat 2 tablespoons vegetable oil over moderately high heat. When hot, add green pepper and onion and sauté, stirring constantly with a wooden spoon, until vegetables are just tender but not browned.

2 Add chili sauce, tomato sauce, lemon juice, Worcestershire sauce and chili powder to sautéed vegetables in saucepan. Bring to a boil over high heat; reduce heat to moderately low; cover and simmer for 15 minutes, stirring occasionally.

3 While sauce simmers, fry tortillas: Add vegetable oil to a small skillet to measure ½-inch deep. Heat oil over high heat until very hot; add one tortilla; soften or cook 20 to 30 seconds, turning once. Do not let tortilla become crisp.

4 Remove fried tortilla from skillet and drain on paper towel. When thoroughly drained, place on a warm platter, cover with aluminum foil and put in a warm oven to keep hot. Repeat with remaining tortillas until all are fried.

5 Melt butter in a large skillet over moderately high heat. Add eggs, 2 or 3 at a time, and cook over medium heat until whites are completely set and yolk is still runny. Remove from skillet and keep warm. Repeat until all eggs are cooked.

6 To serve: Place each tortilla on a serving plate and top with a little sauce and a fried egg. Sprinkle with cheese and garnish, if desired, with slices of green pepper. Serve Eggs Ranchero immediately. Makes 6 servings.

EGGS RANCHERO

RANCHERO SAUCE
2 tablespoons vegetable or olive oil
1 cup finely chopped, seeded green pepper
¼ cup finely chopped onion
1 cup chili sauce

1 can (8 oz) tomato sauce
2 tablespoons lemon juice
1 teaspoon Worcestershire sauce
¼ teaspoon chili powder

EGGS AND TORTILLAS
Vegetable oil
6 corn tortillas

2 tablespoons butter or margarine
6 eggs
¼ cup grated sharp Cheddar cheese
Green pepper slices (optional for garnish)

A SAVORY CHEESE-AND-VEGETABLE TART

The next time you want to serve a simple dinner, prepare this Spinach-and-Cottage-Cheese Tart. Make our homemade pie crust or prepare one from a package. Either way the tart will be delicious with this onion, nutmeg and Parmesan cheese-flavored filling.

1 Prepare Pie Pastry: In a medium-sized bowl, stir flour and salt together; add shortening all at once. With a pastry blender or 2 knives, using a short, cutting motion, cut shortening into flour until mixture resembles coarse cornmeal.

2 Quickly sprinkle ice water, 1 tablespoon at a time, over all of flour mixture, tossing lightly with fork after each addition and pushing dampened portion to side of bowl; sprinkle only dry portion remaining. (Pastry should not be sticky.)

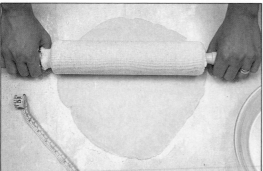

3 Use hands to press and shape pastry into a ball. Flatten with palm of hand and roll out to an 11½-inch circle on a lightly floured pastry cloth, using light strokes from center to edge of pastry, lifting rolling pin as you reach the edge and alternating directions.

4 Fold pastry in half; transfer to a 9-inch pie plate, making sure fold is in center. Unfold pastry; fit into pie plate. Fold under edge of crust and press into upright rim; use fingers to crimp decoratively. Brush pie shell with beaten egg white. Refrigerate until ready to fill.

5 Preheat oven to 375F. Prepare Pie Filling: In medium skillet, sauté onion in hot butter, stirring for about 5 minutes or until golden. Drain spinach in colander; squeeze to remove excess liquid. Add spinach to onion with salt, nutmeg and pepper; mix well.

6 Beat eggs with milk until well blended. Add cottage cheese, Parmesan and spinach mixture; mix well. Turn into pie shell. Bake 35 to 40 minutes or until a knife inserted in center of pie comes out clean. Garnish with sliced cherry tomatoes. Serve warm. Makes 8 servings.

SPINACH-AND-COTTAGE-CHEESE TART

PIE PASTRY
1 cup sifted all-purpose flour (sift before measuring)
½ teaspoon salt
⅓ cup plus 1 tablespoon solid vegetable shortening
2 to 2½ tablespoons ice water
1 egg white, slightly beaten

PIE FILLING
1 cup finely chopped onion
2 tablespoons butter or margarine
1 pkg (10 oz) frozen chopped spinach (thawed)
1 teaspoon salt
⅛ teaspoon ground nutmeg

Dash pepper
6 eggs
½ cup milk
2 cups cream-style cottage cheese
½ cup grated Parmesan cheese

Cherry tomatoes

David Viens

9801-06

McCall's Cooking School

STEP-BY-STEP DIRECTIONS FOR MISTAKE-PROOF RECIPES

McCall's Cooking School Staff:

Editor: Mary Eckley

Associate Editor: Mary J. Norton

Contents 1